BRADSHAW'S
LONDON

BRADSHAW'S
LONDON

George Bradshaw

Edited by John Christopher

AMBERLEY

First published 2014

Amberley Publishing
The Hill, Stroud
Gloucestershire, GL5 4EP

www.amberley-books.com

British Library Cataloguing in Publication Data.
A catalogue record for this book is available from the British Library.

ISBN 978 1 4456 3480 7
EBOOK ISBN 978 1 4456 3501 9

Typeset in 10pt on 12pt Minion Pro.
Typesetting and Origination by Amberley Publishing.
Printed in the UK.

Contents

Introduction to this new edition

George Bradshaw's guide books have enjoyed a remarkable resurgance of interest in recent years, due in no small measure to the popularity of the Great British Railway Journeys television series, presented by Michael Portillo. Born in 1801, Bradshaw happened to be in the right place at the right time when it came to the rapid development of this country's railway network in the early to mid-nineteenth century. He saw that there was a gap in the market for the new breed of travellers and in 1839 he launched his publishing career with the world's first compilation of railway timetables and, in 1863, these were followed by his Descriptive Railway Handbooks. Even though George Bradshaw had actually been dead ten years by then, the distinctive guide books continued to bear his name in an early example of personality branding. The Bradshaw guides covered far more than the railway journeys and in the 1863 *Hand-Book to London and its Environs* he eschewed the railways in favour of a series of walks around central London – a case of the iron horse giving way to Shank's pony – as well as an excursion on the Thames by steamer. As a result it provides the modern reader with a unique insight into the Victorian city of 150 years ago. Armed with this book and the period maps included within its pages, the modern explorer can retrace Bradshaw's steps.

The original Hand-Book is a scarce item nowadays and in order to make this edition more 'pocket friendly' it has been remodelled to a more manageable size. Accordingly, the geographical scope has been confined to the area within the circle of the M25 and some of the further flung 'environs' have been omitted. Furthermore, minor editing has also been carried out on the text, here and here, to smooth out the ride through its pages. If you know London, or if you are a tourist, a newcomer to this fascinating city which was at the centre of the world in Bradshaw's day, this book is the key to your very own time machine. Explore London armed with Bradshaw as your guide and you will see it in an entirely new light.

John Christopher

1863 Preface

The object of this work is to supply a compact yet compendious Guide to the Sights of London, and the chief places of interest and attraction within a circuit of thirty miles, so as to give the greatest amount of information in the smallest compass.

The present edition has been remodelled in the form of an Itinerary, and is divided into such portions or routes through each district of London as the reader will be able to visit in a given time. Every object worthy of attention in the great metropolis is distinctly noticed, and each day's routes are so carefully and clearly arranged that the confusion and unnecessary fatigue incidental to an irregular and discursive wandering hither and thither will be obviated, while each day's walks are varied to diversify the scenes, render them entertaining, and thus enhance the pleasure of a visit to London.

Visitors, however, must be aware that their enjoyments of the most alluring scenes depend, in a great measure, on the frame of mind in which they admire, criticise, or satirise the various objects and peculiarities that come under their notice. A person in good humour always sees the sunny side of every cloud, while another is too prone to be prejudiced by unfavourable impressions. An anecdote is related of the impressions received by two old ladies, who went to receive their dividends at the Bank, which humorously illustrates how different minds are affected by the same circumstances, as noticed by dispositions of a diametrically opposite character.

London as it is:

With A Few Suggestions To Strangers On Their Arrival

Within the last fifty years, London has more than doubled in extent; and, even as we write, is rapidly increasing in every direction. It was happily observed by Herschel, that London occupies nearly the centre of the terrestrial hemisphere – a fact not a little interesting to Englishmen; and, combined with our insular situation in that great highway of nations, not a little explanatory of our commercial eminence. No situation could have been more happily chosen. Though forty-five miles from the sea, it enjoys all the advantages of an excellent seaport, from its position on the Thames. Had it been built lower down the river, it would have been less healthy, and more exposed to hostile attacks; and, had it been placed higher up, it would have been deprived of all the advantages of a deep water harbour. It extends a length of nearly eighteen miles, calculating east and west from beyond Bow to Kew Bridge; and north to south from Holloway to Clapham, may be estimated at a breadth of eight miles. The entire area is computed at thirty-five square miles. The number of houses is upwards of 298,000; and the rental derived from them is so enormous, that only an approximate guess can be made as to the real amount. The money expended by the inhabitants in one year is estimated at £70,000,000. Including the parliamentary boroughs created by the Reform Bill, the metropolis sends eighteen representatives to the Legislature. Of these, four are sent by the City, and two each from Finsbury, Tower Hamlets, Westminster, Marylebone, Southwark, Lambeth, and Greenwich. According to the latest returns, 28,734 vessels have been known in one year to enter the port of London; and the total average value of the property shipped annually on the Thames, is said to exceed one hundred million pounds sterling. The payments into the Exchequer, by the Custom house of London alone, amounts to as much as the net receipts of the other custom houses in Great Britain and Ireland added together.

So vast is the population and magnitude of this metropolis of the world, that if the population of fifty of the principal cities and towns of England were added together, they would not make another London. So rapid is the growth of this queen of cities, that a population equal to that of Exeter is added to its number every eight months; but so overwhelmingly large is the capacity of this leviathan of towns, that, great as this progressive increase is, it is scarcely perceived. It is almost like throwing a bucket of water into the ocean.

The mean annual temperature is 52°, and the extremities 81° and 20°; the former generally occurring in August, and the latter in January. A smaller quantity of rain is said to fall in the vicinity of London than elsewhere in the kingdom. The prevailing wind is the south-west. It may easily be imagined that the vast town, with its dense and busy population accumulated within a circle of twelve miles in diameter, has some palpable influence upon the atmosphere over it. Such is the case. The artificially heated air sends up far more humidity in a state of vapour than the cold air above is capable of receiving, and this moisture being returned, mixed with particles of charcoal and various other infinitesimal ingredients, constitutes that terror of asthmatic country gentlemen called a London Fog. It is curious, however, that its action is found to be beneficial rather than the reverse; for, during its continuance, the fever wards of the hospital are in great part cleared. Though there has been some diversity of opinion on the subject, it is now pretty generally acknowledged that the healthiest parts of London are the northern and north-western. On the elevated ground in Marylebone parish, says Dr Arnott (no mean authority), the air is as pure as Hampstead. The most unhealthy districts include the parishes in the neighbourhood of Whitechapel and Lambeth, whilst – though some allowance ought to be made for its better class of residents – the healthiest parish is St George's, Hanover Square. In Whitechapel, 39 in 1,000 die annually; in St George's, only 17 in 1,000 – being a forcible illustration of the advantages of a more salubrious locality.

The latest returns of the Registrar-General give the average annual mortality of the City as 1 in 40, and that of the East and West London Unions, 1 in 36, (Cripplegate 1 in 32). The mortality of districts adjoining the City, is, for St Leonard's, Shoreditch, 1 in 32; Whitecross Street, 1 in 33; City Road, 1 in 31: whilst the mortality of the healthier districts of the metropolis, is, for St George's, Bloomsbury, 1 in 48; for St John's, Paddington, 1 in 56; Stamford Hill, 1 in 63; and Dulwich, 1 in 91. Talent and ability are now not lacking to give to London all the benefit of its salubrious situation, and make it in reality, what it is comparatively, the healthiest city in the world.

In the midst of the 10,000 acres of bricks and mortar that, according to the latest computation, compose the modern Babylon, there is a plentiful supply of everything that can be required by its 2,336,060 inhabitants. There are 796 board and lodging houses, and for those who dine and breakfast abroad there is a choice of 330 dining-rooms, and 883 hotels and taverns. There are 126 brewers and 66 distillers, and the channels through which their productions flow are amazingly numerous, including 4,340 publicans, 802 beer-shop keepers, eight-eight ale and porter agents, and 770 wine-merchants, besides twenty makers of British wines. For the more intellectual wants, there are 858 private academics, 132 district and parochial schools, 62 British and Foreign, 17 national, and 50 collegiate institutions for granting degrees. Literature is disseminated by 452 printers, 780 publishers and booksellers, and 285 newsvendors. To those who are curious in names it may be worthwhile to observe that the not uncommon patronymic of 'Smith' is borne by no less than 1,412 shopkeepers alone. The annual consumption is estimated at 190,000 bullocks; 776,000 sheep; 250,000 lambs; 270,000 pigs; 120,000 tons of fish; 11,000 tons of butter; 13,000 tons of cheese; 12,000,000 quarters of wheat, besides vast quantities of flour imported; 10,000,000 gallons of milk; 65,000 pipes of wine; 2,000,000 gallons of spirits; 2,000,000 barrels of ale and porter; and 3,000,000 tons of coals.

Having thus prepared the visitor with these astounding statistics to anticipate the magnitude of a place having such marvellous capacities for absorption, we now proceed to supply him with a few other suggestions that may contribute to his accommodation and enjoyment during his stay. On arriving by the train, immediately after seeing to the disposal of his luggage, he should order the driver of the vehicle to convey him at once to the hotel, inn, or boarding-house that choice or private recommendation has rendered preferable. As soon as he has commenced his noviciate in London, wonders begin to accumulate around him.

An observant writer, recoding his early impressions of the metropolis, says, 'How pregnant with instruction to the mind seeking wisdom are the very streets! How curious, recollecting that in fifty years these jostling crowds will, with few exceptions, be mingled with the silent dust, to observe the eagerness with which, as if life and death depended upon a moment, they hurry hither and thither, scarce taking time to see whether they can with safety pass across.' The first and strongest impression received by a stranger entering London, is an idea of its illimitability. It is to him not only a world, but a world without end, spreading its gigantic arms on every side. Miles of narrow dingy streets, that, crammed to repletion with wagons, threaten to crush him between their ponderous wheels and the contiguous walls, indicate the City, whose enormous wealth and splendour are but poorly evidenced by dingy warehouses, dark alleys, and retired counting-houses. Of late years the tradesmen in the leading thoroughfares have vied with each other in generous rivalry, as to the style of their shops and the display of their merchandise, and many of the shops of London glitter with plate-glass and valuable merchandise, almost realising the fabled magnificence of Aladdin's palace. Hence, as from a fountain, the stream of enterprise flows forth, inundating all lands, and returning only to flow forth and fertilise again. Let him advance towards the West-end, and a splendour less real than he has left behind, but more apparent, breaks upon his astonished view. The shops of the goldsmiths, piled from floor to roof with the richest treasures of their art; the shawl-shops, through whose crystal fronts you catch the gorgeousness of their commodities within; the emporiums of art and vertu, where lessons of taste may be had for looking; the vast repositories of learning, appealing eloquently to the eye of the mind; these, and a thousand other evidences of diffusive wealth, lead involuntarily to the belief that all the riches and splendour of the world must be gathered here for show. Whether we take the chaotic multitude that throng the City thoroughfares, all bustle and confusion, the subdued repose of patrician squares, the obscure alley, the princely terrace, the buildings, bridges, churches, halls, markets, theatres, hospitals, or shops, all is alike pregnant with matter meet for reflection and for wonderment, abounding in variety, contrast, novelty, and change.

About nine in the morning, the City streets begin to present and animated scene, for by that hour they are seen thronging with living beings, pouring in from every suburban radius to the great City centre like a walking torrent, until, so numerous appears the mass, London seems to be almost wholly populated by clerks. An hour afterwards, in cab and omnibus, a different class becomes visible, each looking as if the affairs of the universe rested on his individual shoulders; the compressed lip, the steady eye, the furrowed forehead, and the anxiety riding triumphant in every muscle, sufficiently denote them to be the employers. About this time the City may be considered to have received its full complement, and the bustle of the day is fairly commenced.

The whole of the metropolitan police consists of 5,504 men, of whom about only two-thirds can be on duty at one time – and these men have to traverse the extraordinary length of 3,626 miles of streets during the night, and have further to watch over and guard, in the aggregate, 348,907 inhabited houses, 13,305 uninhabited houses, and 5,731 which are built, with a population of 2,336,060 in an area of 700½ square miles. During the period of the Exhibition 8,000 extra police-officers added to the safety of property and persons in the metropolis and its environs.

Beneficent London teems with charitable institutions, hospitals, asylums, refuges for the destitute, the sick, and the lame, and the bind.

Yet though there is scarcely a calamity that miserable humanity is liable to for which Pity in her affluence has not provided a palliative, the streets seem to be thronged with beggars. Without wishing to check the impulse of benevolence, we would recommend the stranger to be cautious in bestowing his indiscriminate charity as he walks along. This beggary is often a mere profession; and for those who happily have the means to spare, it is by far the best plan to make the magistrates of the public police-offices the almoners of their bounty.

In a city of such colossal proportions, it is not wonderful that fires shouldbe numerous – sometimes as many as five or six occurring in one night. To guard as far as possible against the loss of life from these outbreaks, the Royal Society for the Preservation of Life from Fire have been most active, during the last few years, in establishing stations, where fire escapes, with conductors, are placed during the night, ready to be called upon the first alarm of fire. Upwards of 50 such stations are now established in London and its vicinity. No society more richly deserves encouragement, and it would be well if its stations were largely extended. Upwards of 400 lives have been saved by its instrumentality during the last few years. The annual cost of maintaining a station, with its Fire Escape, is £80, in addition to a first outlay of £70, for the machine, etc. The visitor to London will observe, as the dusk of evening approaches, the various Fire Escapes being wheeled to their appointed stations by the conductors. The Institution, like many others of a benevolent character in London, is chiefly supported by the voluntary contributions.

An impartial French writer gives the following account of his impressions of London:

'I warned you,' he writes to a friend, 'not to pay too much attention to my first impressions. I told you that I hated London, and afterwards, that the more I saw of it, the more I hated it. But now that I have seen still more of it, I begin to think it a very fine place. The general aspect of London is quite inferior to that of Paris. London has all the faults of great cities, in a greater degree, perhaps, than any other; and yet it seems to want almost all their redeeming virtues. From its immense extent, there is no consistency, completeness of effect, as the public buildings are so scattered about as to lose all power of producing an impression, except one by one. Yet, notwithstanding all this, London contains in detail much to interest and be admired. I have passed days in wandering about in the vicinity of the parks – though these can scarce be considered as part of London, though they are situated in, and enclosed by it on all sides. London contains also not less than four-and-twenty squares, which are greatly superior to anything else of the kind seen in great cities. None of them are smaller than the Place Vendome, and many of them are nearly as large as the Place de Louis XV.

The noise, the incessant din, the everlasting rumble that is at first so discordant to the ears of one coming from a quiet country place, soon becomes familiar; and it is only in the great thoroughfares, where the murmurs of myriad tongues blend with the hollow roll of the carriages, that it is ever troublesome. Not so the London mud, which, proverbial for the peculiarity of its attributes, stands unrivalled by any plebeian mud yet known. Gluey, well-undisturbed the proud distinction of man over the lower animals – erectness of body. In crossing the streets after rain, the greatest care should be taken to avoid a fall.

The difficulty of selecting points of view whence we may form a correct estimate of the grandeur of London, is great. Views of the bird's-eye kind, like those from the Monument, St Paul's, and the Duke of York's column, are by no means satisfactory, save in giving an idea of the vastness of its extent and the quantity of ground it covers. What with the smoke contending with haze and fog, and the great height by which the streets are narrowed into alleys, the passengers appear to be diminished to the size of ants, and seem merely to crawl along the surface of a spreading brick-red desert of tiles and chimney-pots. Instead of this, or if he will in addition to it, we recommend the individual who wants to see London under its best and most comprehensive aspect, to wend his way to Waterloo Bridge early, in a clear sunshiny morning, and there, leaning upon the parapet of the third such from the Middlesex side, he shall behold a sight to which no other city in the world can afford a parallel.

The thickly clustered houses on every side proclaim the vast population, and the numerous towers and steeples, more than fifty of which, together with five bridges, are visible from this spot, testify to its enormous wealth. One of the best of the suburban views is that from the archway at Highgate. The rural appearance of the road beneath, with the overhanging trees in the shrubbery on the side, and the glad chirp of birds, make a striking contrast with the world of brick and mortar that stretches forward before the eye, evidently fast encroaching upon the few remaining fields in the foreground, and apparently determined to exterminate all that is green and rural. The spires of several modern churches relieve the monotony of the mass of houses, which, at this end of London, are destitute even of the charm of antiquity to render them interesting; and, right before the eye in the distance, St Paul's rears its well-known colossal form: a misty line beyond denotes the course of the river, and the range of the Surrey hills forms the background.

We account it needless to caution strangers against the pretended smugglers, the mock auctions, the gambling-houses, and the other nefarious places with which London, like all great cities, abounds. If he be a man of sense, his own discretion will prove his best Mentor; and, if the reverse, all the cautions in the world would never prevent his occasionally getting entangled in some one or other of the lures set in the metropolis to catch the unwary. We would have him, however, by all means avoid a crowd, which proves such a fertile source of emolument to the pickpockets. The directions of the main streets follow the course of the river Thames from east to west, and the cross streets run for the most part in a direction from north to south. This remembered, will facilitate the stranger in his progress from one point to another.

The plan we have adopted for description will be found, we believe, at once novel and advantageous. We take St PAUL'S and the CITY as the starting point, and then divide London into its four divisions of EAST, WEST, NORTH, and SOUTH. By this arrangement the visitor will find his task of observation much simplified, and a facility for reference given that has never been before imparted to works of a similar description …

A busy Ludgate Hill with St Paul's in the background, *c.* 1905. The artist Gustav Doré had portrayed the same scene with the streets clogged with people and horse-drawn vehicles. *(CMcC) Below:* By Bradshaw's time the Thames had become little more than a fetid, open sewer, its foul stench giving rise to the notorious 'Great Stink'. This *Punch* cartoon from 1858 depicts 'The Silent Highway-Man' doing his rounds.

PART ONE

The City

First Day's Route

DISTRICT 1

The centre of our great commercial transactions – the heart, as it were, of London – is that place of mighty import, the CITY, which has been not inaptly termed the Bank for the whole world. Here are situated the banking-houses, the counting-houses of the bullion, bill, and discount brokers, the offices of stock and share brokers, and the huge establishments of those wealthy individuals, who under the title of 'merchants,' without any other specific designation, carry on those extensive operations which give vitality to the most remote region where the foot of man has ever penetrated. There are 336 stockbroking establishments, many of them firms with two or more partners; 37 bullion, bill, and discount brokers, 248 ship and insurance brokers, and about 1,500 'merchants,' – all of whom have their places of business concentrated within a five minutes' walk of the Royal Exchange. And this is without reckoning the bankers, the general and commercial agents, the colonial, cotton, silk, and wool brokers, the corn and coal factors, the solicitors and notaries, the tradesmen and shopkeepers, and the great insurance, railway, and steam-packet companies, who have all located themselves within the same neighbourhood. Truly may we point out this thickly populated section of the metropolis as one having no parallel on the globe, and the immense amount of wealth here concentrated as equal to the entire revenue of many European States.

Since the time of the Great Fire of 1666, London has not been so greatly changed as it has been during the last quarter of a century; and it is gratifying to note that these changes distinctly show the onward progress of the nation, both in taste and wealth. It is curious to compare in an architectural point the places of business, such as banks, insurance offices, shops, taverns, &c., of the times to which we refer, and the structures intended for similar uses at the present day. The new squares, streets, and warehouses look like palaces by the contrast. This beneficial change ins most visible in the City, in Threadneedle Street and Cornhill, for instance, where several noble buildings have been erected by side of old ones, which render the contrast most notable.

So far back as the reign of Edward I, the City was divided into twenty-four wards, to each of which an alderman, chosen by the livery, was assigned, to be assisted in his duties by the common councilmen, who were chosen as at present, by the freemen of the City. The livery is a numerous body, elected by their respective guilds from amongst the freemen. These guilds, or companies, are known to have existed in this country very soon after the Norman Conquest; but the date of the charter of the Goldsmiths' and Skinners' Companies, the oldest now extant, only reaches as far as the year 1327. We need hardly say that their original object was to preserve their original object was to preserve their respective arts, trades, or mysteries, from the exercise of non-freemen. The City is now divided into twenty-six wards, the aldermen representing which constitute, with the Lord Mayor and 236 elected members, the court of common council, and have the privilege of making bye-laws, and disposing of the funds of the corporation. The Lord Mayor is chosen from the aldermen, generally by seniority, on the 29th of September, and enters upon his office on the 9th of November following. He is assisted in the legal duties of his office by two sheriffs similarly chosen. The Recorder is appointed for life, and is the first law-officer to the City. The Aldermen are also perpetual justices of the peace for the City. The revenue of the corporation, which is derived from sundry dues, rents, interests of bequests, and other sources, may be averaged at about £200,000 annually, which is generally met by an equal expenditure. Within the last few years vast alterations have been made in this quarter of the metropolis, and the old crumbling warehouses in which the citizens of the last century amassed their well-earned wealth are rapidly giving place to handsome structures of proportionate magnitude, and the spirit of improvement that has at last penetrated these haunts of commercial enterprise has gone hand in hand with taste and liberality. There are yet, however, vestiges of those closely-built neighbourhoods that form the prominent characteristics of the City, which would convince the most sceptical, that every inch of available ground has here its corresponding value. In many places the houses still appear to shoot up in gaunt and gloomy rivalry of each other, screening the cheerful sunlight from their narrow pathways, and flinging a dusky obscurity over the bustling thoroughfare, as though the outspread wings of Mammon has enveloped its votaries in eternal shadow. The establishment of omnibuses has gone far to accelerate these alterations; for the citizen is now enabled to study his health as well as his pocket, and, whilst enjoying the fresher air of his cottage in the suburbs, can as conveniently present himself at his counting-house in the City at the accustomed early hour.

The City companies are eighty-three in number, and forty-one of these are without halls. Some exist merely for the sake of the charities at their disposal, and for the annual dinners on the 9th of November, which the bequests of members, anterior perhaps to the Reformation, enable them to discuss. Others exist but nominally, like the Bowyers, Fletchers, and Long Bowstring-makers, and some, like the Patten-makers, owing to the smallness of the fees which they exact from those who are obliged to take up the freedom of the City. Of the twelve great companies, as they are called, upwards of two-thirds are rich, not from what they make, but from what they possess. The acting companies are really very few in number. The Goldsmiths' is regarded as the chief, and the Stationers', though not one of the most ancient, (for printing was a late invention), is certainly one of the most important.

The plan we have proposed to follow out for the convenience of the stranger, will enable us, under a description of the City, to commence with an account of its principal buildings, and of these St Paul's will form an appropriate subject with which to inaugurate our survey. Thence we shall take the reader with us along that busy thoroughfare, leading eastward from the cathedral, and having terminated our gossiping companionship with a summary of all that claims mention in this quarter, proceed to a description of the other portions of the metropolis. For the bodily as well as the mental refreshment of the sight-seeker, nearly every street provides the means of gratification; and it should not be forgotten that the City dining rooms enjoy almost a world-wide celebrity for the excellence of their fare, and the recognised reasonableness of their charges. The chief inconvenience experienced by a countryman in threading the streets of London, arises from the constant jostling of the crowd of passengers, who may sometimes seem to have unanimously entered into a league to impede his movements. This is easily obviated by observing the rule adopted by the experienced Londoners, who maintain along their crowded pavements two district streams of passengers flowing in opposite directions; and it is unwise for a stranger to deviate, even for an instant, from the course pursued by the throng with which he finds himself identified. A little tact and good temper will enable the pedestrian to discover that he can move as comfortably through the most frequented thoroughfares as with the same essentials he can make his way in the world, where the occasional jostling encountered involve a more extensive area for their exercise. This premised – and such seeming trifles will be found in reality matters of no minor importance – we assume our privilege of companionship, and invite a pause before the solemn dome and massive grandeur of that majestic building, which, centred in the very heart of London's traffic, is consecrated to the national worship as the largest Protestant Church in the world.

St Paul's Cathedral – Among those who do not wholly repudiate the spirit of poetry and romance which associates itself with the musty records of antiquity it has been long a favourite opinion that here stood the ancient Temple of Diana, probably as early as the second century. Situated just where the Hermin Way led the hunter forth from the northern gate immediately upon the surrounding forest, and which was plentifully stocked with wild animals, it is natural to imaging that here the ancient votary of the chase made his oblation to Diana ongoing forth, and that, on returning, he here offered up his spoils as a tribute in sacrifice to the tutelary deity of his pursuits. It is a singular fact, as if the custom itself had outlived the memory of its origin, that for centuries afterwards, the offering of a fat doe in winter, and a buck in summer, was annually made at the high altar on the day of the saint's commemoration, and was solemnly received by the dean and chapter, attired in their sacred vestments, and crowned with garlands of roses. As late as the reign of Elizabeth, this offering was made in lieu of twenty-two acres of land in Essex, belonging to the canons of the Church. Long before the Reformation, Old St Paul's was renowned for its embellishments; and massive basins of gold, silver candlesticks, silver crosses, gold cups, and other ornaments of the most costly and sumptuous description, sparkled on its altar, which displayed the most extravagant workmanship, and was inlaid with precious jewels. In front of the cathedral stood the famous Paul's cross, a wooden pulpit, in which the most eminent divines preached ever Sunday forenoon. For many years the old cathedral was a place of common resort, and converted into a general thoroughfare. The chapels and chantries were tuned into workshops for mechanics, who pursued their business during Diving service; the vaults were made wine-cellars; shops and houses were built against the outer wall of the cathedral, and even 'a playhouse' is said to have been among the erections with which the exterior was disfigured. At last the great fire took place, and put a stop to these abominations, entirely consuming in a few hours that splendid pile that had cost, for so many centuries, so much money and labour in its erection and adornment.

The important task of rebuilding the cathedral was confided to Sir Christopher Wren, who found the preliminary removal of the gigantic walls, in many places standing eight feet in height, and five in thickness, a colossal undertaking. His skill and perseverance, however, surmounted all difficulties; and on the 21st of June, 1675, the first stone of the new cathedral was laid. Divine service was performed here for the first time after the fire on the 5th of December, 1697; but it was not until the year 1710, when Wren had arrived at his 78th year, that his son placed the highest stone of the lantern on the cupola. Notwithstanding it was thirty-five years building, it was finished by one architect and under prelate, Henry Compton, Bishop of London. The expense of the building was £736,752, but the entire cost has been estimated at a million and a half. It stands upon two acres and sixteen perches of ground. Its entire length from east to west, within the walls, is 500 feet; its breadth from north to south, 286 feet; the circuit of the entire building, 2,292 feet; and the height to the summit of the cross, 404 feet. A beautiful view of the upper portion of the Cathedral is obtained from the new street, now in course of construction, leading from Clerkenwell to Farringdon Street, to be called Victoria Street ...

At a quarter before 10 a.m., and at a quarter past 3 p.m., the choral service is performed, and there is also divine service every week-day morning at 8 o'clock. On these occasions the body of the cathedral is of course open gratuitously to the public. On Sundays, and on every Wednesday and Friday, during Lent, sermons are preached by the dean and canons residentiary. In May and July, the anniversaries of the 'sons of the clergy,' and 'the charity schools,' generally take place; and being celebrated with as much care and splendour, present the cathedral under additionally attractive aspects.

The Count de Soligny, in his 'Letter on England,' expresses his admiration of St Paul's Cathedral in the following manner: 'I have just come from seeing St Paul's Cathedral. I had been reading something about it last night, and this morning I by accident found myself on the bridge of Blackfriars, from which, as I have learned since, there is the best view of it that can be had anywhere, though even from that point it is seen to great disadvantage, as the whole of its lower order is concealed by the surrounding buildings. I have not, of late, been apt to be surprised; but I was so, and to a very fine effect, by the first unexpected view of this most stupendous temple. I had passed half over the bridge before I saw the cathedral, or knew that it was in sight; but turning on the left hand to look at the scenery on the banks of the Thames it stood before me with a look of grandeur and beauty of which I had formed no previous idea. After having passed all the rest of the day in examining it from every point of view, I do not hesitate to tell you that, as a whole which can be taken in by the eye at once, I think the cathedral of the city of London must be the finest thing in the world! Perhaps the finest that ever has been seen in the world. In saying this, I do not forget that the Parthenon once existed, and that St Peter's still does exist. I am disposed to rank the cathedral of London before the latter, for St Peter's is too large for all its parts to conduce to one general effect.

St Paul's, I repeat, is perhaps a finer work, with reference to itself, than the Parthenon was. I should think the latter was looked at with one single feeling of intense, but tranquil pleasure – a full, total unmixed delight. St Paul's calls up feelings of a more elevated, a more impressive, and a more lasting character. These feelings vary from time to time as you continue looking, till at last they resolve themselves into a lofty but indefinite admiration, which lifts you above yourself and the earth, and inspires you with the moral assurance of the possibility of something infinitely greater, better, and happier. I cannot help being amused at fancying what the Londoners would say to my praises of their cathedral. I am sure they would think them quite extravagant, if they did not say so. They do not seem to have any idea even of its comparative size. I dare say, not ten among the tens of thousands who pass by it every day, have ever looked at it at all; and those who have, seem to want either taste to perceive its beauties or enthusiasm to admire them. They go to Paris and stare and everything in stupid wonder, and then come back and pass by their own magnificent cathedral, without seeming to know it stands there, though Paris contains nothing of the same kind that can approach to a comparison with it. There is, to be sure, one excuse for this. St Paul's is so hideously clogged up on all sides with houses, that it may be passed by without being observed, if it is not looked for. It would certainly be worthwhile to establish a despotic monarchy in this country for one twelvemonth, if one could be sure the holder of it would have the taste enough to employ part of the time in battering down all the buildings that stand within a few hundred yards of St Paul's on every side. I cannot think of any mischief he would be able to do in the rest of the time, for which this would not compensate.'

Having bestowed a glance of recognition on the statue of Queen Anne, which is seen in front of the portico facing Ludgate Hill, and obtained an entrance by the door of the northern portico, now freely open to all visitors, we are permitted to enjoy the feelings of veneration and delight which the striking and impressive view of the building is sure to induce. Eight immense piers, each of them forty feet at the base, support the great dome of the central area, exhibiting a spacious concave embellished by Sir James Thornhill. Through some fine open screenwork may be obtained a view of the place where the usual services are performed, and which is highly decorated with dark oaken carved work. Around are the monuments of the illustrious dead, who have left to this country the legacy of names with which worth, honour, learning, and patriotism have been associated. We should probably save some misapprehension if we first inform the reader, that but few persons are buried here whose monuments have been erected in the cathedral; and, to show how recent is their introduction, the first statue erected in St Paul's was that of the burly lexicographer, Dr Johnson. There are about fifty monuments altogether, the finest as a work of art being generally admitted to be that by Westmacott, to the memory of Sir Ralph Abercrombie. The monuments to Nelson and Howe by Flaxman, and those to various generals by Chantrey, are also finely wrought. From these the eye will naturally be raised to an inscription more emphatic than any of the rest, which is seen on a plain marble slab over the entrance to the choir. The Latin, by frequent quotation, as become almost as familiar as the vulgar tongue, but we give the translation in preference: 'Beneath lies Sir Christopher Wren, the builder of this Church and City, who lived upwards of ninety years, not for himself but for the public good. Reader, seekest thou his monument? Look around!' Above is the organ built by Schmidt, in 1694. It has 2,132 pipes, and cost £20,000. On each side of the choir is a range of fifteen stalls, with the Episcopal throne near the altar, occupied only on state occasions. The stall for the bishop may be recognised by the pelican and the mitre, and the Lord Mayor's stall opposite by the City sword and mace.

On leaving the monuments we proceed from the entrance across the cathedral to a door in the south aisle, which leads us to the outer galleries. Here a person supplies tickets, which are obtained by paying sixpence each. We may therefore appropriately remind the visitor of what he will have to accomplish. There are 280 steps to the whispering gallery round the bottom of the dome; 254 more to the gallery at the top of the dome; and 82 from that gallery into the ball. The total number is thus 616, which will forcibly impress the truth of Beattie's line – 'Ah! Who can tell how hard it is to climb?' – upon the mind of the ambitious traveller towards the top. When half-way to the whispering gallery, the visitor will see on the right the door leading to the Library, which is attained by passing through a long gallery. It is a handsome room about fifty-feet by forty, having shelves crammed with about 7,000 goodly volumes, among which are some Latin manuscripts beautifully written by the monks 800 years ago, and an illuminated English manuscript, 600 years old, containing rules for the government of a convent. The portrait of Bishop Compton is seen over the fireplace. The most curious object is, however, the oaken floor, curiously inlaid with 2,376 small square pieces, without a nail or peg to secure their adhesion.

We are next introduced to the geometrical staircase, originally intended as a private way to the library, and which appears to be suspended without visible support. Passing the greatest western window we enter the Model Room, in which is preserved Wren's original model of the cathedral. Admirably designed as it was, this model was rejected on the absurd ground, that it differed too much from the preconceived notion of cathedrals; and, to the great chagrin of the architect, he was compelled to complete his plan in the form we now see it. Near the library door are the stairs leading to the great bell, and in the turret at the top, the great bell itself is seen suspended nearly forty feet from the floor. It is ten feet in diameter, ten inches thick, and weighs 11,470 pounds. The hammer of the clock strikes the hours on this bell, the deep sonorous tones of which may be heard at a great distance. This mighty tocsin is only tolled on the demise of any members of the royal family, the Archbishop of Canterbury,

Bishop of London, or the Dean of St Paul's. It is advisable to visit this part of the cathedral between twelve and one, at which time any further explanations required can be given by the man in attendance, who superintends the gigantic machinery of the clock. There are two dial-plates, each of them fifty-seven feet in circumference; the minute hands are nine feet eight inches in length, and weight seventy-five pounds; and the figures are two feet two and a half inches long. The fineness of the workmanship, and the unfaltering accuracy of its stupendous movements, combine to render this clock one of the greatest curiosities in the world. The visitor is next introduced to the Whispering Gallery, 140 yards in circumference, situated just below the dome. A stone seat extends round the gallery in front of the wall. On the side directly opposite the door by which visitors enter, several yards of the seat are covered with matting, on which the visitor being seated, the man who shows the gallery whispers with his mouth near to the wall, when, though uttered 140 feet distant, the voice is heard in a louder tone, and as if close to the listener's ear. The effect is by no means so perfect if the visitor sits down half-way between the door and matted seat, and is still less so if he stands near the man who speaks, but on the other side of the door, the mere shutting of which produces a sound like a peal of thunder rattling and rolling among the mountains. From this gallery the marble pavement of the church looks extremely beautiful, and the paintings by Sir James Thornhill, illustrative of the life of St Paul, are here viewed to the most advantage.

Hence we go to the Outer Gallery, from which the immense extent of the metropolis and the circling panorama of the environs form a prospect of peculiar interest and variety. The vast lines of buildings spreading out in every direction, the busy aspects of the diminished streets immediately below, the mapped-out city looking like a fairy towy in which the world is shown in mocking miniature, and the sinuous path of the Thames, crossed by its numerous bridges, and winding between banks on which the noblest of British worthies have lived, flourished, and died, make this a scene which engrosses the attention of the mind, as much as it enchains and enchants the wandering gaze. Poets, painters, and philosophers, statesmen, and politicians, novelists, dramatists, and gallant patriots, have given a deep and enduring interest to nearly every street and alley we survey; and the eye can scarcely fix itself upon a spot that is not hallowed by some association of the past, or contemplate an object that is not identified with some glorious triumph of human learning or noble generosity.

After leaving the gallery, the payment of one shilling and sixpence will procure admission to the ball and cross. The ball is capable of holding twelve persons, and is thirty feet below the summit of the cross. It was from this spot that the ordnance survey of 1849 was made, a scaffolding being thrown around the cross for the purpose. Returning to the basement of the cathedral, those who feel disposed may obtain access to the Crypt, or vaults beneath, for which a charge of one shilling is made. These dreary silent mansions of the dead are lighted at intervals by grated windows, which afford partial gleams of light, with broad intervals of shade between. The vaults are divided into three avenues by immense arches and pillars, some of them forty feet square. The middle one under the done is perfectly dark, and a portion of the north aisle at the east end is dedicated to St Faith, where are preserved the few monumental statues that escaped the ravages of the fire. Shrouded by a flat stone sunk into the pavement, lies the body of Sir Christopher Wren; and here also repose the remains of Lord Nelson, Collingwood, and the Duke of Wellington, in close proximity; and the eminent painters, Reynolds, Barry, Opie, Fuseli, West, and others who have earned the tribute of those funeral honours that a grateful country could bestow.

The open area in which the cathedral stands is called St Paul's Churchyard, and the names of the streets and lanes branching therefrom, give token of their former connexion with the religious structure and its clerical attendants. On the southside an open arched passage leads to DOCTORS' COMMONS, and the offices attached to the ecclesiastical courts and on the northern side the courts communicate with PATERNOSTER ROW, the great literary market, where booksellers and publishers have established themselves from a very early period, and in tall and sombre houses that little indicate the constant busy traffic going on within. Upwards of 20,000 new volumes are hence distributed annually over all parts of the world.

At the eastern end of the cathedral is ST PAUL'S SCHOOL, founded by Dean Colet in 1510, for the gratuitous education of 153 boys, several of whom are transferred afterwards to the universities. The Mercers' Company have the management of the school. The rules are very minute, and were drawn up by the founder.

The Post Office, in St Martin's-le-Grand, reached by turning to the left from the cathedral, next demands our notice and admiration, not only as a fine specimen of architecture, but also for the important object that it serves in receiving and distributing the epistolary intercourse of the world. It was built under the superintendence of Sir Robert Smirke, and was first opened for public business on the 23rd September, 1829. The whole edifice is of stone, and measures 390 feet in length. Beneath the central portico is the entrance to the great hall, which is eight feet long, sixty feet wide, and fifty-two feet high, and is supported by six Ionic columns of Portland stone. On the north side are the newspaper, inland, and foreign offices, and on the opposite is the London post department. Against the walls on the western side

The Post Office was a vital centre of communications in Victorian London, and accordingly Bradshaw describes it at some length. The scene in a typical London Post Office is shown *opposite*. (CMcC) The Penny Black, *left*, was the world's first adhesive postage stamp when it was issued in May 1840. The idea of pre-paid postage stamps was part of Rowland Hill's reforms for the British postal system. The Blacks were only in use for about a year because the red cancellation marks were hard to see and their ink was too easily removed by the unscrupulous.

28

will be found boards giving a list of persons whose address cannot be ascertained, from either erroneous or imperfect superscriptions. Beneath the hall is a tunnel uniting the two grand divisions of the building, and furnished with some ingenious machinery to facilitate the conveyance of letters from one department to another. Machinery is also employed for supplying water and fuel to the upper parts of the building, as well as for other purposes. Immediately under the portico are two large gasometers, that feed the many gas-burners required by the establishment. The entire business of the MONEY ORDER OFFICE is transacted in a building erected for the purpose in Aldersgate Street, a little above the Post-Office, and on the opposite side the way. For the attainment of exact and rapid delivery in the metropolis, London and its environs are divided into Ten Districts, each treated in many respects as a separate town, and to render this arrangement effectual correspondents are requested to add after the address the initials of the district for which the letter is intended. Books at the various post offices are sole at 1d each, containing a list of the several street, with the proper initial appended after them; and to give some idea of the enormous amount of business regularly transacted here, with a rapidity and accuracy almost incredible, it

may be mentioned that on the 14th of February, 1850, the letters thus passed through the office for the district post alone, amounted to 187,037, exclusive of those for the provinces and places beyond sea. The increase of correspondence that has taken place since the adoption of the cheap and uniform rate of postage is as gratifying as it is remarkable. Under the old system, in 1889, the number of letters that passed through the post was 76,000,000; in 1840, when the present rate came into operation, the number was enlarged to 162,000,000. Although the business is now exactly four times and a half more than it was in 1839, the expenses of management have only doubled. In the former year the cost was about £690,000; in 1849, it was £1,400,000. The number of newspapers passing through the Post-Office is estimated at not less than 70,000,000 per annum. Of late years the broadsheet has materially increased in size and weight, each paper now averaging five ounces; so that 9,765 tons weight of papers annually, or 187 tons weekly, are thence scattered to the uttermost ends of the earth. The posting of the newspapers here at 6 p.m., the latest period at which they can be posted without fee, is one of the sights of London, and cannot fail to astonish the visitor.

In Foster Lane, at the back of the Post Office, is GOLDSMITHS' HALL, a spacious structure in the Italian style, built on the site of the old hall, which it has replaced. The principal front, which is almost screened from observation by the surrounding buildings, consists of six handsome Corinthian entablature of great beauty. Here are assayed and examined the gold and silver articles manufactured in London, which have then the 'hall mark' impressed upon them as a guarantee of their being genuine. The interior of the building can only be viewed by an order obtained from a member of the court.

Deviating into CHEAPSIDE, which originally received its name from Chepe, a market, as being the first great street of splendid shops, we shall find how well its present condition justifies its former repute. The fine statue of Sir Robert Peal is erected on the site of the ancient cross and conduit. On the south side, easily distinguished by its projecting clock, is the ancient Church of ST MARY-LE BOW, erected by Sir Christopher Wren in 1673, and considered one of his greatest masterpieces. The steeple, which is of Portland stone, is much admired. Some few years since the church underwent considerable alterations, the tower and spire were rebuilt after the original design; and when the dragon which forms the vane was elevated to its accustomed lofty station, one of the workmen bestrode its back, to the astonishment of an admiring multitude. Connected with this famous heraldic monster there is a curious story afloat. An ancient prophecy announced, that when the Bow Dragon and the Gresham Grasshopper should meet, on England's throne no king should sit. The prophecy was singularly verified; the late Royal Exchange and Bow Church being under repair at the same time, and their respective vanes being sent to the same artificer for re-gilding, they were actually placed side by side, in the first year of her present Majesty's reign. In this Church the Boyle Lectures are annually delivered, and the Bishops of London consecrated. Here, too, are the 'Bow bells' that recalled Whittington, and those born with the sound are still avouched to have just claim to the epithet of 'Cockney.'

The City of London School lies at the back of the houses facing Bow Church, and was first opened in 1837. John Carpenter, its original founder, was town clerk of London in the reigns of Henry V and VI. The present clear annual value of the estates he left for this purpose is not less than £900. It is a fine building of the Elizabethan style, and comprises nine class-rooms and a library, rooms for the masters, a theatre for lecturers, and other apartments. Besides the four boys who are on the foundation, and who are maintained, educated, and endowed with £100 each towards their advancement in life, the sons of freemen are admitted under certain regulations. Four scholarships have been founded in accordance with the will of the founder, and the education imparted is of an acknowledged high character.

The Guildhall is seen at the end of King Street, which runs northward from Cheapside. This is the civic palace, where the principal business of the corporation is conducted, and the magnificent banquets given that have made the City Feasts famous in history. The building was erected at different periods, an irregularity which it betrays in its architecture. The Gothic front, with the City arms in the centre, was finished in 1789, but it has been since frequently repaired. The hall, which is accessible without charge, contains some fine monuments, the principal ones being those erected in memory of the Earl of Chatham, William Pitt, and the illustrious Duke of Wellington (recently finished), and at the western end, raised on pedestals, are the two colossal figures of Gog and Magog, said to represent an ancient Briton and Saxon. This is one of the largest rooms in London, and can accommodate about 3,500 at dinner. It is 153 feet long, 48 feet broad, and 55 feet high. On the windows at each end, beautifully represented on stained glass, are the Royal arms, the insignia of the Bath, St Patrick, the Garter, and the City arms. The other apartments are decorated with various paintings and monuments of historical interest, to view which a small fee to the official in waiting will generally be all the introduction required. In the east wing are the City Courts of law, and opposite is the Guildhall police office, where an alderman attends daily to hear and decide cases. The Church of St LAWRENCE, close by, was built from the designs of Wren, in 1671. Here lies Bishop Wilkins, who endeavoured to explain the art of attaching wings to the shoulders of mankind; and the register records the marriage of Archbishop Tillotson with Elizabeth French, niece to Oliver Cromwell, on the 23rd of February, 1663, and his death and burial here in 1694.

In Cheapside is SADDLERS' HALL, rebuilt 1823, and a little farther on towards the Poultry is MERCERS' HALL, distinguished by a richly sculptured front, adorned with emblematic figures of Faith, Hope, and Charity, and containing some curious relics of Whittington, thrice Lord Mayor of London. Not fewer than 62 mayors were of this Company, from 1214 to 1762. The narrow street called the OLD JEWRY took its name from the great synagogue which stood there till the persecuted race were expelled from the kingdom in 1291. The GROCERS' HALL stands nearly on the side of the original Jewish temple. Diverging southwards from Cheapside, at this point, is Bucklersbury, that took its name from one Buckle, who had there a manor-house. In Stow's time it was the chief residence of grocers and apothecaries; but it is now chiefly occupied by the proprietors of dining-rooms. Here an excellent repast can be made for one shilling, and a positively luxurious one for double the amount.

Threadneedle Street with the Bank of England on the left, and the Royal Exchange building to the right. The statue is of the Duke of Wellington. *(LoC)*

DISTRICT II

The widening of the streets and the other architectural improvements recently added, where no less than seven great thoroughfares converge towards one central point, have made the present aspect of the busy region in front of the Royal Exchange worthy of the grandeur and importance of the first city in the world. The cluster of public buildings here surrounding us renders a detailed description necessary of each.

The Mansion House, the official residence of the Lord Mayor during his year of civic sovereignty, is a building of Portland stone, with a Corinthian portico of six columns in front, resting on a low basement. This edifice, which has some emblematic sculpture on the pediment, stands on the site of what was anciently called Stocks-market, the great market o the city during many centuries. A flight of steps leads to the door beneath the portico, which is the grand entrance, and to the left is the office where the police charges are taken and adjudicated. Besides an extensive suite of domestic apartments, it contains a number of State-rooms for the reception and entertainment of company, and these when lit up present a magnificent appearance. The principal is the Egyptian-hall, a loft room of considerable splendour. The Lord Mayor has an allowance of £8,000 for his year of Mayoralty, but this income is often considerably exceeded by the expenditure. The use of a State coach and a superb collection of plate is also a privilege which is extended to the period of his official occupation of the Mansion House. Adjacent to the Mansion House is seen the Church of St Stephen's, Walbrook, acknowledged to be the masterpiece of Sir Christopher Wren, for the beauty of proportion his architectural skill has imparted to the interior. It was erected in 1675. The altar-piece, by West, represents the interment of St Stephen, and was placed there in 1776. The rood of the church is supported by Corinthian columns so disposed as to produce a grander effect than the dimensions of the church seemed to promise. Deacon's Coffee-house, close by, is worthy of mention for the quantity of newspapers, metropolitan, foreign, and provincial, provided for the visitors. The files of newspapers here kept can all be examined for a small gratuity.

The Bank of England is seen nearly opposite, bounded by Princes Street on the west, Lothbury on the north, and the new Royal Exchange on the south. Is screened by a long stone wall, handsomely ornamented; but the windows being blank, the principal front presents by no means a lively appearance. The structure was first commenced by Mr George Sampson, in 1733, afterwards embellished by Sir Robert Taylor, and finally brought to its present unity of design by the late Sir John Soane. It occupies an irregular area of eight acres; and, as there are no windows in the exterior, the light is admitted to the various departments by nine open courts. The chief entrance is in Threadneedle Street, and leads direct to the Rotunda, a spacious circular chamber with a lofty dome, fifty-seven feet in diameter, crowned by a lantern, the divisions of which are formed by the architectural figures called caryatides. This dome is, of its class, one of the most striking works of art in the metropolis. Herein are paid half-yearly the dividends or annual interest of the national debt. The recipients frequently attend in person, ladies as well as gentlemen, acting as their own agents in the pleasant business of receiving money. In each week certain days are appointed for the transfer of stock, which is mostly effected by brokers. When an actual bargain has been made, the parties go into the bank, and the particular clerk, on whom the duty devolves, examines the books to see if the seller actually has the stock which he proposes to sell. When all is ascertained to be correct, the transfer is made out, the books are signed, and the business being completed, the purchaser is, from thenceforth, until he parts with his right, in possession of 'money in the funds,' that is, he is entitled to receive certain half-yearly sums of money called 'dividends,' and may attend at the Rotunda himself to have them paid to him. Should the visitor select a 'dividend day' for his visit, he will be much interested in the animated scene presented, and the dexterous celerity with which the business we have indicated is carried on. The 'telling-room' presents an appearance of extraordinary activity; clerks counting up and weighing gold coins, porters passing constantly to and fro, and crowds of tradesmen and others negotiating business at the counters. There is an ingeniously constructed clock in a building over the drawing-office, which indicates the time on sixteen different dials, striking the quarters as well as the hours. The other and more private portions of the bank can only be seen by an order from one of the directors, and chiefly consist of the bullion-office, in a vaulted chamber beneath, an armoury, library, treasury, and the apartments in which the notes of the bank are manufactured. The bulk of the note is printed from a steel plate, the identity of which is secured by the process of transferring. The paper is moistened for printing by water driven through its pores by the pressure of the air-pump. In this way 30,000 double notes are moistened in an hour. The printing-ink is made from linseed oil, and the charred husks and veins of Rhenish grapes. The numbering and cipher-printing are executed by the ordinary press. The tenacity of the paper used in the manufacture has been satisfactorily proved by experiment; for in its water leaf, or unsized condition, a bank note will support 36 lbs, and when one grain of size has been diffused through it, it will 56 lbs. There are above

800 clerks employed, and the salaries and pensions amount to about £220,000 annually. Except on holidays, the Bank is open every day from nine till five, and during these hours it is accessible to strangers. This great national establishment was first incorporated in 1694. It is governed by a court of twenty-four Directors, eight of whom go out of office every year, when eight others are elected.

The New Royal Exchange is now before us, and the splendour of the architecture, and its adaption to the purpose designed cannot fail to arrest the attention of the observer. In the open space opposite the western front is a fine equestrian statue, in bronze, of the late Duke of Wellington. It was cast, by Chantrey, from the metal of guns taken in the various victories gained by the hero of Waterloo, and cost £9,000, exclusive of the material, valued at £1,500 more. The former building which occupied its site was destroyed by fire on the night of the 10th of January, 1838. On the 17th of January, 1842, the foundation stone was laid by Prince Albert, and on the 28th of October, 1844, the Exchange was opened with great ceremony by Her Majesty in person. The extreme length of the building, which stands east and west, is 309 feet; the inner quadrangle is 170 feet by 112 feet, and the height of the tower to the top of the vane 177 feet. It is scarcely necessary to remind the intelligent reader that, in 1564, the first building on this spot owed its origin to Sir Thomas Gresham; and the gilt grasshopper, the crest of the Gresham family, is still observed to perpetuate his memory. This is literally the place where 'merchants most do congregate.' The area appropriated to them is very spacious, and highly ornamented with emblazoned decorations. About three o'clock is the time to see the place to advantage, as at that hour, among the concourse assembled, will be found the most eminent men in the mercantile world, who here provide the sinews of that commerce which has proved to us the foster-mother of literature and the arts, and the dispenser of luxuries, comforts, and enjoyments, to all classes of the community. In the centre of the open space is a statue of Queen Victoria, but it is hardly worthy the place in which it has been deposited. Several shops of showy exterior, and some public offices connected with the assurance companies are arranged round the building. A conspicuous part of the building is assigned to LLOYD'S, familiar abbreviation of the important society of underwriters meeting at Lloyd's Subscription Coffee-house. There are two suites of rooms, one open to the public, and the other specially reserved for subscribers. Signal service has been rendered to the maritime world by the establishment of insurances at Lloyd's. The society has agents in all the principal ports of the world, and through their means the commercial and shipping intelligence is published daily, and received with a confidence which for more than a century nothing has ever occurred to destroy. Communications respecting the arrival and departure of ships, of the existence and fate of vessels in every part of the globe, reports from consuls and commissioners resident abroad, newspapers and gazettes from every country, and other publications connected with the shipping interest, are here arranged in such perfect and convenient order, that the actual machinery by which the movements of the commercial world are regulated, seems to be placed within the hands of the directors of Lloyd's.

The Stock Exchange will be found opposite the east end of the Bank, and at the upper extremity of a narrow passage called Capel Court. It is a kind of commercial sanctum sanctorum, open only to its members, who are elected by ballot and who are compelled to find sureties for honourable conduct in the discharge of their monetary obligations. Should they be unable to meet their engagements, or be proved guilty of any nefarious transaction, they are publicly posted as defaulters and excluded, and then, in the peculiar language of the Stock Exchange, they are denominated 'lame ducks.' The Stock Exchange is governed by a committee of twenty-four members, who are also elected annually by ballot; but the business of stock-jobbing is not entirely confined to the members, there being hosts of persons called 'outsiders,' who, being inadmissible to the Exchange, assemble in Bartholomew Lane, immediately in front of it, and, though in many instances of very questionable means, they talk as coolly of hundreds and thousands of pounds as tough the whole wealth of the neighbouring edifice, the Bank of England, was at their command. To the uninitiated the business here carried on is as unintelligible as the jobbers themselves. Their transactions chiefly consist in the purchase and sale of government securities, railway and mining shares, and other properties of the same nature. Time-bargains form a very considerable part of the business, and are thus effected: One broker will agree to purchase of another a certain quantity of any particular stock, at a given price, on a certain day. These days, which occur at stated intervals, are called settling days. In the meanwhile, the stocks either rise or fall in value, and when the period for completing the bargain arrives, a settlement is made without the transfer of stock, the losing party paying merely the difference, or, if mutually agreed on, the affair may be carried over to the next settling-day. The sellers of time-bargains are technically termed bears, the buyersbulls, the object of the former of course being to depreciate the value of the stock sold – of the buyer, to increase it. To effect this object the most ingenious tricks are devised, false reports likely to affect their price are invented and spread abroad, and every possible ruse which cunning can devise is brought into play. We may here mention, for the benefit of those unversed in such subjects, that the national debt is divided into various classes under different names, bearing different rates of interest. The largest class is that termed the 'Three per cent Consols,' the latter word being a contraction of consolidated, the fund having been formed by the union of three funds, which had been kept separate. The rate of interest is indicated by its name. There are probably more than 2,000,000 persons directly concerned in the receipt of this annual interest; for though the debt stands in the names of only about 280,000 individuals, most of these are merely trustees or managers acting for societies and institutions. In Lothbury, that great banking region, is situated the central office of the ELECTRIC TELEGRAPH COMPANY, whence the wires, that have a subterranean communication with all the railways termini in London, receive and diffuse intelligence with astounding rapidity.

CORNHILL, where the glitter of the jewellers' shops, and the prosperous look of those having quieter attractions, will be sure to attract the passengers' eye with terrible provocations to become a purchaser, leads us direct to LEADENHALL STREET, where the fine massive building of the East India House appears upon our right. This stately-looking edifice, with its projecting portico, supported by six lofty Ionic columns, was originally built in 1726, and enlarged in 1799. The front, composed of stone, is 200 feet in length. On the apex of the pediment is a statue of Britannia, at the east corner a figure of Asia seated on a dromedary, and at the west another of Europe on a horse. Here there is a grand court-room for the directors of the Company, large sale-rooms for the disposal of tea and other goods, and offices of various kinds, and in this building all the general and official business of the Company is transacted. The grand court-room contains a fine bas-relief in white marble, representing Britannia, attended by Father Thames, while three female figures, emblematical of India, Asia and Africa, present their various productions. Other principal rooms are adorned with portraits and statues of various persons who have distinguished themselves in the Company's service, and with paintings chiefly of Indian scenery. The library contains an extensive collection of Oriental manuscripts, Chinese printed books, drawings, and copies of almost every work relative to Asia that has been published, and a fine copy of the Koran, formerly belonging to Tippoo Said. The museum is open on Tuesdays and Thursdays by directors' tickets, and on Saturdays without any restriction. The hours of admission are from eleven till three. Leadenhall Market, the City market for meat, poultry, leather, hides, etc., lies to the right of the great thoroughfare from which it takes its name. Turning into Bishopgate, the first building that deserves mention is CROSBY HALL, now chiefly appropriated to purposes of public entertainment as a lecture and concert room; but, among other illustrious characters, it once belonged to Richard, Duke of Gloucester afterwards Kig Richard III. After being the abode of many wealthy citizens and noblemen, it was subsequently converted into a Dissenters' meeting house, and ultimately into a packer's warehouse. From this state of degradation it has been rescued within the last few years, and by means of a public subscription a great deal has been done towards restoring it towards its original beauty. Near here will be found the London Tavern, and othe well-known hotels, of City reputation. In Threadneedle Street is the SOUTH SEA HOUSE, where the official business of the South Sea Company was conducted, byt more recently the office of the notorious British Bank. Returning through Lothbury, we enter Gresham Street, which in 1846 swallowed up the ancient thoroughfare of Lad Lane. The 'Swan with two necks', that used to be the great booking office for coaches to the north, is still a most comfortable hotel. In Milk Street, close at hand, was born Sir Thomas More, and in the Old Jewry is held the Lord Mayor's Court. Here also died the celebrated Professor Porson, in 1808, in a room of the London Institution, of which he was the Librarian. In Wood Street, Cheapside, should be noticed the fine old elm tree and decayed rookery which stands just without the main thoroughfare, in a little enclosed churchyard, this neighbourhood will be found the great emporium of the wholesale woollen and drapery establishments. A fine building at the corner of Wood Street, at its junction with Gresham Street, was erected in 1849, for the Messrs. Morley, hosiers, and glovers ...

London was the backdrop for many literary classics including some of Charles Dickens' most celebrated stories. Bradshaw refers to *Little Dorrit* which was first published in serial form between 1855 and 1857. *Left:* His public readings, both at home and in the USA, were hugely popular, giving rise to the phenomenom of the ticket tout.

Second Day's Route

DISTRICT III

We again start from St Paul's, taking a south-easterly direction through Cannon Street, leading therefrom towards King William Street and London Bridge. The money provided for these new City improvements (£200,000) was raised on bonds at interest, on the credit of the City revenues and estates. The relief afforded by this new artery to the crowded thoroughfare of Cheapside is most acceptable and beneficial; and it contains some of the finest warehouses in London.

Doctors' Commons, a nest of brick buildings, entered by the archway on the right of St Paul's Churchyard, derived its name from the civilians communing together as in other colleges. Here are the offices where wills are registered and deposited, and marriage licences granted. The maritime and ecclesiastical courts held here, consist chiefly of the Admiralty, the Arches, the Probate, and the Consistory Courts, in all of which the business is principally carried on in writing by the doctors and proctors. At the Prerogative Office searches for wills are made, chargeable at one shilling each, and copies, which are always stamped, are to be had on application. They are registered from the year 1383.

THE COLLEGE OF ARMS, of Herald's College, is on Bennett's Hill, on the east side of Doctors' Commons. The corporation, founded in 1484, is under the control of the Duke of Norfolk, as Hereditary Earl marshal; the present building, a plain brick structure, with Ionic pilasters, was erected in the reign of Charles II. Their office is to keep records of the genealogical descent of all noble families in the kingdom, and to search for coats of arms, &c. Strangers may view the court on application. The fees are generally moderate. Knight-rider Street was so called from the gallant train of knights who used to pass this way from the Tower Royal to the gay tournaments at Smithfield.

Southwark Bridge – Passing down Watling Street, which the ancient Roman road, we come to Queen Street, which gives a direct communication between Cheapside and Southwark Bridge, immortalised by Charles Dickens, in 'Little Dorrit.' This bridge was first opened at midnight in April, 1819, having occupied five years in construction, at an expense of £800,000. Its centre arch has a span of 240 feet, and the two side ones measure 210. If we except the abutments and piers, the whole of the bridge is of cast iron, and the height of the centre arch above low water mark is 55 feet, whilst the weight of the cast-iron used for the bridge is computed at about 5,780 tons. There is a toll of one penny to foot passengers, but those who disembark from the steamboats that call at the bridge-pier pass over without charge.

The cross streets about here, with their narrow causeways and long lines of lofty warehouses and dark offices, are worth turning into for the signs of busy traffic they present, and the picturesque old-mansion appearance which many of the houses still retain. The venerable churches and church-yards, coming upon us unexpectedly in the very heart of a dense cluster of buildings, and the palpable struggling after vegetation of some smoke-blackened tree, putting forth a few withered green leaves at yearly intervals about the spot, tend to invest this region with some noticeable characteristics peculiarly its own. That the visitor may know something of the objects that lie around him, we here group together a few of the more interesting, that will furnish him with an excuse for deviating a little from his direct course.

Queenhithe, at the bottom of Queen Street, and to the right of the bridge, was formerly one of the most generally used landing-places on the banks of the river. The term hithe (signifying a wharf or landing-place) takes back its history to Saxon times ... It was first called Queen's hithe in the reign of King John, out of compliment to his consort. Opposite is the Church of ST MICHAEL'S, built in 1677 by Wren.

Vintners' Hall, distinguished by the figure of Bacchus striding his tun, is close by in the Upper Thames Street. In the great hall is a good picture of St Martin dividing his cloak with a supposed beggar ... The vintners were first incorporated in the reign of Edward III, when the best red wine was sold at fourpence a gallon!

Thames Street is about a mile in length, and extends from Blackfriars to the Tower, along the river bank. That part of the street below London

Bridge, is called Lower Thames Street, and that part of it above the bridge, Upper Thames Street. In the middle of the 18th century it was remarkable for the number of Cheesemongers' shops in it. In the part of the vintry known as GARLIC-HITHE will be seen St James's Church, built in 1676, and admitted to be the worst specimen of Wren's architectural abilities in London. Over the clock is a figure of the saint. The place derives its name from the quantity of garlic that used to be sold near the church. On College Hill, the next turning past Queen Street, stands St Michael's Paternoster Royal, which was made a collegiate church (hence the name) by the executors of Sir Richard Whittington, the renowned Lord Mayor. The almshouses he founded stood on the north side of the church, but they were removed a few years ago to Highgate. This church was also one of those rebuilt by Wren after the great fire. The altar-piece was presented to the church by the directors of the British Institution in 1820, and represents Mary Magdalene anointing the feet of our Saviour. It is curious that Whittington, who was thrice Mayor, was in this church thrice buried – first, by his executors, who erected a handsome monument to his memory; then in the reign of Edward IV, when it was taken up by one Mountain, the incumbent, who supposed that great wealth had been buried with him; and finally, by the parishioners, in the next reign, who were compelled to take up the body to re-encase it in lead, of which it had been despoiled on the former occasion. In this neighbourhood was the Tower Royal, a large building of considerable strength, wherein at one time the Kings of England resided, and which, with many another palatial structure, graced the banks of the river in days gone by.

Returning to Cannon Street, by way of Dowgate Hill, we shall emerge nearly opposite ST SWITHIN'S, another of Wren's churches, but more remarkable for having preserved on its outer wall, all that remains of the famed 'London Stone,' concerning the original purpose of which there has been so much speculation. There is evidence of a thousand years having passed away since it was first set up; but we must still say with Stowe, 'the cause why this stone was there set, the very time when, or memory thereof is there none.' Whether it was an ancient British relic, whether it marked the spot where proclamations were published, or whether it was a Roman milliarium whence distances were measured, is still uncertain, and probably will remain so. At the time when Stowe wrote, it stood on the south side of Cannon Street, then called Candlewick Street. In December, 1742, it was removed to the curbstones on the north side of the street; and in 1798, it was enclosed within a modern case of an altar form, and placed in its present position, the better to preserve it. In the adjacent thoroughfare of Suffolk Lane, and on the eastern side, is the celebrated seminary of 'Merchant Tailors' School,' founded by that company in 1561. The present building, which is a plain massive structure, was rebuilt immediately after the great fire, and comprises a spacious school-room, a house for the head-master, a library, and a chapel. About 250 scholars are here educated, many of whom are sent to St John's College, Oxford.

We now approach King William Street, at the northern extremity of which is the statue, by Nixon, of William IV, placed there in 1844. It is of granite, and stands, with the pedestal, 40 feet in height. The MONUMENT is now seen to raise its lofty head above us, rising from an open area on Fish Street Hill. It is almost superfluous to tell the reader it was erected in 1677, in commemoration of the Great Fire of London, which began at the distance of 202 feet eastward from the spot, and its height has on that account been made 202 feet. It is a fluted Doric column built of Portland Stone, designed by Wren, and executed under his superintendence, at a cost of £15,000. The pediment is 40 feet high and 21 feet square, and the column is surmounted by a blazing urn of gilt brass 42 feet in height. The north and south sides of the pedestal have each a Latin inscription, one descriptive of the destruction of the city, and the other of its restoration. Within is a spiral staircase of black marble, having 345 steps by which the visitor may ascend to the summit, enclosed by an iron railing, and obtain an extensive view of the mighty city, with its suburbs stretching miles away beyond. It is open every day from nine till dusk, except Sundays, at a charge of sixpence each person.

In Great Eastcheap, on the site now occupied by the statue of William IV, stood the Boar's Head Tavern, the scene of Falstaff's memorable vagaries, as recorded by Shakespeare. The original tavern was destroyed in the great fire, rebuilt immediately afterwards, and finally demolished to allow of the new London Bridge approaches in 1831. The church seen nearer the bridge is St Magnus, erected by Wren between 1676 and 1705. The cupola and lantern has been much admired. Miles Coverdale, who lies here buried, was the rector, and under his direction, in 1535, was published the first complete English version of the Bible.

On the western side ofthe bridge is FISHMONGERS' HALL, a handsome structure of Portland stone, erected in 1833. On the right of the grand staircase leading to the interior is the statue of Sir William Walworth, whose hand grasps the identical dagger with which he slew Wat Tyler. The fishmongers were once the most powerful, and perhaps the wealthiest of the City companies. The widening of the approaches to London Bridge considerably improved the value of the ground in this locality, and seven guineas per food has been paid for frontage in King William Street. At the eastern foot of the bridge is the Government Emigration Office. So great is the traffic at this point, that on a careful inquiry, in April, 1850, it was found that in one day there passed along King William Street, from eight in the morning till eight in the evening, 11,022 vehicles, being at an average of 971 an hour, or sixteen a minute; and on the same day it was calculated that within the same space of time there passed 54,432 foot passengers, giving an average of nearly eighty a minute.

LONDON BRIDGE, with its approaches, cost about two millions, and was seven years building, being commenced in 1824, and finally opened by King William IV and Queen Adelaide on the 1st of August, 1831. It have five elliptical arches, and presents to the eye not only a substantial and solid specimen of architecture, but a scene of bustle and traffic unsurpassed by any bridge probably in the world. It connects the heart of the City, where the mercantile world is so busily occupied and so densely concentrated, with the almost equally thickly populated Borough. A century ago, old London Bridge afforded the sole passage from one bank of the Thames to the other, and it formed the only entrance into town from the south, as it had done for eight

'London Bridge at Noonday', an engraving from *The Illustrated London News*, 1872. The bridge was the main crossing point for a constant stream of traffic going to and from the Surrey Commercial Docks on the south side of the river. Marc Brunel's Thames Tunnel, passing under the river between Rotherhithe and Wapping, had been intended to alleviate the congestion, but the money ran out and the access ramps for the horse-drawn vehicles were never constructed.

centuries before. The first bridge was a wooden one, built between the years 993 and 1016. The first stone bridge was constructed in the reign of King John (1209), and an old tradition asserts that the foundation was laid upon woolpacks – a report manifestly arising from a tax on wool having contributed towards its expense. It was much injured by a fire in the Borough that broke out four years afterwards, when 3,000 persons perished. It had a drawbridge for the passage of ships to Queenhithe, and until the middle of the last century was crowded with houses, at one time mostly tenanted by booksellers, and at another, by pin and needle makers. There was a chapel on the bridge, and a tower whereon the heads of all unfortunate offenders were placed. An old map of the city, in 1587, represents a terrible cluster. The wharfs along the Middlesex side are chiefly devoted to the embarkation and disembarkation of passengers for Greenwich, Woolwich and Gravesend.

Pursuing our course eastward along Lower Thames Street, we next reach the New Coal Exchange, built at the corner of St Mary at Hill, and opened in November, 1849. It includes a circular area for the meeting of the merchants, 60 feet in diameter, with three galleries running round it, and the area is covered by a glazed dome 74 feet from the floor. At the angle of the two fronts is a circular tower 100 feet high, and forming a conspicuous object from the river. The entire cost of the structure was £40,000.

Billingsgate, the great fish-market of London, is nearly opposite. It was established in 1699, and is held every day except Sunday, when mackerel are, however, vended by permission within its precincts. In November, 1849, was laid the foundation of a new market, to include an architectural frontage of 172 feet, extending from the Customhouse Quay to Nicholson's Wharf.

The Custom-House is next, presenting an extensive and rather handsome river frontage 484 feet in length, and 100 in breadth. Besides the warehouses and cellars there are nearly 180 distinct apartments in which the various officials transact their business. The interior may be visited daily from nine till three. On the first floor is the long room, which is 190 feet in length, 66 feet wide, and 50 feet high. There is a good promenade before the building, which affords a lively view of the constant traffic of the Thames. The present building was erected in 1817. On St Dunstan's Hill adjoining is the church of St Dunstan's in the East, noticeable for the peculiarity of its construction. From the square tower springs a lantern of singular form, having arches that support the spire, and of this flying steeple, Wren, the architect, was extremely proud.

In Mark Lane, a thoroughfare diverging northward into Fenchurch Street, is the CORN EXCHANGE, a large plain building in which the greater part of the sales of corn take place. Monday is the principle market day, when the greatest bustle prevails. Close by is the London Terminus of the Blackwall Railway.

We now approach the Tower, with its memories and associations of early times and struggles – its varying history as a fortress, a palace, and a prison, and its deeply stirring records of the wise, the virtuous, the daring, and the unfortunate, who have found a lodging within its walls and a death-place within its shadow. The earliest associations of this spot carry us back to the remote period where our annals merge into the twilight region of mythic fable and obscure tradition. A host of names rush into the memory; but our task is rather to describe the present than chronicle the past, else might we dwell upon the recollections here up-called of the patriot Wallace, the adventurous Raleigh, the revengeful Richard, with his helpless nephews, Clarence drowned in the Malmsey butt, the good Sir Thomas More and the chivalrous Earl of Surrey, Lady Jane Grey and her young husband, the ruthless Mary and the 'Virgin Queen,' besides a host of innocent victims, sacrificed in the dark days of despotism and tyranny, that 'pass like veiled phantoms on before the mind.' The very streets that introduce us to the spot, remind us of the city in its olden days, before gaslights and the new police had made the ways clear and the paths safe – when each house had its sign dangling in the palpable obscure of after-dark, their outlines ever and anon rendered more distinctly by the smoky glare of the linkboy's light as he piloted some bibbing citizen to his domicile, or the sudden assemblage of the swinging lanterns of horn, at the familiar cry of Watch.

The Tower is now known to have originated with the Romans, but the principal foundations were laid by William the Conqueror, to maintain his authority over the city. Subsequent monarchs built, enlarged, and reconstructed the various buildings from time to time, and the fire that consumed the grand storehouse, or small armoury, on the night of October 30, 1841, has caused some portions of the interior to assume a modern aspect. Within the outer wall the buildings cover a surface of twelve acres, surrounded by a ditch, which, though now drained and exhibiting a grassy slope, was not many years since the repulsive receptacle of stagnant water and filthy mud. The entrance is through four successive gateways, which are opened at daylight every morning, with all the forms and ceremonies of a garrisoned fortress. The appearance of the warders and yeomen, in their beefeater costume, with their large sleeves and flowing skirts ornamented with gold lace, the official badge, and their flat round caps tied about with bands of parti-coloured ribands, give a characteristic interest to the place directly we enter. At the Armoury Ticket Office within the entrance gate, a warden is in attendance to conduct parties through, from 10 till 4. A fee of one shilling is paid for viewing the Regalia and the Armoury. To the left is the Bell Tower, said to have been the prison of Queen Elizabeth and now containing the alarm-bell of the garrison. Near where that sentry's bright bayonet glitters in the sunshine, you may see a stone arch under the esplanade. That is the water-way to the celebrated Traitor's Gate, through which offenders were conveyed, seldom to these unfortunates being other than a gate of death. A boat, securely guarded, almost unnoticed, and beyond the reach of mob or rescue, bore the prisoner swiftly down the stream. Once under the shadow of that arch, the huge gates opened to receive the victim, and as they closed again upon him, the world and hope were alike shut out. Beyond the gate a flight of stone steps was washed by the tide, and stepping ashore, the offender was within the fortress and readily consigned to any of its numerous dungeons. The last prisoner taken through Traitor's Gate was Arthur Thistlewood, afterwards hanged for the Cato Street conspiracy. Passing beneath the gateway of the 'Bloody Tower,' so called from it being the supposed scene of the murder of the two infant princes by their uncle Richard III, we find ourselves under the walls of the White Tower, and in front of the spot where the grand storehouse, or small armoury, stood, which was destroyed by the fire before mentioned. On this site the Waterloo Barracks have been erected. To the left is the Tower Chapel, or Church of St PETER AD VINCULA. In front of the altar are buried Anne Boleyn and Catherine Howard, the ill-fated wives of Henry VIII; in the same grave with his turbulent and ambitious brother, Lord Seymour, and side by side with his powerful rival Dudley, the proud Duke of Northumberland, was interred the protector Somerset. Here also lie the remains of Thomas Cromwell, the rival of Wolsey; Devereux, Earl of Essex, Elizabeth's favourite; Lady Jane Grey; her husband, Lord Guildford Dudley; and under the communion table, James, the unfortunate Duke of Monmouth. Besides these and other bygone celebrities, whose names are handed down by history, and occasionally revived in the pages of romance, here will be found many of those devoted adherents who lost their lives in the cause of the Stuarts. In one grave were interred the Lords Balmerino, Kilmarnock, and Simon Lord Lovat.

The White Tower presents a large square irregular outline, and exhibits architecture as ancient as any now remaining among us. It consists of three lofty stories, under which are spacious vaults. At the south-west corner is the entrance to the HORSE ARMOURY, which is comprised in a single apartment, 150 feet by 33. The floor is lined by a series of equestrian figures, twenty-five in number, and clothed in the armour of various reigns, ranging from that of Edward I to James II. The figures in this romantic collection are arranged in chronological order; each is mounted inthe full field costume of its respective era, and placed beneath an arch, in the left column of which is affixed a banner displaying in letters of gold the name, rank, and period of the illustrious personages beneath, who look like animated portraits borrowed from some Illustrated History of England. A small room to the right contains in addition specimens of the various kings of fire-arms that have been in use since the invention of gunnery. Here will be noticed, among other trophies, three swords, a helmet, and a girdle, once belonging to TippooSaib, and some curious Chinese dresses and accoutrements captured in one of our recent victories at Chusan. Nor should we omit to direct attention to Henry the Eighth's walking-staff, with three matchlock pistols in it, and a short bayonet in the centre of the barrels, with which trusty companion the portly monarch is said to have perambulated the streets of London in disguise after nightfall.

At the north-west corner of the Horse Armoury is the staircase leading to Queen Elizabeth's Armoury, which contains specimens of those weapons in use before the introduction of fire arms. Here figure the partisan, the pike, the boar – spear, the bill, the glaive, the ranseur, the spontoon, the battle-axe, and other formidable arguments of a like description, with which our ancestors were wont to settle disputed questions. Here, too, are sundry instruments of torture, the thumb-screw, and the 'scavenger's daughter,' which make the blood run cold to look at. At the entrance the attendant will point out the apartment which was the prison of the gallant Raleigh. The lower portions of the White Tower are occupied as store-rooms for the Ordnance Department, and the upper portion as a repository for the national records.

THE JEWEL OFFICE is generally the next place visited. The crown jewels were formerly kept in the Martin Tower, but in 1841 the present building was prepared for their reception. Here will be seen the gorgeous regalia with which our monarchs have been invested at their coronation. The most conspicuous among them is the Imperial Crown, modelled for George IV, and said to be the richest diadem in Europe. It is made of rich velvet, enclosed with silver hoops, and covered with diamonds. In the front is a large Jerusalem cross entirely frosted with brilliants, having in the centre a beautiful sapphire of the purest and deepest azure; at the back is another cross, similarly frosted, and enclosing the rock ruby worn by Edward the Black Prince, and by Henry V, at the battle of Agincourt. These matchless jewels are separated by four large diamond flowers, set between the arches, and the whole rests upon a double fillet of large pearls, enclosing several diamonds, emeralds, rubies and amethysts of surpassing brilliancy. Besides the crown there are shown about forty other objects of curious interest, some remarkable for the amazing splendour of their ornaments, and others uniting great antiquity to dazzling lustre. They are all displayed within enclosures lined with white cloth, and fronted with large squares of plate glass. The jewels are valued collectively at nearly three millions sterling, notwithstanding the recent decision in our law courts with respect to the crown jewels of Hanover, which has had the effect of removing a portion of them to that kingdom.

Opposite the church, and on the south-west corner of the Tower Green, the ancient place of execution, is the Governor's residence, in which is the COUNCIL CHAMBER, where there is a record kept of the Gunpowder Plot, the conspirators having been examined here. The BEAUCHAMP TOWER stands half-way between the Governor's residence and the church. It was the ancient state prison, and consisted of two stories, the walls of which, with their carved memorials, bear sad testimony to the dismal thoughts of those who were imprisoned. North of the Beauchamp Tower is the DEVELIN TOWER, and to the eastward are the remains of the BOWYER TOWER, the reputed scene of Clarence's death in the Malmsey butt, the FLINT and the BRICK TOWER, where Lady Jane Grey underwent her imprisonment. The upper storey of the WAKEFIELD TOWER is pointed out as the spot where Henry VI was murdered. Before leaving these venerable precincts, the visitor should ascent the parade, look at the old batteries, where the cannons are happily rusting away in peaceful inaction, and having explored the short streets and court-yards, which give this remarkable spot the appearance of a little fortified town, let him make his exit by the postern, on the eastern side, and contrast the advantages of our present happier condition with the evidence that has been afforded him of the brutal tastes and sanguinary pursuits of the nation, when kings upheld their thrones by the tyranny of bloodshed, and the people were taught to regard their brethren across the Channel as their natural enemies. Let him, stand by the loft dock-walls of St Katherine, and view the thronging herd of ships that crowd upon the Pool, and he will behold a scene of true glory which the world cannot equal – a sight which is alone and unparalleled in the history of nations, a spectacle which neither Greece in her refined enlightenment, nor Rome in her imperial power, could boast. A channel left in mid-stream is lined on each side with shipping, the hulls lying darks and solid upon the water, the rigging mingling into one long-continued web, a mesh in interlacing ropes and spars. Ten thousand masts stretch tapering to the sky in token of England's commerce with each corner of the globe; the flags of all countries spread their colours to the breeze, the tongues of all nations mingle in one busy clamour, which still tells that every clime sends to this chosen haven the choicest products of their several lands, giving wealth almost beyond calculation, to be centred in the Pool, the docks, and the tall warehouses around. Such is a visible sign of the wonders wrought by popular progress, and a brilliant contrast in its picture of peaceful industry to the dark evidence of the horrors of the past, shrouded within the venerable walls of the Tower.

Before quitting the neighbourhood, there are two buildings by Tower Hill which should not escape observation. The one on the north side is the TRINITY HOUSE, a handsome structure of Portland stone, which is the seat of the Trinity Corporation, founded in 1512. Here are examined the masters of ships, and besides appointing pilots to the Thames, the government of lighthouse, harbour-dues, buoys, &c., all falls under their cognisance. To the eastern side of the hill is the MINT, a fine stone building erected from the designs of Smirke, and possessing vast mechanical aids within for executing the coinage of the United Kingdom, which is all issued from this great money manufactory. The buildings in which the coining is carried on are a series of neat workshops situated in the courts behind. The machinery is exceedingly interesting, and the whole is a model of ingenuity and exactness. Strangers can only be admitted by the special introduction of some superior officer connected with the establishment.

DISTRICT IV

Proceeding northward from St Paul's towards Newgate Street, we again traverse the great bookselling district, in the heart of which, standing back from a passage leading from Ludgate Hill to Paternoster Row, is STATIONERS' HALL, where the works of all authors are entered to secure their copyright. The gross amount of magazines and other periodicals, sold on the last day of the month, in Paternoster Row, has been estimated at 500,000 copies. The annual returns of periodical works alone are rated at 300,000, and this, notwithstanding the wonderful cheapness of price at which they are issued, so that some idea may be formed of the extensive nature of the business here transacted. Threading the tortuous thoroughfare of WARWICK LANE, which derives its name from the mansion of the Earls of Warwick having been there situated in the days of yore, we pass on our left the COLLEGE OF PHYSICIANS, where the golden globe on the dome 'seems to the distant sight a gilded pill.' The business of the college is now removed to a much finer building in Pall Mall East; and the ground floor of the old College is occupied by the butchers, who could not find room in the confined space of Newgate Market. Other manufactures are carried on in the upper floors of the building. At the back of this building, and in the midst of a densely-populated area, is NEWGATE MARKET, which is productive of considerable inconvenience to the public, from its ill-chosen situation. On market-days it frequently happens that the streets in the vicinity are completely blocked up by the butchers' carts. In thirteen slaughter houses here, there are as many as 600 sheep, and from 50 to 110 bullocks slaughtered every day. It will, certainly, be a great public convenience, if Old Smithfield, which is close at hand, as suggested, be converted into a dead meat market.

In Newgate Street, nearly opposite the entrance to the market, and standing back a little from the main thoroughfare, is seen the south front of CHRIST'S HOSPITAL, familiarity called the 'Blue Coat School.' From the peculiar costume worn by the boys. This noble institution, founded by Edward VI occupies the site of an ancient monastery of Grey Friars, and was first opened for the reception and education of boys in 1552. The present annual revenue is about £50,000. About a third part of the children are educated at an auxiliary branch of the institution, at Hertford, whence they are transferred to town. Besides other endowments, Charles II founded a mathematical school for forty boys, and another, by Mr Travers, provides a mathematical education for thirty-six more. Four boys are annually sent to Oxford and Cambridge, and there are likewise two scholarships of £30 each, one founded by the Pitt club, and the other by the proprietors of the Times newspaper. The buildings of the institution embrace several structures of large dimensions, chiefly ranged round open courts with cloisters beneath. The Great Hall, which occupies the first floor, is 187 feet long, 51 feet broad, and 47 feet high. In this magnificent apartment the boys take their meals, and on the eight Sunday evening preceding Easter Sunday, the public suppers that take place, at 6 p.m., constitute one of the most interesting sights in London. Strangers are admissible by tickets, which can only be obtained from those connected with the school. The management of the institution is vested in a body of governors, composed of the Lord Mayor and Corporation, together with all benefactors to the amount of £400 and upwards... Many a bright name on England's muster-roll of celebrities has been first recorded in the books of this truly valuable institution. At the end of Newgate Street, and forming a sombre angular junction with the Old Bailey, will be seen the prison of NEWGATE, the name of which occurs so frequently in the chronicles of crime. It is a gloomy massive structure, of a quadrangular form, built in 1777, and being considerably injured by the riots in 1780, was afterwards efficiently strengthened and repaired. Within the last few years many improvements have been made; and it is a cheering reflection that in the present prison, with its clean, well-whitewashed, and well-ventilated wards, its airy courts, its infirmary, its humane regulations, and its strict but intelligent officers, the myriad miseries of the old jail have been utterly abolished. The condemned cells are at the north-east corner next to Newgate Street, and those doomed to expiate their offences on the scaffold are consequently not more than a few feet from the bustling tide of population ever streaming past. These dark and narrow dungeons have but a small grated aperture in each, letting in light from the court-yard on the other side. The executions take place in front of the debtors' door. Those desirous of inspecting the arrangements of the prison, must obtain an order from the Sheriffs, or one of the other competent City authorities.

Further on, down the Old Bailey, is the CENTRAL CRIMINAL

COURT, for the trial of criminal offences, there are two court-rooms called the 'Old' and the 'New Courts,' and to these a third has been recently added. In the Old Court, the Crown judges sit during the Sessions, and here the more serious cases are tried. In the New Court, the lighter kind of offences are disposed of by the Recorder and the Common Sergeant. A fee, ranging from one to five shillings, according to circumstances, will enable a stranger to procure admission into the gallery to hear the trials.

St Sepulchre's Church, the solemn tolling of which is so associated with the knell of the murderer, stands on the north side of Snow Hill, nearly opposite Newgate. It was from this spot that a solemn exhortation was generally given to the prisoners appointed to die at Tyburn.

St Bartholomew's Hospital presents a handsome stone front on the south-east side of Smithfield, and has a fine entrance under an arched gateway, which leads into a spacious square court beyond, where the principal buildings connected with the institution are situated. It was originally a priory, founded in 1102 by Rahere, minstrel or jester to Henry I, and who became the first prior of his own foundation. The present building was erected in 1729, and the great staircase was embellished by Hogarth gratuitously with such appropriate subjects as the 'Good Samaritan,' the 'Pool of Bethesda,' 'Rahere laying the Foundation Stone,' and 'A Sick Man carried on a Bier, attended by Monks.' At the head of the staircase is the hall, a very large room, ornamented with a full length of Henry VIII, and some other portraits of benefactors. Tradition asserts, and from recent discoveries, not without reason, that a subterranean passage led from the crypts below to the house of the priors situated at Canonbury. The arrangements of the wards, and the professional attendance, merit the highest commendation. All indigent persons, maimed by accident, are received at all hours of the day and night, without charge or ceremony; and, as a practical school of surgery for medical students, this hospital ranks among the highest. Lectures by eminent professors are delivered at stated periods. The annual expenditure is about £32,000. Crossing Smithfield, and passing up St John's Street, we may direct the stranger's attention to a fine old vestige of ancient London, seen at the extremity of a narrow lane of the left, leading to St John's Square. This is ST JOHN'S GATE, consisting of a large pointed arch, with a Gothic window over it, and a large tower on each side. This is all that remains of a magnificent structure erected in 1110, and which was the sumptuous priory of St John of Jerusalem, belonging to the warlike order of the Knights Hospitallers, instituted by Godfrey of Boulogne. The buildings covered a vast extent of ground, and are now occupied by St John's Square. Adjoining the gate was the residence of Cave, the publisher of the 'Gentleman's Magazine,' and the spot is further rendered interesting by its association with Dr Johnson, and other literary celebrities of the past century, who either habitually visited the spot, or took up their abode in this locality. Aylesbury Street, beyond, covers the site of the grounds formerly attached to the mansion of the Earls of Aylesbury.

Retracing our steps to St John's Street, Charter House Lane will bring us to the CHARTER HOUSE, founded by Sir Walter Manny in 1370 as a Carthusian Monastery, from which it derives its name. After the dissolution it was, in 1611, sold for £13,000 to Thomas Sutton, who converted it into a magnificent hospital, comprising a master, a preacher, head schoolmaster, and second master, with forty-four boys, and eighty decayed gentlemen, to defray which he endowed it with lands at that time worth £5,000. The pensioners, many of whom have distinguished themselves in the world by their talents, if they have failed in securing a stronger claim upon the favours of fortune, are allowed £14 per annum each, besides chambers, provisions, fire, and a cloak. The arrangements, though sometimes savouring of monastic quaintness, still display the charitable intentions of the founder, and effectually minister to the comfort of the unfortunate, who find here a peaceful retreat for their declining age. The School in connection with this foundation is an admirable one, and contributes to our universities some of the finest scholars. The privileges and scholastic perquisites enjoyed are very extensive.

Turing into Aldersgate Street, we may notice a fair specimen of ornamental street architecture in the facade of the former City of London Literary and Scientific Institution, which was rebuilt at a cost of £5,000, in 1839, the institution, now the home of the Young Men's Christian Association, was founded in 1825, and has enabled many to acquire intellectual improvement at a small expense. The library contains many thousand volumes. Jewin Street will lead the curious explorer into that region familiar to the debtors, under the name of the Whitecross Street. THE DEBTORS' PRISON is a substantial structure, built in 1815, for the reception of those debtors who had been previously incarcerated indiscriminately with criminals in Newgate and the Compter. There is accommodation for about 400 prisoners, access to whom is readily granted every day, at stated hours ...

If we again make our way into Newgate Street, the visitor should not pass Panyer Alley, the width of three streets from St Paul's, without noticing a flat stone placed against the wall of a house there, on which is sculptured a naked child sitting upon a pannier or basket, with the following doggerel inscription, which had more truth when placed there than it has now: 'When you have sought the city round, yet still this is the highest ground. August the 27th, 1688.'

Continuing our way along Skinner Street, we shall come to the foot of Holborn Hill, where the old Fleet River, that now forms the sewer underground, was once spanned by a bridge, and bore upon its surface the broad barges of the merchants. It was filled up in 1733, and finally built over. Here will be noticed a new street, communicating with the northern suburbs, and advantageously substituting a commodious thoroughfare for the nests of vice and crime that until very lately occupied its site. FARRINGDON MARKET lies a little to the west of the street so called, and occupies a space of an acre and a half. There is a roofed avenue with shops all round, but vegetables form the chief commodity sold within its precincts. The Market itself having proven an utter failure, this spot, with other waste spaces in the same neighbourhood, are spoken of as likely to form the terminus of the Metropolitan Railway, an Act for which has been passed.

On the left, as we ascend Holborn Hill, is St Andrew's Church, which was rebuilt by Wren in 1686, and is further noticeable for a fine painted window over the altar, representing the Lord's Supper and the

Ascension. In the register of burials, under the date August the 28th, 1770, is recorded the name of Chatterton, the most wonderfully gifted youth the world has ever known. Here was interred another suicidal poet, Henry Neele, the young and imaginative author of the 'Romance of English History,' etc.

ELY PLACE, nearly opposite, was for many years the residence of the Bishops of Ely; and Hatton Garden marks the spot where the Lords Hatton had their dwelling from the time of the renowned Sir Christopher , who, as some historians assert, danced himself into the favour of the capricious Queen Elizabeth. THAVIEW INN was a residence for students as long back as the days of Edward III, and was granted in fee to the Benchers of Lincoln's Inn. STAPLE'S INN was so called from its being the place where the wool-staplers used to assemble, but it gave shelter to law students possibly before the reign of Henry V. FURNIVAL'S INN, the chief now of a formidable array of law-courts that once flanked Holborn, was in old times the town abode of the Lords Furnival, a title that became extinct in the reign of Richard II.

At Holborn Bars the City boundary terminates, and hence, by Fetter Lane and Fleet Street, we may retrace our steps to St Paul's.

DISTRICT V

We now proceed from St Paul's west-ward, and, to vary the route a little, we may suggest a digression towards the TIMES PRINTING OFFICE, situated in Printing-House Square – a small quadrangle at the back of Apothecaries' Hall, and easily reached by taking one of the tortuous thoroughfares leading southward from Ludgate Hill towards the water-side. A visit to the office during the time the huge machine is at work, casting off its impressions at the rate of 170 copies a minute, will present a sight not easily to be forgotten. From five till nine in the morning this stupendous establishment, employing nearly 300 people daily on its premises, is to be seen in active operation. The average daily circulation is 32,000; and the value of the advertisements is estimated at £110 per page of six columns. The first number of the Times appeared on the 1st of January 1788. The duties paid to Government for paper, advertisements, and stamps, alone, amount to £95,000 annually... Besides an extensive corps of editors, contributors, and reporters, for the collection and arrangement of local intelligence, correspondents at a liberal salary are stationed at all the principal places on the globe; and scarcely an event can occur anywhere, of which its emissaries are not prepared to supply the earliest and the fullest account.

APOTHECARIES' HALL, built in 1670, is next encountered on our way from Printing-House Square to Bridge Street, Blackfriars. Those who desire to have drugs unadulterated, may place the most implicit reliance on the articles here sold. The famous botanic garden at Chelsea, founded by Sir Hans Sloane, belongs to the Apothecaries' Company, who have the privilege of granting certificates to those desirous of vending chemicals, and for which they must pass a previous examination.

We now emerge upon Bridge Street, at the end of which is BLACKFRIARS' BRIDGE, forming an important link of communication with the opposite side of the river. Blackfriars' Bridge was commenced in 1760, and completed in November, 1769. The immense sums necessary for its construction were raised by loan, the City guaranteeing their payment by tolls to be levied on the bridge; but Government ultimately bought the tolls, and rendered it free. The entire expenditure was not less than £300,000; but it has been repaired since, at a cost nearly equal to the original amount. The bridge consists of nine arches, and, from wharf to wharf, is 995 feet in length and 42 in width. The removal of the balustrades, and the substitution of a plain parapet, somewhat spoiled its architectural beauty. The steamboat pier on the eastern side is the most important accommodation of its class; it has no pretension to ornament, but considerably promotes the convenience of the many thousand passengers who daily embark and land at this point. From the fourth arch of the bridge, one of the best views of St Paul's Cathedral can be obtained.

BRIDEWELL, a City house of correction, has its entrance on the western side of Bridge Street. The building consists of a large quadrangle, one side of which is occupied by a spacious hall. The prison affords accommodation for seventy male and thirty female prisoners, who are incarcerated in single cells. The sentences vary from three days to three months. The treadmill is kept in inactive operation. In 1849, there was here received, under the commitments by the Lord Mayor and the Aldermen, 812 disorderly persons who had been subjected to hard labour; twenty-five apprentices sent by the Chamberlain for confinement; and 287 vagrants who had been found begging about the streets of the City; making a total of 1,124.

Near here, now represented by a plain and unpretending pump, was one of the 'holy-wells' with which London anciently abounded, and which were supposed to possess peculiar properties and virtues if taken at certain specified times. It was named, after the saint to whom the neighbouring church was dedicated, St Bride's Well, and

Blackfriar's two bridges, road and rail, with St Paul's in the background. *(LoC)*

gave its name to the adjacent hospital founded by Edward VI, and which we have above described under its modern aspect as a house of correction. The churchyard at the east end of the church, or at the end of Bride Lane, is considerably elevated above the road, and the iron pump visible in the niche beneath, indicates the spot where the trusting dames of yore came to quaff the blessed waters of St Bridget. 'Cogers' Hall', a well-known debating tavern, is situated in Bride Lane; the society was first founded in 1756. The London house of the Bishop of Salisbury was near the church, and the name is retained by the adjoining square. Near to the end of Dorset Street, leading from Salisbury Square towards the Thames, was situated the 'Whitefriars' Theatre;' probably one of the earliest buildings erected in the metropolis for dramatic entertainments. It was destroyed in 1580, re-erected in 1629, and finally suppressed by the Puritans in 1648. The ancient sanctuary of Whitefriars, the Alsatia of James the First's day, and re-peopled by Scott in his 'Fortunes of Nigel', was about the spot now occupied by the City Gas-Works, which, with their gigantic gasometer, will be noticed on the west side of the bridge stretching along the river bank.

ST BRIDE'S CHURCH was originally destroyed by the same fire, in 1666, that consumed so many other public buildings, and was rebuilt by Wren in 1680, at a cost of £11,430. The steeple was then 234 feet in height; in consequence of which great elevation, coupled with the want of proper precautions, it was twice seriously injured by lightning. On the first of these occurrences, in June 1764, so much damage was done that it was found requisite to take down eighty-five feet of the spire. A more recent opening of the paved court affords a fine view of the church on its northern side. A house in the little quadrangle overlooking the churchyard, was one of Milton's London residences. It may be appropriately mentioned in this place, that the two obelisks at the Farringtdon Street end of Fleet Street, are respectively memorials of the notorious politician John Wilks, once alderman of Farringdon Without, and Alderman Waithman.

Passing up FLEET STREET towards Temple Bar, we shall find the courts and narrow outlets of this busy thoroughfare replete with interesting associations of the past. To the left are numerous avenues leading to the Temple; and on the right or north side will be noticed BOLT COURT, where Dr Johnson died (in the back room of the first floor of No.8); JOHNSON'S COURT, where he lived for some time, though it was not named after him; and CRANE COURT, where the SCOTTISH HOSPITAL is situated. This benevolent institution originated from a society formed a short time after the succession of James I, and materially contributes to the relief of distressed natives of Scotland who apply to it for assistance. The number of applicants is about 300 monthly. A few paces in advance of Anderton's Hotel (No. 164), a fine view of the western front of St Paul's is to be obtained; nearly opposite (No. 59) is the metropolitan depot and publishing office of Bradshaw's railway publications.

ST DUNSTAN'S-IN-THE-WEST will be observed on the right hand side. The demolition of the old church that stood here took place in 1830, and the present one, built by Mr Shaw, was consecrated July, 1838. The curious figures that struck the quarters on the projecting clock of the old church were bought by the Marquis of Hertford, and are now at the villa in Regent's Park. The tower rises 130 feet above the base. The interior is remarkably light and elegant, with some handsome stained windows. On the eastern side is a statue of Queen Elizabeth, placed in a niche, and which was brought from the western side of Ludgate, when that gate was taken down in 1766 ... These and the other architectural accessories are in the style of the time of James I, and form a very pleasing composition, harmonizing with the embellished house to the west. It was at this point that the Great Fire of London ceased its ravages westward. Two taverns in Fleet Street, 'The Cock' and 'The Rainbow', are worth mentioning on account of the reputation they have enjoyed under the same name for more than two centuries; the latter was the first coffee-house in London, and was established in 1657.

CHANCERY LANE, the well-known thoroughfare of legal repute, contains the official abode of the Law Society, founded in 1827 and incorporated 1845, at which time the present substantial structure was erected. Attorneys and solicitors are here registered. In Southampton

Buildings, at the Holbourn end of Chancery Lane, is the Mechanics' Institution, founded by Dr Birkbeck in 1823. The ROLLS liberty is a parish of itself. The Rolls, or records of the Court of Chancery, from the reign of Richard III to the present time, are here deposited, under the control of the Master of the Rolls. The Chapel dates back to the time of Edward III, but there is nothing now suggestive of antiquity in the appearance of the building. CLIFFORD'S INN, at the back of St Dunstan's Church, is an inn of Chancery appertaining to the Inner Temple. An old oak case in the hall, or antique workmanship, contains the ancient records of the society. It may give additional interest to a saunter through the courts about there to mention, that in GOUGH SQUARE, No. 17, on the north-west corner, Dr Johnson and his six amanuenses compiled the dictionary that bears his name. The whole of this neighbourhood is studded with large printing establishments.

Temple Bar, the western boundary of the City, was built from Wren's design in 1670. Statues of Queen Elizabeth and James I are placed in niches on the eastern side, and on the western are those of Charles I and Charles II. The interior is leased from the City by Messrs Child, the oldest bankers in London, as a repository for their ledgers and cash-books. The heads of persons executed for high treason were formerly placed on this gate, and many a mangled trunk has been here exhibited as a sacrifice to the cause which conscience had recommended the unfortunate victim to defend. The last heads exposed here belonged to the ill-fated participators in the rising of 1745, and one remained even as late as 1773. To show the power of the Lord Mayor, the ponderous gates of the civic barrier are shut upon all occasions of royal visits to the City. The herald then sounds a trumpet, and the mayor and corporation within demand by their marshal to know the monarch's pleasure, which, being communicated, the City sword is presented, the barrier flies open, and the cavalcade proceeds.

The Inner Temple Gate was erected in the fifth year of the reign of James I, the house above the entrance being decorated with the Prince of Wales' father, the symbol of the promising Prince Henry. It is now a hairdresser's, with an erroneous inscription alleging it to have been formerly a palace belonging to Henry VIII and Cardinal Wolsey. The

The imposing west face of St Paul's Cathedral.
Designed by Sir Christopher Wren to replace the previous cathedral building, which was destroyed in the Great Fire of London in 1666, St Paul's Cathedral has become an iconic symbol of the city. At the height of the Blitz, Winston Churchill gave special instructions that it was to be protected at all costs. This image from the 1890s shows the Cathedral darkened by the dirt and grime which covered so many of the city's buildings in the days of smog and coal fires. *(LoC)*

Above: Looking up into the great dome of St Paul's Cathedral. To obtain and support the weight of the high dome Wren's design makes clever use of three domes sitting one inside the other. *(Johnny Greig)*

Left: The statue in front of St Paul's is of Queen Anne. Note that the tower in the background has a blank opening while in the corresponding position on the other tower there is a clock. *(Man vyi)*

Opposite: One view of St Paul's that the Victorians didn't get to enjoy: looking north from the London Millennium pedestrian bridge which crosses over the Thames, leading to the Tate Modern on the south side. *(JC)*

Commercial London

Above: Cheapside – the name is derived from the Old English term for a market place – which connects with Threadneedle Street and the Bank junction.

Left: Looking past the corner of the Bank of England towards the Royal Exchange building. Designed by William Tite it was opened by Queen Victoria in 1844 and trading commenced in the following year. *(LoC)*

Covent Garden. London.

Covent Garden Market
Formerly a slum area, the square at Covent Garden was created by Inigo Jones as an open piazza, and became a fruit and vegetable market from the mid-seventeenth century. The current market building, designed by Edward Barry, was completed in 1858. *(CMcC)*

Oxford Circus, on the junction with Regent Street
In 1811, John Nash drew up plans for a strictly commercial thoroughfare. Regent Street was built between 1814 and 1825, with some major rebuilding taking place at the end of the nineteenth and beginning of the twentieth centuries. Today, every building on Regent Street is listed to at least Grade II. *(CMcC)*

OXFORD CIRCUS. LONDON.

The Palace of Westminster
After the old Palace burned down in 1834, its replacement was built in the richly decorative Perpendicular Gothic style contrived by the architect Sir Charles Barry with detailing by Augustus Pugin. The work was still underway when Bradshaw's Hand-Book was published and wasn't completed until 1870. *(LoC)*

Above: Westminster Steps and Bridge, looking southwards across the River Thames to St Thomas' Hospital. The bridge was, as Bradshaw points out, illuminated by lime lights which burned an oxy-hydrogen mixture to 'present a most brilliant appearance'.

Right: Westminster Abbey. In keeping with the Victorian's love of religious architecture, Bradshaw devotes several pages to an in-depth description of the Abbey. He refers to it as 'a magnificent edifice' and 'one of the principal features of London ... eminently deserving a most careful and elaborate examination'. *(LoC)*

Trafalgar Square

It was King George IV who engaged the architect John Nash to redevelop and improve this area of Charing Cross in the 1820s. The design of the present square is due to Sir Charles Barry and was completed in 1845. The 170-foot-high column was constructed between 1840 and 1843 to a design by William Railton. The statue to Nelson, the hero of the Battle of Trafalgar, is by E. H. Bailey. The square is the property of the Queen.

In this photograph, *c.* 1900, the National Gallery is shown on the left. *(LoC)*

Scotland Yard

Top right: The headquarters of the capital's Police force was originally located on Whitehall Place, with a rear entrance on Great Scotland Yard which is how the name came about. A bigger version was built on the Embankment overlooking the Thames in the 1890s. The Met moved to its current headquarters at 10 Broadway in 1967.

'Town Life' in Bond Street

This postcard, *right*, depicts some of London's dedicated followers of fashion doing what they do best – going shopping. *c.* 1905. *(CMcC)*

Kensington

Bottom right: The Earl's Court Road at the turn of the century.

Hyde Park

Above: Apsey House, on Hyde Park Corner, was the home of the Duke of Wellington. When combined with Kensington Gardens on its western side, Hyde Park covers 630 acres. Henry VIII had it enclosed to create a deer park and hunting ground. In 1851 it was the site of the Great Exhibition held in Joseph Paxton's Crystal Palace.

Middle: Rotton Row running along the southern edge of the park – the name is thought to come from 'rotteran', meaning to muster. Created as a private road by William III, it became a popular place for wealthy socialites to ride.

Bottom left: The last monarch to live at Kensington Palace was George II. *(LoC)*

The Albert Memorial
Situated in Kensington Gardens, directly north of the Albert Hall, the memorial was commissioned by Queen Victoria in memory of her husband, Prince Albert, who died of typhoid in 1861. Funded by public conscription, the memorial was designed by Sir George Gilbert Scott in the highly ornate Gothic Revival style. It took ten years to complete and stands 170 feet tall. *(LoC)*

London's railway termini

It was the rapid expansion of Britain's railways in the 1830s and 1840s that prompted George Bradshaw to publish his successful timetables and guide books. As to be expected, London sat at the hub of the network and the railway companies vied with each other to build prestigious terminus buildings which reflected their status and soilidity. The style of architecture varied enormously. King's Cross, *above*, opened in 1852 and featured two business-like spans in a plain style which appears surprisingly modern, whereas its immediate neighbour, St Pancras – a relative late-comer – was all about flamboyance and show. The difficulties in obtaining permissions and land to construct the lines into the city led several companies to share sites, as happened at Victoria station, *below*.

Above: William Powell Frith's painting 'The Railway Station' features a broad gauge train about to depart from Platform 1 at the Great Western Railway's Paddington station. The painting was first put on display in 1862, shortly before Bradhaw's *Hand-Book of London* was published, and its narrative style, suggesting the individual stories of the assorted passengers – from a bridal party to an apprehended fugitive – was hugely popular.

LONDON BRIDGE STATION.

London Bridge station was variously the terminus of the London & Greenwich Railway, the London & Croydon Railway, the South Eastern Railway and the London Brighton & South Coast Railway. Following the regrouping of the railways in 1923, it came under the ownership of the Southern Railway.

Going Underground
The Metropolitan Railway was the first underground railway in the world when it opened in 1863. Following the line of the Euston Road it was built by the cut-and-cover method by which a deep trench was excavated, lined with brick and roofed over to create a sub-surface line. The steam locomotives made condition almost unbearable for the passengers and they were later replaced by electric traction.

Fleet Street
Famed as the centre of the newsaper trade, this long street takes its name from the River Fleet which once ran to the walls of the City but was contained within an underground conduit in Victorian times. It is one of several rivers and streams that flow unseen, deep beneath the pavements of London.
Left: The *News of the World*'s offices. Most of the Fleet Street newspapers have moved their premises to Wapping or Canary Wharf. *(LoC)*

City churches
London is reknowned for its fine Wren churches. *From the top:* Temple Church, which he refurbished, St Andrew, Holborn, which escaped the Great Fire of 1666, and St Dunstan-in-the-East, which he repaired. Both of the latter two were gutted in the air raids of the Second World War. St Andrew has been refitted, but the main body of St Dunstan remains as a ruin with the grounds made into a public garden. *(JC & CMcC)*

The British Museum
The Victorians had an insatiable appetite for the new discoveries being brought to the hub of the Empire from the far flung corners of the world. The Egyptian Saloon at the British Museum houses a fascinating collection of ancient artifacts, inluding this large statue of Amenhotep III.
(A. Parrot)

Raphus Cucullatus
The extinct and flightless Dodo, found on the island of Mauritius in the Indian Ocean. 'A bird now supposed to be extinct, and only known by a few scanty remains.'

history of the Temple, which is perhaps more rife with interest and richer in old associations than any other locality in the metropolis, may be thus briefly condensed within our limits:

The Temple owes its designation to the 'Knights Templars,' who used to dwell within the precincts of the place, and who removed from their former residence in Holborn to the Temple in 1184, in the reign of Henry II when it was called the 'New Temple.' In 1313, at the downfall of the Templars, Edward II gave it to Aymer de Valence, Earl of Pembroke, after whose demise it passed into the hands of the Knights of St John, from whom the premises of the Inner Temple were soon after leased by the common law students, while those of the outer were leased by Walter Stapleton, Bishop of Exeter. On the dissolution of religious houses, the Temple became the property of the Crown, and remained so until, in 1608, King James granted it to the students of law, who have ever since retained it in undisputed possession. Their government is vested in the benchers, who comprise the most eminent members of the bar. Before any person can be admitted as a student, he must furnish a written statement giving his age, residence, and condition in life, with a certificate of his respectability, signed by himself and a bencher of the society or two barristers. No person in priest's or deacons orders can be called to the bar. The cost is for the Middle Temple, £34; and £100 must be deposited as security with the treasurer, to be returned without interest on being called to the bar. The hall attendances, including the dinners, cost about £1, 10s each term, or £6 per annum. You must eat, or at least sit down to, three dinners in each term, and you must pay for fourteen, whether you eat them or not. The call to the bar costs £86. Attorneys and attorneys' clerks are inadmissible as such, which of course is a virtual prohibition of any emolument being derived from the law while a student. The buildings are chiefly laid out in courts and terraces, and every floor forms one or more sets of chambers, occupied by different tenants, and in every worm-eaten rafter and crumbling brick there is a volume of bygone romance, rich in antique association, and teeming with historic lore.

There is in the tranquil retirement of these buildings, more especially such as look down upon a patch of greensward or strip of garden, embowered by shadowing trees, and enlivened by the cool melodious plash of the well-known sparking fountain, an appearance of the most delicious quietness and study-inviting solitude, contrasting all the stronger with the noisy region which we have just quitted ...

The Middle Temple entrance from Fleet Street is by a plain building with stone facings, built by Wren in 1684, in place of the old gate-house, which was built by Sir AmiasPaulet, who put Wolsey, when a lad, into the stocks for drunkenness and riot at a fair. Wolsey curiously revenged himself afterwards, by shutting Sir Amias up for several years in the same place. Here he re-edified his prison, and sumptuously garnished the outside with cardinals' hats, and arms, and sundry devices.

The Middle Temple Hall was built in the ear 1572, when Plowden, the great jurist, was treasurer. The rood of the hall is said to be the finest piece of architecture extant in London. The screen is an early and elaborate specimen of the transition style, quite out of keeping with the roof and everything around it, but well deserving notice. There is a general impression to the effect that this screen was formed from the spoils of the Spanish Armada; but the records of the Society show that it was set up thirteen years previously to the Armada putting to sea. In taking up the floor of the hall in 1764, nearly one hundred pair of dice were found, which on different occasions had dropped through the crevices in the flooring.

The whole area of the Temple is consecrated to the recollection of some of our greatest men who here took up their residence. It was here that the stern and uncompromising Hampden studied. Glance yonder at the dark winding staircase on the south-east angle of Hare Court, and you will be gazing on the very spot where, some two centuries bygone, the ambitious Oliver Cromwell occupied a dull and gloomy chamber at the summit. In the quiet nooks about the Middle Temple the brilliant old Chaucer wrote, and the wise and valiant Sir Walter Raleigh enriched his capacious mind; whilst in later days we find Congreve, and afterwards Oliver Goldsmith, occupying the same abode, No. 2, Brick Court, on the right, up two pair of stairs, and where he died, April 4, 1774. Coke and Selden, Christopher Hatton, Beaumont the poet, Edmund Burke, Dr Johnson, Cowper, Charles Lamb, and many other distinguished ornaments to their country's literature, were likewise inhabitants of this ancient seat of learning.

The Temple Church is the place of worship for both the Inner and Middle Temple; but through the original round church was built in the year 1185, the beautiful proportions of the building alone remain, and no era save the present is represented. A few years since the exterior and interior underwent a complete repair, at a cost of £70,000, and the old monuments of the Knights Templars were so redecorated and shorn of their ancient and interesting appearance, that the dust of time no longer remains on those figures. The fine old organ, made by Father Schmidt, on which Blow and Purcell played in long-contested rivalry, has vanished. The choral services, however, are now extremely well conducted every Sunday, and the visitor to London should not fail to be present on one of these occasions at least. The round of the church is open to all, but the choir is reserved for the benchers and students. The Temple Gardens, a large green parterre by the river side, surrounded by gravelled walks, trees, shrubs, and flowers, are historically commemorated by Shakespeare in his Henry VI (Part I); for here were plucked the two emblems under which the houses of York and Lancaster depopulated half the country. The rose has long since failed to put forth a bud in this locality. The range of Elizabethan structures on the eastern side, is called 'Paper buildings,' and occupies the site of a more ancient row, destroyed a few years back by fire. Fronting the garden-gate, which is open in the summer evenings, at 6 p.m., to the public, there is the Hall of the Inner Temple, possessing no features worthy of detailed notice. Its foundations were laid in the reign of Edward III.

The Temple is a thoroughfare by day, but the gates are closed at night, and admission is only granted to those passing to the chambers within.

With this we may appropriately close our walks round the City, and extend our next excursion to the busy maritime districts lying eastward of St Paul's.

London's docks have been described as the living 'heart' of the city, and in Victorian times they handled every manner of trade from all corners of the British Empire. Until the construction of new purpose-built docks to the east of the city, the ships came up the Thames to dock at the 'Pool' in central London. This continued right up to the 1960s and the advent of containerisation. *(LoC)*

PART TWO

The East

Third Day's Route

DISTRICT I

The eastern division of London will be found to present a marked contrast to the other portions of the metropolis, and will amply repay the stranger for any inconvenience he may experience in his visit to this thronged and busy region. Either by boat or omnibus he may accelerate his progress towards the Docks; andwe shall commence our description with an account of these vast repositories of our commercial wealth.

St Katherine's Docks, as the nearest, claim priority of notice. The most direct way is to pass at the back of the Tower, and through the entrance by the Mint. These docks, which include a space of twenty-five acres, ten of which are occupied by the water, were opened October 25th, 1828, the cost of construction having been £1,700,000. In the warehouses, vaults, sheds, and covered ways, there is accommodation for 110,000 tons of goods. There is the East and West Dock, a basin, and a connecting lock canal, which communicates with the river, and is so capacious that vessels of 700 tons burthen may enter at any time of the tide. A portion of the frontage is used as a steam-packet wharf. In clearing the ground to obtain the requisite space, 1,250 houses were bought and pulled down, including the ancient Hospital of St Katharine, to which it owes its appellation, and a population of 11,300 persons had to find 'a local habitation' in another locality. The capital thus employed was £1,350,000; but it has proved a highly profitable investment. Upwards of a thousand merchant vessels can be here congregated at one time. It is impossible to witness this scene of busy activity without being forcibly reminded that it is to commerce that England owes her pre-eminence in the scale of nations.

The London Docks, to which the entrance at the opposite end of St Katharine's will conduct us, were commenced in 1802, and opened 1805. The docks comprise an area of ninety acres, and cost upwards of four millions of money. The outer walls alone cost £65,000. In 1845 some new tea warehouses were erected, capacious enough to contain 120,000 chests. An excellent description by Henry Mayhew, as the Morning Chronicle Commissioner, supplies us with the following graphic details, which cannot fail to interest the visitor: 'As you enter the dock, the sight of the forest of masts in the distance, and the tall chimneys vomiting clouds of black smoke, and the many-coloured flags flying in the air, has a most peculiar effect; whilst the sheds with the monster wheels arching through the roofs, look like the paddle-boxes of huge steamers. Along the quay you see, now men with their faces blue with indigo, and now gaugers with their long brass-tipped rule dripping with spirit from the cask they have been probing; then will come a group of flaxen-haired sailors, chattering German, and next a black sailor with a cotton handkerchief twisted turban-like round his head. Presently, a blue-smocked butcher, with fresh meat and a bunch of cabbages in the tray on his shoulder; and, shortly afterwards, a mate with green parroquets in a wooden cage. Here you will see sitting on a bench a sorrowful-looming woman with new bright cooking-tins at her side, telling you she is an emigrant preparing for her voyage. As you pass along this quay, the air is pungent with tobacco; at that, it overpowers you with the fumes of rum. Then you are nearly sickened with the stench of hides and huge bins of horns; and, shortly afterwards, the atmosphere is fragrant with coffee and spice. Nearly everywhere you meet stacks of cork, or else yellow bins of sulphur, or lead-coloured ore. As you enter this warehouse, the flooring is sticky, as if it had been newly tarred, with the sugar that has leaked through the casks; and, as you descend into the dark vaults, you see long lines of lights hanging from the black arches, and lamps flitting about midway. Here you sniff the fumes of the wine, and there the peculiar fungous smell of dry rot. Then the jumble of sounds as you pass along the dock, blends in anything but sweet concord. The sailors are singing boisterous negro songs from the Yankee ship just entering – the cooper is hammering at the casks on the quay – the chains of the cranes loosed from their weight rattle as they fly up again – the ropes splash in the water – some captain shouts his orders through his hands – a goat bleats from some ship in the basin, and empty casks roll along the stones with a dull drum-like sound. Here the heavy laden ships are down far below the quay, and you descend to them by ladders; whilst in another basin they are high up and out of the water, so their green copper sheathing is almost level with the eye of the passenger; while above his head a long line of bowsprits stretches far over the quay, and from them hang spars and planks as a gangway to each ship.' This immense establishment is worked by from one to three thousand hands, according to the 'brisk' or 'slack' nature of the business. One of the most extraordinary and least-known scenes of London life is presented at the dock-gates at half-past seven in the morning. Congregated within the principal entrance are masses of men of all grades, looks, and kinds – a motley group of all who want a loaf and are willing to work for it; for the London Dock is one of the few places in the metropolis where men can get employment without either character or recommendation. The Tobacco Warehouses, rented by Government at £14,000 a year, are situated close to a dock of above an acres in extent, called the Tobacco Dock, and contain accommodation for 24,000 hogsheads of the Indian weed, each hogshead averaging 1,200 lbs. Near the north-east corner is a door inscribed 'To the Kiln.' Here the damaged tobacco is burned, the long chimney which carries off the smoke being facetiously denominated the Queen's pipe. The vaults beneath are appropriated to the reception of wines, and present in their long, dark, winding passages all the appearance of a subterranean town. The vast cellarage is arched with brick, and extends about a mile in one continuous line, with diverging branches of even greater length. There is stowage for nearly 70,000 pipes of wine and spirits. To furnish some idea of the quantity usually deposited here, we may mention that in June, 1849, these vaults contained 14,783 pipes of port, 13,107 hogsheads of sherry, 64 pipes of French wine, 796 pipes of Cape wine, 7,607 cases of wine containing 19,140 dozen, 10,113 hogsheads of brandy, and 3,642 pipes of rum. A tasting order may be procured from a wine merchant who has pipes in bond, or from the secretary at the London Dock House, in New Bank Buildings. Ladies are not admitted after 1 p.m.; and it is generally considered advisable for the uninitiated to preface their visit with a repast of substantial character, the very atmosphere of this vinous region having an intoxicating property. The entrances to the Docks from the Thames are three, viz., Hermitage, forty feet wide; Wapping, forty feet wide; and Shadwell, forty-five feet in width.

We can leave the Docks either by Pennington Street or Wapping. If the former, it should not be forgotten that in the Swedish Church, Princes Square, Ratcliffe Highway, Baron Swedenberg, founder of the well-known sect which bears his name, was buried in 1772. WAPPING presents all the characteristics of a seaport, the inhabitants being generally connected with the shipping interest; shipbuilders, sailors, and shop-keepers dealing in commodities for the supply of seafaring men, give a lively aspect to the place. Wapping was nothing more than a marsh till the time of Elizabeth. Execution Dock was the place where pirates were formerly hung in chains.

The Thames Tunnel, two miles below London Bridge, connects Wapping with Rotherhithe onthe opposite side the river. Cylindrical shafts, of 100 steps each, give the means of descent and ascent, and each foot-passenger pays a toll of one penny. This stupendous work is 1,300 feet long, and was completed in 1843, at a total cost of £614,000, having been commenced in 1825, and executed, after various delays, in about nine years of active labour. It is a magnificent monument of the skilful engineering of Sir [Marc] Isambard Brunel, the original projector. The principal apparatus was the shield, a series of cells, in which, as the miners worked at one end, the bricklayers built at the other, the top, sides, and bottom of the tunnel. With all the perils of the engineering, but seven lives were lost in the work, whereas forty men were killed in building the present London Bridge. The two arched passages are each sixteen feet four inches in width, with a path of three feet for pedestrians, and the whole is brilliantly illuminated with gas. The annual amount of tolls is averaged at £5,000 not sufficient to more than defray the expenditure for repairs. As an exhibition, the Tunnel is deservedly one of the most popular; and during the Fancy Fair that was held here under the Thames, in the week before Easter, 1850, it was visited by no less than 59,251 persons in five days.

Shadwell is next, and between the houses and the river bank there are numerous small docks and building yards; so that the passenger is often surprised by seeing the prow of a ship rising over the street, and the skeleton framework of new ones appearing at the openings. The Church of St Paul's Shadwell, was erected in 1821. LIMEHOUSE, where there is a pier at which the river steamboats call, had the interior of its fine old church destroyed on the morning of Good Friday, March 29th, 1850. At Limehouse begins the REGENT'S CANAL, which after several windings and tunnels through the northern part of London, joins the Paddington Canal. This Canal is the last link near London of the chain connecting that city with Liverpool. It has two tunnels; one at Maida Hill, 370 yards long; and the other under Islington, 900 yards long. The entire length is about nine miles, and it has a fall of ninety feet by twelve locks. It is now chiefly used for supplying coal to the northern districts. What is called the Pool terminates at Limehouse Reach.

The West India Docks extend along the banks of the Thames from Limehouse to Blackwall, and cover 295 acres. They were commenced in 1800, and partially opened in 1802. Warehouses of enormous extent are ranged along the four quays. There are two docks and a canal; the northern one, for unloading vessels, having accommodation for 300 West Indiamen; and the southern one, for loading outward-bound ships, receiving 200. They are now less exclusive than formerly, and ships from all parts of the world will be found together. The capital employed in construction was £1,380,000. At the highest tides the water is twenty-four feet deep, so that vessels of 1,200 tons burthen can enter. The whole space is enclosed on every side; all the buildings are fireproof, and the premises are well guarded by watchmen, so that the system of pilfering, formerly carried on to a great extent in this part of

The building of iron-hulled ships continueed at the Blackwall shipyards throughout the nineteenth century. This is the launch of the screw-ship *Himalaya* in 1853.

the river, is completely abolished. The carts or wagons which convey goods to town, are loaded from the backs of the warehouses without entering the dock-gates. Some admirable contrivances recently adopted, preserve the purity of the great body of water in the docks, and prevent the accumulation of mud … and the free transit of vessels ensured without inconvenience.

Blackwall, with its fine view of the reach of the river and the pleasant uplands towards Shooter's Hill, is an agreeable termination to a progress eastward. To the large taverns here, epicures flock from May till August to eat whitebait, caught in the glittering shoals about this part of the river, and turned within an hour out of the Thames into the frying-pan. With the usual accompaniments of cayenne and lemon juice, brown bread and butter, and the equally important beverage of iced punch, they make a delicious refection. A vast amount of iron shipbuilding is carried on in the district, being an art of not more than twenty years' growth. Here will be seen the clanking boiler works, the cyclopean foundries and engineering workshops, in which steam is the principal motive power. The Brunswick Wharf was opened July 6, 1840, and the constant arrivals and departures of the

Gravesend steamboats make it a very animated promenade. This is also the terminus of the LONDON AND BLACKWALL RAILWAY. Great improvements have recently been made at the Fenchurch Street Station. Some idea of the immense outlay upon this line which is only four and a half miles long, may be formed form the circumstance, that the portion between the Minories and Fenchurch Street (450 yards) cost £250,000. The EAST INDIA DOCKS are situated at Blackwall, covering a space of thirty-two acres. They were opened in 1806. The dock for loading outward bound Indiamen in 780 feet in length, and 520 in width. The gates are closed at 3 p.m. in winter, and 4 p.m. in summer. It is proposed to construct docks of vast extent, nearly three miles long, on the margin of the Thames, from a point a little below the Blackwall steamboat pier down to the Eastern Counties station, opposite Woolwich. The land is already in the possession of the promoters. The cost of the docks is estimated, with the projected warehouses, at £1,500,000 …

A locomotive on the Millwall extension of the London & Blackwall Railway. This line was originally built on a string of viaducts through East London, going from Fenchurch Street station, on the edge of the City, to the wharves at Blackwall. Much of the line has been incorporated within the new Docklands Light Railway.

DISTRICT II

ALDGATE, to which an omnibus from any of the main thoroughfares will serve as a conveyance, may be taken as a suitable point at which to renew our pilgrimage in this direction. The place derives its name from the 'old gate' that here guarded the entrance to the City, and which was taken down in 1606. The fictitious bank recognised as Aldgate pump, will be seen at the commencement of Aldgate High Street. Beneath the pavement is a curious chapel or crypt, presumed to have been a part of the Church of St Michael, and built in 1108. The whole addition of soil since its commencement is supposed to have been twenty-six feet. The inn on the left, called the 'Three Nuns,' is as old as the days of De Foe, and is mentioned by him in his history of the Plague. Northward from Aldgate Church are HOUNDSDITCH, BECIS MARKS, and DUKE'S PLACE, the great quarter of the Jews, and here they have settled in large numbers ever since the days of Oliver Cromwell. The MINORIES, a communication with Tower Hill, derived its name from nuns of the order of St Clare, or minoresses who had been invited into England by Blanch, Queen of Navarre, who here founded a convent for their reception. There are now several spacious shops; amongst which, the showy finery of Moses and Sons' establishment appears conspicuous. GOODMAN'S FIELDS, now a thickly populated region, are at the back of the Minories. Stow, in his quaint fashion, tells us that, in his time, one Trollop, and afterwards Goodman, were the farmers there, and 'that the fields were a farm belonging to the said nunnery; at which farm I myself,' he says, 'have fetched many a halfpenny worth of milk, and never had less than three ale pints for a halfpenny in the summer, nor less than one ale quart for a halfpenny in the winter, always hot from the kine.' The theatre in Goodman's Fields was where Garrick first appeared, October 19, 1741; and here he drew such audiences of gentry and nobility, that their carriages filled up the road from Temple Bar to Whitechapel. The theatre in which Garrick appeared was burned down in 1746 ... Whitechapel has nothing by the butcher's shambles to boast of as a characteristic feature. The church has no features of either architectural of historical interest. In the JEWS' BURIAL GROUND in Whitechapel Road, Rothschild, the great millionaire, lies buried.

The London Hospital, seen on the right of the road, was instituted in 1740 for the relief of maimed and invalided persons who are, from the nature of the avocations, subject to casualties. The patients are chiefly those employed about the docks and the shipping. In Beaumont Square, Mile End Road, is the 'Beaumont Literary and Philosophical Institution,' founded by Barber Beaumont, who died in 1841, and endowed it with £13,500.

Bancroft's Almshouses are on the north side of the Mile End Road, and were erected in 1735, for twenty-four poor men of the Drapers' Company, and a school for 100 boys. Bancroft was an officer of the Lord Mayor's court, and is said to have acquired his fortune by acts of extortion. He ordered in his will his body to be embalmed, and placed 'on a coffin made of oak, lined with lead; and that the top or lid thereof be hung with hinges, neither to be nailed, screwed, locked down, or fastened in any way, but to open freely and without trouble, like the top of a trunk.'

Bethnal Green. Passing up Globe Lane we can reach Bethnal Green, a large district chiefly populated by the silk-weavers of Spitalfields. Ten churches have been erected here within the last ten years; and model lodging houses have materially contributed to the comfort of the poorer denizens. The houses generally are miserably small, and densely inhabited. The line of the Eastern Counties Railway traverses the very heart of this squalid region. Bonner's Fields derived their name from the hall of Bishop Bonner, close by, and which was removed in 1845, to make way for the new Victoria Park. This Episcopal palace of the sixteenth century had been divided into five separate dwellings, but its general character was that of a substantial old English hall. Underneath the east wing was a small cell, where it was said that certain of Bonner's guests, whose theological tenets were not in harmony with his own, were wont to experience unwelcome hospitality. More probably, however, this cell was a cellar, containing the wherewithal to cheer the spirits of those who sat at the board above stairs.

Victoria Park is a most desirable and ornamental addition to this quarter, and presents a prettily-planted pleasure ground of 290 acres. It is bounded on the north by fields, on the south by the Lea Union Canal, on the west by the Regent's Canal, and on the east by Old Ford Lane, leading to Hackney Wicks. A handsome Elizabethan lodge has been built at the entrance, and an iron bridge of light and elegant construction adds to the general effect. A vote of £100,000 was granted by Parliament to defray its expenses. We can hence make a circuit round by the Hackney Road towards Shoreditch, or thread the mazy thoroughfares of Bethnal Green.

Shoreditch, notwithstanding its present uninviting appearance, was once a genteel district, much inhabited by the players of the court and those connected with the 'Curtain' and the 'Blackfriars' theatres. The parish church of St Leonard's, built by Dance, the City architect, in 1740, presents nothing exteriorly remarkable; but in the burial ground several distinguished personages are interred. Here the parochial register records the interment of Will Somers, Henry VIII's famous jester; Tarlton, the celebrated clown of Shakespeare's days; Burbage the actor, and many other original personators of our great bard's creations. In Shoreditch is the spacious terminus of the EASTERN COUNTIES RAILWAY. NORTON FOLGATE, a continuation of Bishopsgate Street Without, has nothing requiring notice but the City of London Theatre, built in 1838; and in Bishopsgate Street Without, has nothing requiring notice but the City of London Theatre, built in 1838; and in Bishopsgate Street we need only direct the observer's eye to a tavern called the 'Sir Paul Pindar,' and which was formerly the house of a generous merchant of that name, who gave largely towards the restoration of St Paul's. The Church of ST BOTOLPH, close by, contains a monument to his memory. The church was built in 1728; and the living, in the gift of the Bishop of London, is more valuable than any other in the City.

In London Wall was opened, in January 1850, the new GREEK CHURCH, the first ecclesiastical structure erected by the Greek residents in London. The exterior is plain, except at the north or entrance front, which is divided into two stories by a bold and enriched moulding, the lower story having an arcade of three arches, whence admission into the church is obtained. The interior is very loft, and in its general form differs widely from the usual arrangements. The cost was £10,000 – evidence of great liberality on the part of the Greek residents, as there are not more than thirty families residing in the metropolis. There is one service every Sunday, commencing at eleven o'clock.

Finsbury Square, built in 1789, and reached by London Wall, a vestige, in name at least, of olden London, brings to recollection its original appellation of Fens-bury, from the marshy nature of the soil before it was drained. FINSBURY CRCUS has on its northern side the London institution, originally established in the Old Jewry in 1806. The present building was erected in 1819. The library, which contains upwards of 56,000 volumes, is open from 10 in the morning till 11 at night, except on Saturdays, when it closes at 3 p.m. At the corner, by East Street, is the Moorfields Roman Catholic Chapel. Here was buried Weber, the composer; but in 1844 his remains were removed to Dresden. The service in this cathedral is of a remarkably impressive character. Hence we may pursue our way by the Pavement again into the City ...

Below: The Strand, the main thoroughfare eastwards through the City, *c.* 1900. *(LoC)*

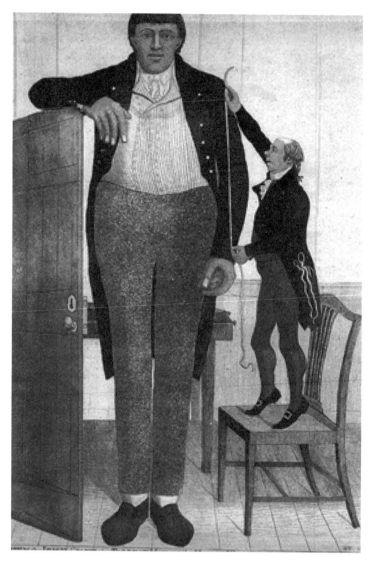

The Irish Giant: Celebrated as a curiosity in London in the 1780s, Charles Byrne's height was much exaggerated with claims that he was over 8 feet tall, but as Bradshaw confirms his skeleton is on display at the Royal College of Surgeon's museum in Lincoln's Inn. This reveals that he was a mere 7 feet 7 inches. *(LoC)*

PART THREE

The West

DISTRICT I

We proceed from Temple Bar westward, and enter the Strand. Before us is the Church of ST CLEMENT'S DANES, rebuilt in 1682 by William Pierce, who received the design from Wren. There was a church here before the arrival of the Danes, who destroyed it by fire. The poets Otway and Lee are buried here. On the right, by the pillars, is the entrance to CLEMENT'S INN, an inn of Chancery belonging to the Inner Temple. The hall was built in 1715. It was a residence for students in the reign of Henry IV if not before; and Shakespeare makes Falstaff say, 'I do remember him at Clement's Inn, like a man made after supper of a cheese-paring.' The inn is chiefly inhabited by professional persons not engaged in the law, and the rents of chambers are moderate, varying according to the altitude of the location. The kneeling figure of the negro in the garden was presented by Holles, Earl of Clare. Holywell Street is chiefly tenanted by newsvendors, second-hand book-sellers, and renovators of faded garments.

Essex Street, leading down to the river, where there is a pier at which the steamboats call, stands partly upon the site of Essex House, which the talented but rash and unfortunate Earl of Essex fortified against the authorities when he fell under the shadow of Queen Elizabeth's displeasure. The story of his favour, his imprisonment, and death upon the scaffold, it is unnecessary to repeat. A little beyond on the left hand side, is the STRAND THEATRE, a small establishment devoted principally to the production of burlettas and burlesques. The Whittington Club, which formerly occupied the premises originally known as the Crown and Anchor Tavern, being destroyed by fire a few years since, has been rebuilt upon the same spot, but the chief entrance is in Arundel Street. Adjoining is the entrance to Strand Lane, into which it is worthwhile deviating to see the Old Roman Bath, a genuine work of the Romans, built up for many years, and only opened at a recent period, when it was found exactly as it now appears. The sides are formed of layers of brick placed edgeways, and the bottom is paved with flat bricks, having over them a thin coating of stucco, and a thick basis of cement and rubble. The spring which supplies the bath, flows up directly from the earth at the upper end, and the action of the water having worn a deep hole there, a section of the pavement is visible. The water is pure and cold, and no doubt flows from the ancient 'Holy Well' of the opposite side of the Strand. The chamber which contains this remarkable piece of antiquity is one of a series of large vaulted apartments, of Roman structure, indicating considerable antiquity, notwithstanding the alterations since made.

The Church of ST MARY-LE-STRAND, or the 'New Church,' as it is sometimes called, though the present one was built by Gibbs in 1717, stands on the site of the ancient maypole. Although of small dimensions, it is elegantly constructed, and possesses architectural features of much merit. At the back of the church, in Wych Street, stands the OLYMPIC THEATRE, originally built by Astley in 1805, out of the timbers of an old man-of-war, burnt down in March 1849, and rebuilt and re-opened in the December following. The new theatre has the form of an elongated horse-shoe, with but few projections, so as not to present any interruptions to either sight or sound. The height from the pit floor to the highest part of the ceiling is 37 feet ... In Newcastle Street is LYON'S INN, so called from an old inn called the 'Lion,' which stood here, and was purchased by the law students in the time of Henry VIII.

Somerset House, which is now devoted to the business of Government, was the successor of a palace which was commenced by the Protector Somerset in 1546, and fell, after his death, into the hands of the Crown. The present building was erected by Sir William Chambers, and was completed in 1786. It is built in the form of a quadrangle, with wings, and has a fine entrance archway from the Strand. Opposite will be noticed Bacon's bronze allegorical sculpture of Father Thames, which with the statue of George III cost £2,000. The Venetian front, towards the river, is of striking magnificence, and its balustraded terrace affords a fine view of the river. This portion of the building is seen to the greatest advantage from Waterloo Bridge. Here are the Offices of Stamps and Taxes, the Audit Office, the office of the Duchy of Cornwall for managing the estates of the Prince of Wales, the Admiralty, and the General Registrar's Office. Nearly a thousand Government officials are employed at Somerset House, from 10 till 4 every day, at an aggregate annual cost of about £280,000. Under the open arches, at the principal entrance, are on the left the apartments of the Royal Society and the Society of Antiquaries; and on the right, those of the London University. The Government School of Design, which was originally held here, has been amalgamated with the South Kensington Museum.

King's College, established in 1833, is on the eastern side of Somerset House, and is an institution similar in its nature to the London University College, in Gower Street, but stricter in its theological character. Every pupil must produce, before admission into the school, a certificate of good conduct, attested by his last instructor. The age is from nine till sixteen. In the Museum of the College is placed the celebrated calculating machine, invented by Mr Babbage.

Waterloo Bridge, next seen, at the end of Wellington Street, is deserving a detailed notice, as a bridge which has been justly called the noblest in the world. It was built at the enormous cost of above one million of pounds, raised by a company incorporated in 1809, under the title of 'The Strand Bridge Company.' It was planned by the famous John Rennie, and opened on the anniversary of the battle of Waterloo, June 18, 1817. The bridge, formed of granite, has nine elliptical arches of 120 feet span and 35 feet high. The entire length is 2,456 feet, and its breadth within the balustrades 42 feet. The roadway on the summit of the arches is level on a line with the Strand, carried on by a gentle declivity on the opposite side. Foot-passengers pay a toll of one halfpenny. The increase in the number of vehicles passing over to the terminus of the South Western Railway, on the opposite side, has materially benefited the company's revenue. The view of London from this bridge is remarkably fine and strikingly suggestive. The features of the south bank of the river are comparatively flat and uninteresting, there being little else besides coal and timber wharfs and tall chimneys, that pour forth their volumes of smoke by night and day. But on the north shore numberless objects of interest attract the wandering eye. In the foreground Somerset House stretches magnificently along the river bank. Further on, the Temple Gardens, with their trees and verdure down to the water's edge, contrast refreshingly with the masses of brick and stone around. Glancing over the elegant steeple of St Bride's, the huge cupola of St Paul's is seen towering with majestic dignity above the angles of surrounding buildings; and behind these, among a cluster of spires and towers, rises the Monument, and further on the Tower, whilst the extreme distance shows us a bristling forest of masts dwindling into the hazy perspective of the Pool. Turning westward there is seen, on the Lambeth shore, the Shot Tower and Goding's lion-surmounted brewery, with the sombre dome of Bethlehem Hospital behind. On the opposite side is the Savoy, the beautiful chapel of which still remains, the graceful suspension bridge, the aristocratic-looking Whitehall Gardens, and the summit of the Nelson Column and the venerable towers of Westminster Abbey; whilst in a favourable state of the atmosphere, a misty line of hills may be traced onward, reaching to the very heart of the most picturesque and pastoral portion of Surrey. Waterloo Bridge affords, in fact, a complete panorama for the sight-seeker ...

On the north side of the Strand, in Upper Wellington Street, is the LYCEUM THEATRE, built by Beazley on the site of an older one, and first opened in July, 1834. The portico forms the entrance to the boxes; the pit entrance is in the Strand. The interior is very handsomely decorate, the shops which we now pass on our progress westward, are generally devoted to the exposition of some one of the multifarious shapes of art. To give some idea of the valuable nature of the objects placed in this way before the gaze of the street-lounger, we may mention that, in one establishment for the sale of pictures, near Exeter Hall, works of the old masters are frequently exhibited in the shop window, estimated to be worth £30,000. Mr Barratt, the proprietor, is, we believe, insured in one of the offices to more than double that amount. Savoy Street, on the opposite side, indicates the site of the Savoy, alternately a palace, hospital, and prison. The chapel of St Mary-le-Savoy was originally built in 1505, but it has since been frequently altered and embellished. Al that remained of the other portion of the Savoy was cleared away when Waterloo Bridge was erected.

Exeter Hall, where May Meetings are generally held, and some of our best concerts given, was built in 1831. The large hall will accommodate about 4,000 persons. A little further, towards Charing Cross, is the ADELPHI THEATRE, recently rebuilt, under the direction of Benjamin Webster, Esq., its present proprietor. At the back of the theatre is Maiden Lane, with a noted place of late-hour entertainment, called the 'Cider Cellars,' originally opened as a concert-room, underground, in 1730.

On the opposite side of the Strand is John Street, leading to the ADELPHI TERRACE, a large pile of buildings, built by the brothers Adam in 1768, on the site of old Durham House, and the 'New Exchange.' The terrace front is a conspicuous object from the river, and the spacious subterranean vaults and arcades beneath, give evidence of the extreme depth of the foundations. In John Street is the SOCIETY OF ARTS, first established in 1754, and removed here in 1774. There is gratuitous admission to see the pictures any day but Wednesday, between 10 and 4. The object of the Society is to promote the arts, manufactures, and commerce of the kingdom, by the judicious distribution of honorary or pecuniary rewards. The prizes are generally awarded at the end of May. BUCKINGHAM STREET has an old water gate at the end, built by Inigo Jones, the only remnant left of a princely mansion, built for George Villiers, the second and last duke of that family, whose name will be found perpetuated in the neighbouring streets, and an alley called 'Of,' to make this streetological title complete.

Hungerford Market, opened in July, 1833, occupies the site of an older market of the same name. Fruit and vegetables are sold in the avenues above, and the lower portion next the river is appropriated to the sale of fish. This is the direct entrance to HUNGERFORD SUSPENSION BRIDGE, which crosses to the Belvidere Road, on the Lambeth side. The steamboat-pier at this point is the great focus of the smaller steamboat navigation; upwards of a million passengers embarking and disembarking annually. Hungerford Suspension Bridge was constructed under Brunel's direction, and was first opened April 18, 1845. It consists of three arches, the span of the middle one being 676 feet, 6 inches, and in the centre is 32 feet above high-water. It is only second to the suspension bridge at Fribourg, in Switzerland; and

One of Landseer's four monumental lions in Trafalgar Square, *c.* 1900. *(LoC)*

the total cost, including the purchase of property, law, parliamentary, and other expenses, was £110,000. The quantity of iron employed is estimated at 11,000 tons. A toll of one halfpenny is paid on crossing the bridge. The length of the footway is 1,440 feet.

Lowther Arcade – Nearly opposite the entrance to the Market is the Lowther Arcade, a bazaar-like avenue, where shops seem to be turned inside out, and the stalls are crammed with French and German goods, interspersed with a prodigal display of Mosaid finery. It is 245 feet in length, and 35 feet in height, and was built in 1831. The improvements that took place at the same time in this part of the West Strand, have given a modern aspect of magnificence to the adjacent thoroughfares. CHARING CROSS HOSPITAL, at the corner of King William Street, was built in 1833 by Decimus Burton. The annual revenue is about £2,500; and in 1849, 9,000 necessitous patients were relieved through its agency.

Trafalgar Square – We now arrive at Trafalgar Square, occupying the site of the old Royal Mews, and a newest of wretched courts, that were all cleared away in 1829. The fine portico and Church of St Martin's forms a conspicuous object on the eastern side. The original Church of St Martin's – no longer meriting its parochial addition of 'in-the-Fields' – was erected in 1535. The first stone of the existing building was laid down in 1721, and it was completed by Gibbs in 1726, at the cost of £36,891, 10s 4d. The portico has eight Corinthian columns, and supports a pediment in which are the royal arms. The interior is richly decorated. The present burial-ground is at Pratt Street, Camden Town; but in the old burying-ground, now covered by the pavement along the side of the church, was interred, among many celebrated personages, the notorious house-breaker Jack Sheppard.

Northumberland House, seen at the south-west corner, by Charing Cross, was built in the reign of James I, and is the town residence of the Duke of Northumberland. The front is surmounted by a lion, the crest of the Percys; and in the magnificent apartments within are many valuable paintings by the old masters. The grounds at the back reach to the very verge of the river.

The Nelson Column, designed by Mr William Railton, afforded

an opportunity to both architect and sculptor to combine their efforts in perpetuating the memory of Trafalgar's hero. Baily's statue on the summit is eighteen feet high, and was set up November 4, 1843. The column is built on clay; the granite was brought from the coast of Devon; the figure is of Craigleith stone; and the entire cost of the monument was £28,000. The height is nearly 177 feet, and the pedestal alone has an altitude of thirty-six feet. On the four sides of the pedestal, represented in bronze bas relief, are sculptures of 'The Death of Nelson,' by Carew; 'The Battle of the Nile,' by Woodington; 'St Vincent,' by Watson; and 'Copenhagen,' by Ternouth. The relieve was cast in five pieces, and the thickness of the metal is about three-eighths of an inch.

The equestrian statue of George IV, at the angle of the square, is by Chantrey, and was originally intended to surmount the marble arch in front of Buckingham Palace. The cost was 9,000 guineas. Monuments in memory of the celebrated warrior, Sir CHARLES NAPIER, and of JENNER, the friend of his species, the discoverer of vaccination, are likewise erected on this spot. The fountains, with their granite basins, have been made the subject of much ridicule. They are supplied by an artesian well, sunk to a considerable depth at the back of the National Gallery.

The National Gallery extends along the whole of the north side of the square, and originated in the purchase by Government of the Angerstein collection of pictures for the sum of £40,000. The present structure was designed by Wilkins, and finished in 1838. The length is 461 feet, and the greatest width is 56 feet. The central portico is the main feature of the building, and the Corinthian columns are the same which used to support the portico of old Carlton House. The Gallery is open without charge to the public every Monday, Tuesday, Wednesday, and Thursday, and on Friday and Saturday to artists. The hours are from ten till five. During the last two weeks of September and the month of October the Gallery is wholly closed. Although inferior to the great continental galleries, this is still a highly valuable collection. There are many works of the ancient masters, with some fine specimens of our own Hogarth, Wilkie, Gainsborough, Reynolds, and Lawrence. As there are so many cheap catalogues, from one penny upwards, to be had at the doors, we consider an elaborate enumeration of the pictures to be quite unnecessary ...

The Royal Academy occupies the eastern end. It was constituted, December, 1768; opened its first exhibition in Somerset House, May, 1780; and removed from Somerset House, and opened its first exhibition in Trafalgar Square, May, 1838. Its principal objects are set forth as being the establishment of a well-regulated school of design for students in the arts, and of an exhibition open to all artists of distinguished merit, where they might offer their performances to public inspection, and acquire that degree of reputation and encouragement which they should be deemed to deserve. The Society consists of forty royal academicians, including a president, twenty associates, and six associate engravers. The whole of the funds are derived from the produce of its annual exhibition, which always opens on the first Monday in May. The receipts amount now to nearly £6,000. The average number of paintings and pieces of sculpture is 1,500.

Fourth Day's Route

DISTRICT II

Charing Cross, though now one of the busiest scenes in the metropolis, was, not more than two centuries and a half ago, within bowshot of the open country, all the way to Hampstead and Highgate. The Haymarket was a country road, with hedges on each side, running between pastures; and from old St Martin's Church there was a quiet country lane, leading to St Giles's, then a pleasant village sheltered by clumps of fine trees. The place exhibits at the present time far different features. On the side now occupied by the statue stood one of the numerous memorials of the affection of Edward I for his beloved Queen Eleanor, the cross pointing out the last spot on which her body rested. It was destroyed by the Puritans in 1647. The equestrian statue of Charles I was cast by Huber le Soeur n 1633, but it was not placed in its present situation until 1674. The pedestal is the work of Grinling Gibbons. Everybody remembers the story, how the statue was condemned by Parliament to be sold, and how John Rivet, the brazier, bought it and buried it under ground, making for his own profit a vast number of handles of knives and forks in brass, which he sold as made of the supposed broken statue, and which were eagerly bought by the Royalists from affection to their monarch, and by the Roundheads as a mark of triumph. It is not, however, so well known that the horse is without a girth, and that the king's sword was stolen by some felonious madcap when Queen Victoria went to open the Royal Exchange in 1844.

At the entrance to Craig's Court is Cox and Greenwood's, the largest army agency office in Great Britain. At the back of the buildings at this part is SCOTLAND YARD, so called from the kings of Scotland having been formerly lodged here. It is the headquarters of the metropolitan police, and was also the site of the PALACE COURT, removed here from the Marshalsea in 1801, and finally abolished on the 1st of January, 1850. On the opposite side is a range of public buildings of considerable importance, which we shall notice successively.

The Admiralty, built in 1726, contains the house and offices of those who superintend the marine department, and here a vast amount of correspondence connected with our naval affairs is received and directed. The two telegraphs that stood at the summit of the building, one communicating with Deal, and the other with Portsmouth, have been quite superseded by the quicker agency of the electric telegraph. Adjoining are the offices of the Paymaster-General.

The Horse Guards, a fine spacious stone building, with an arched opening into St James's Park, is easily recognised by the two mounted sentinels that no duty in the small recesses on the side. Here are the offices for the Commander-in-Chief, the Military Secretary, the Quarter-Master-General, and the Secretary of War. The War Office is also here situated, and from this source all army intelligence can be obtained.

Whitehall, nearly opposite the Horse Guards is merely the vestige of a royal palace, in existence from the days of Henry VIII to William

III, and of which the present building was the banqueting hall, built by Inigo Jones in 1622. It was on the scaffold erected in front of Whitehall, facing the park, that Charles I was executed. In the reign of George I it was converted into a chapel, which it still is, though never consecrated; and on every Maunday-Thursday the distribution of the Queen's bounty-money to poor aged men and women furnishes an additional temptation to visit the interior. The ceiling is lines with pictures on canvas, painted by Rubens in 1635, and representing the apotheosis of James I. there is a fine organ at the end over the entrance door, and lofty galleries are on each side. At the back of the building is a fine statue in bronze of James II, the work of Grinling Gibbons. In Privy Gardens adjoining was the mansion of Sir Robert Peel, whose untimely death, July 2, 1850, the nation had to deplore. In Whitehall Yard is the UNITED SERVICE MUSEUM, which may be gratuitously inspected every day by an order from a member of the institution.

The Treasury, with its fine massive exterior, built by Barry in 1847, is a spacious building reaching from the Horse Guards to Downing Street. Here are the offices of the BOARD OF TRADE, the HOME OFFICE, and the PRIVY COUNCIL. The COLONIAL OFFICE and the FOREIGN OFFICE are both in Downing Street. Sixty-five millions of pounds sterling are annually received and paid in this focus of government influence. Hence are fulminated decrees that sway the fortunes of countries afar off; and in its vast and busy chambers are projected the influential plans that affect the Legislature of our own. A voice from Downing Street has its echo at the Antipodes.

At the end of PARLIAMENT STREET is an opening to WESTMINSTER BRIDGE, built in 1750, and now in course of removal to give place to the new iron bridge, the southern half of which, alongside, was opened on the 1st of March, 1860, for heavy traffic. Besides the great advantage it possesses over the old bridge in being very nearly level with the approaches on both sides, a tramway for omnibuses and wagons has been laid down, and must, doubtless, afford great relief to the heavily loaded draught horses. A portion macadamised, is reserved for light carriages and saddle horses, whilst foot passengers, for the present, use the serviceable portion of the old bridge yet standing.

This bridge, when completed, will equally deserve a critical visit, after one to Waterloo, as both bridges will be remarkable for their level surface, and as points interesting to visitors for the views they afford. The old bridge was 44 feet wide, the present one, inclusive of the parapets, will be 85 feet; the span of the centre arch is 120 feet. Each arch, complete, will contain fifteen ribs, besides the decorative facing.

The space occupied by the numerous houses and buildings that have been, and that remain to be pulled down, will render the approaches of ample and unusual width to display this latest work of engineering skill, and afford a point of view whence the Houses of Parliament, and especially the clock tower, will be displayed to the greatest advantage.

The stranger should observe that the completed portion of the new bridge is lighted by the lime light, lately introduced. Ten lights, about one-third of the number of the old gaslights, present a most brilliant appearance. It is most interesting to know that in the lime light Newton's assertions are fully corroborated. The oxy-hydrogen flame burns the constituents of water, and water is the only product of such combustion. The chief feature and improvement in these lamps is the adaption of lime as the reflecting surface on which the jet of flame from coal gas plays, and which becomes intensified to an extraordinary degree, and makes the old gas burners, in close proximity, appear dull, as though they were burning in the day time.

New Palace Yard, the open space opposite Westminster Hall, derives its name from the ancient palace that stood here from the reign of Edward the Confessor to that of Queen Elizabeth, and of which Westminster Hall and the crypt of St Stephen's Chapel are the old portions remaining. OLD PALACE YARD, a little further towards the Abbey, was the place of execution for Guy Fawkes and the other Gunpowder Plot conspirators. The bronze statue of Canning, by Westmacott, in the little enclosure opposite, cost £7,000.

Westminster Hall, now the focus of our superior law courts, was originally the hall of a palace built by William Rufus in 1097, and considerably altered by Richard II in 1399. Around the hall will yet be seen on the stone moulding that the king's favourite crest, the white hart couchant. The law courts have been established here since 1224. The Hall is said to be the largest unsupported by pillars in the world, and is 290 feet long, 68 feet broad, and 90 high. The roof consists of ancient oak, and has an air of solemn grandeur. Within these walls, a king (Charles I) has been tried and condemned to death, the chivalry of England assembled at the banquet-table, and the coronation fetes celebrated of England's monarchs. To the right are the entrances to the courts of law, which are open to those who wish to witness the proceedings, and are thus to be distinguished: The COURT OF CHANCERY, the highest court of judicature in the kingdom, next to the Parliament; the COURT OF QUEEN'S BENCH, in which are tried matters determinable at common law between the sovereign and her subjects; the COURT OF COMMON PLEAS, for causes between subject and subject; and the COURT OF EXCHEQUER, for the trial of those questions relating to the revenue.

St Margaret's Church, opposite, and within a few yards of the north side of Westminster Abbey, was originally founded by Edward the Confessor (1061), rebuilt in the reign of Edward I, and frequently repaired since. It is the church of the House of Commons. The east window is a fine specimen of glass painting, and was a present from the magistrates of Dort, in Holland, to Henry VII, by whom it was intended for his neighbouring chapel. Having frequently changed hands, it was finally bought by the parish for the sum of 400 guineas. It represents the crucifixion, with, in the lower panels, figures of Arthur Prince of Wales, eldest son of Henry VII, and his bride Catharine of Aragon. The figure of St George, with the customary national emblems, make up an impressive and striking tableau. Caxton the printer, Skelton the poet laureate, Sir Walter Raleigh and some other persons of note, were here buried.

Westminster Abbey is open to public inspection between 11 and 3, and in the summer months between 4 and 6 p.m. The nave, transept, and cloisters are free. The charge for admission to the rest of the abbey is sixpence. The entrance is by POET'S CORNER, at the south transept. As one of the principal features of London, and eminently deserving a most careful and elaborate examination, we devote a proportionate degree of space to its description. The general dimensions are: length from east to west, 375 feet; breadth from north to south, 200 feet; height from the floor of the nave to the roof of the interior, 101 feet; height from the choir to the lantern, 142 feet.

A Latin cross, the favourite form in early times, marks the general outline of this wonderful structure; but the cloisters and numerous chapels added to the main building, take greatly from the original simplicity of the plan. The western front is formed of the entrance porch, stretching far inward and vaulted, and two square towers. A magnificent central window, shields, and other sculptural ornaments, invest this portion with an aspect of great splendour; but architects discover in its faults which can be defended by no rule of their art, and Sir Christopher Wren, to whom the charge of conducting its repair was entrusted by the Government, is accused of having erred in an attempt to combine the Gothic with the dissimilar style of Grecian architecture. The other portion of the architecture, with the exception of Henry the Seventh's Chapel, is early English.

The origin of this magnificent edifice is traced to a very remote period, and it is said to have been founded by Sebert, King of the East Saxons, in 616. This spot of ground was then a small insulated tract, surrounded by the Thames, and called Thorny Island. Edward the Confessor, and afterwards Henry III, enlarged and rebuilt it; and in January, 1502, Henry VII laid the first stone of the superb chapel which bears his name, granting to the Abbey numerous estates, which increased its wealth in proportion to the growth of its importance. Henry VIII appropriated a large portion of its revenue, and converted the Abbey into a cathedral, and Westminster into a city. Wren made extensive repairs at the beginning of the eighteenth century; and, since then, a complete restoration of this ancient structure has taken place, at various times, which has preserved it to us in its existing splendour.

POET'S CORNER is usually the first place that engages the attention of the visitor, and here it is advisable to wait until a sufficient party is formed for the guide to serve as a cicerone through the building. For this purpose a verger is always in attendance, at the stated hours ... It is here that the choicest genius of the land has received from admiring ages the acknowledgment of its worth. Here it is that our British poets seem to be still looking upon the world which they delighted and improved by their song; and he would scarcely deserve to share in the good diffused by the elevated strains of these mighty men who could stand in the midst of this chamber of soul – breathing imagery without a deep and generous emotion of thankfulness that such men have been given to his country. We select a few of the monuments deserving notice:

CAMDEN, the eminent antiquary (d. 1623), and for some time master of Westminster School, where Ben Jonson was one of his pupils. In his left hand is a book, and in his right hand are his gloves resting upon the altar.

GARRICK (d. 1779). Garrick is throwing aside a curtain, which reveals a medallion of Shakespeare, allegorically indicating the power he possessed of unveiling the beauties of the bard of all time. Tragedy and comedy are seen personified with their appropriate emblems.

ADDISON (d. 1719). A fine sculpture by Westmacott. The statue of our great essayist appears on a circular basement, surrounded by small figures of the muses.

HANDEL (d. 1759). The figure of this eminent composer, by Roubiliac, is elegantly wrought, and the features bear a faithful resemblance to the original. The left arm is resting on a group of musical instruments; the attitude expresses rapt attention to the harp of a seraph in the clouds above, and the oratorio of the 'Messiah' lies open at the sublime and appropriate passage, 'I know that my Redeemer liveth.'

GOLDSMITH (d. 1774). This consists simply of a bust of the poet, in profile, in high relief, in a medallion; and is placed in the area of a pointed arch, between the monuments of Gay and the Duke of Argyle. It was executed by Nollekens. Dr Johnson wrote the epitaph, which is inscribed ona white marble tablet beneath the bust.

GAY (d. 1732): Rysbrach. A winged boy exhibits a medallion portrait; and masks, musical instruments, and a dagger, are grouped around as devices, showing the various styles of writing in which he excelled, from fables to satire.

THOMSON (d. 1748). The figure of the poet is resting the left arm on a pedestal. In basso relieve, on the pedestal, the 'Seasons' are represented, a boy pointing to them, and offering as the reward to genius a wreath of laurel.

SHAKESPEARE (d. 1616): Scheemaker. The bard is shown leaning on a pedestal, the bust of Queen Elizabeth indicating the period in which he flourished. The flowing epitaph of Milton deserves to be read at leisure; it is a glorious sonnet, worthy of the genius of both; and as such its transcription in this place will be readily forgiven:

What needs my Shakespeare for his honour'd bones?
The labour of an age in piled stones
Or that his hallow'd relics should be hid
Under a starry-pointing pyramid?
Dear son of Memory! great heir of Fame
What need'st thou such weak witness of thy name?
Thou, in our wonder and astonishment
Hast built thyself a livelong monument;
For whilst, to the shame of slow-endeavouring art,
Thy easy numbers flow, and that each heart
Hath from the leaves of thy unvalued book
Those Delphic lines with deep impression took,
Then thou, our fancy of itself bereaving,
Dost make us marble with too much conceiving,
And so sepulchred in such pomp dost lie
That kings, for such a tomb, would wish to die.

SOUTHEY (d. 1843). A monument by Weekes, deservedly commemorative of this great critic, poet, and historian.

PRIOR (d. 1721). On one side of the pedestal stands Thalia with a flute on the other Clio with her book closed. Between them, on a raised altar, is a bust; and over that a pediment, with boys on each side; one with an hourglass in his hand, the sand run out; the other holding a torch reversed. Prior left £500 for the erection of this monument, which was designed by Gibbs, the architect of St Martin's.

GRAY (d. 1771). This is a fine monument by Bacon. The lyric muse is exhibiting a medallion of Gray, and, at the same time, pointing to the monument of Milton immediately above.

SPENSER (d. 1598). This is an exact copy of the original monument, which was of Purbeck stone, and so decayed in 1778 that its removal was determined on, and the present placed there as its substitute …

MILTON (d. 1674). A bust and tablet by Rysbrach, with a lyre beneath, encircled by a serpent holding an apple. It is peculiarly suggestive of Dryden's graceful panegyric:

> Three poets, in three distant ages born,
> Greece, Italy, and England did adorn;
> The first in loftiness of though surpass'd,
> The next in majesty, in both the last –
> The force of nature could no further go;
> To make the third she join'd the other two.

BEN JOHNSON (d. 1637). This monument, which was not erected until about a century after the poet's death, is a neatly sculptured tablet, by Rysbrach, with a head in relief, and emblematic devices. The expressive epitaph, 'O! Rare Ben Jonson,' is the more forcible for its quaint brevity.

Besides those poets we have mentioned, will be found monuments to Campbell, Rowe, Anstey, Dryden, Cowley, Chaucer, Phillips, Michael Drayton, Mason, Shadwell, and Samuel Butler, the witty author of Hudibras; whilst some others who have been buried in the Abbey on account of their rank, valour, or patriotism, have their names here perpetuated by some 'storied urn or monumental bust.'

THE CHAPEL OF ST BENEDICT is generally the first chapel shown. The principal tombs are those of Langham, Archbishop of Canterbury (d. 1376); the Countess of Hertford (d. 1598), sister of the Lord High Admiral Nottingham, engaged in the defeat of the Spanish

Armada; and several of the Deans. Close to the gate of entrance is the ancient monument of Sebert, King of the East Saxons (d. 616), and of his Queen Athelgoda (d. 615).

THE CHAPEL OF ST EDMUND contains twenty monuments, among which the most important are: John of Eltham (d. 1334), second son of Edward II, and born in Eltham Palace; a small tomb with two alabaster figures representing William of Windsor and Blanche de la Tour, children of Edward III, who died in infancy; Lady Elizabeth Russell, of the Bedford family, traditionally alleged to have died from the prick of a needle, and Lord Russell, her father (d. 1584), represented in effigy within a recess formed by Corinthian columns; William de Valence (d. 1296), Earl of Pembroke, and half-brother to Henry III. The effigy is of oak, and was originally covered with thin plates of gilt copper, exhibiting the earliest existing instance of enamelled metal being used for the purpose. Here there is also a gravestone to the memory of the celebrated Edward Lord Herbert, of Cherbury, who died in 1678. A fine bust of Richard Tufton, son of Sir John Tufton, and brother of the Earl of Thanet (d. 1631), is seen to the right as we leave the chapel.

THE CHAPEL OF ST NICHOLAS contains monuments to Lady Cecil, (d. 1591), a lady of the bed-chamber to Queen Elizabeth; Duchess of Somerset (d. 1587), wife of the Protector Somerset; Lord Burleigh's magnificent monument to his wife Mildred and his daughter Anne; and the Marchioness of Winchester. The large altar-tomb in the centre of the chapel is to the memory of Sir George Villiers and his lady, the father and mother of the celebrated Duke of Buckingham of the time of James I.

THE CHAPEL OF HENRY VII, which is the next visited, has been called the wonder of the world, and never, perhaps, did the genius of art, combined with the power and resources of wealth, produce a nobler specimen of architectural skill. It was commenced in 1502, the first stone having been laid in the presence of the monarch, and was completed in about ten years. King Henry lived to see the building nearly completed, and was buried in the sumptuous tomb which had been prepared according to his command for the reception of his remains. The splendour of this building, when its gates were first opened to crowds of devout worshippers, forms a favourite theme with the antiquary, whose imagination might well be moved at the pictures drawn of the altars covered with gold, of the cross of the same metal, the beauteous marble pillars, and the image of the Virgin bedight with sparkling jewels. With the exception of the plinth, every part is covered by sculptural decorations, giving to stone the character of embroidery; the buttress towers are crested by ornamental domes, and enriched by niches and elegant tracery; the cross-springers are perforated into airy forms, and the very cornices and parapets are charged even to profusion with armorial cognizances and knotted foliage. How magical must have been the effect when in the days of yore the sun's rays beamed through the orient colours and imagery of its painted windows, and tinged the aerial perspective with all the gorgeous hues of the prism and the rainbow.

The entrance is by a flight of twelve steps leading through the porch, which is upwards of twenty-eight feet in width, to the brazen gates of the chapel itself. Upon the summit of the small pillars are Henry's supporters, viz, the lion, the dragon, and the greyhound; in the spandrils of the middle arch are his arms, and in those of the small arches his badges. The architecture of the nave is equally beautiful and rich in ornament. A long range of statues imparts a grace and animation to the rest of the decorative appliances; and the noble arch which extends its magnificent span over the nave from north to south, forms in itself a splendid object for the eye to contemplate. The chapel consists of a central aisle, with five small chapels at the east end, and two side aisles, north and south. The principal object of admiration, both for its workmanship and its antiquity, is the tomb of Henry VII and Elizabeth his queen. It stands in the body of the chapel, enclosed in a chantry of crass, admirably designed and executed, and ornamented with statues of saints. Within, on a tomb of black marble, repose the effigies of the royal pair in their state robes. At the head of the chantry rest the remains of Edward VI, who died in 1552. In the north side are the monuments of Queen Elizabeth; the murdered princes, Edward V and his brother Richard; Sophia and Maria, infant daughters of James I, and George Saville, Marquis of Halifax. In the south aisle are monuments of Mary, Queen of Scots; Catharine, Lady Walpole; Margaret Beaufort, Countess of Richmond, the mother of Henry VII; and a monument on which lies a lady finely robed, the effigy of Margaret Douglas, the mother of Lord Darnley, husband of Mary, Queen of Scots. At the east end of the south aisle is the royal vault, as it is called, in which the remains of Charles II, William III, and Mary his consort, Queen Anne, and Prince George, are all deposited. In the vault beneath the centre of the nave, King George II and Queen Caroline, Frederick, Prince of Wales, the father of George III, and the Duke of Cumberland, of Culloden celebrity, are all interred. It will be interesting to mention that the remains of King George II and his Queen lie mingled together, the monarch having expressly desired that a side should be taken from each coffin expressly for the purpose. In 1837, when the vault was opened for the last time, the two sides which were withdrawn were seen standing against the wall. The stalls on each side of the nave are formed of oak, and are surmounted by richly carved canopies. These stalls are now appropriated to the Knights of the Bath, whose names and arms are fired at the back on plates of gilt copper. At the grand installation which took place in 1818, silken banners were hung round the chapel, bearing the arms of the distinguished men who then belonged to the order.

THE CHAPEL OF ST PAUL follows next in rotation. On the right as you enter, is a fine altar-tomb to LodowickRobsart, the standard-bearer to Henry V at the battle of Agincourt; Sir Thomas Bromely (d. 1587), who was privy counsellor to Queen Elizabeth, and sat as Lord Chancellor at the trial of Mary Queen of Scots; his hands are clasped in the attitude of prayer, and his eight children are kneeling at the base. There is also, among others, a colossal statue, by Chantrey, of James Watt (d. 1819), who is represented seated on an oblong pedestal, with compasses, and forming plans …

THE CHAPEL OF ST EDWARD THE CONFESSOR is the sixth, and by many considered the most interesting. It occupies the space at the back of the high altar, at the eastern end of the choir. The screen which divides the chapel from the choir was placed there in the reign of Edward VI, and though sadly dilapidated, is justly regarded as one of the most interesting remains of ancient art. It is decorated with a frieze, divided into fourteen compartments, and representing in elaborate sculpture the traditionary events of the Confessor's life. The first three are merely historical; the fourth represents King Edward alarmed by the appearance of Satan dancing upon the money collected for the payment of Dane-gelt; and in the next we have Edward's generous admonition to the thief who was purloining his treasure. The rest of the representations are so remarkably, that the curious in historical traditions will be amply repaid by tracing the events they display. The tomb of the monarch occupies the centre of the chapel, and the translation of his remains to this superb shrine was for nearly three hundred years commemorated as a grand festival. Offerings of the richest kind, gold and jewels, were presented at the altar; and the shrine itself, constructed of the most precious materials, is said to have presented, before it was despoiled at the Reformation, a specimen of the most sumptuous art. By order of James II, the coffin which contains the saint was enclosed within another, made of planks two inches thick, and bound together with iron. Surrounding this magnificent mausoleum of the Confessor are the tombs of Edward I, Henry III, Queen Eleanor, Henry V, Queen Philippa, Edward III, and Richard II. Each of these shrines affords some proof of the luxurious taste which prevailed in the periods when they were raised, and of the pious reverence with which the remains of the great and good were regarded by their followers; but on none does the eye rest with more pleasure than on that dedicated to Queen Eleanor, the consort of the adventurous Edward I. in all the dangers of that monarch's long and valorous career, she was ever at his side; and a tradition, that we hold it heresy to disbelieve, adds, that when in the Holy Land he lay almost in the agonies of death, she saved his life by sucking away the poison that had been infused by the dagger of the Saracen. When the tomb of Edward I was opened in 1774, the body of the king was discovered almost perfect, with a tin gilt crown upon his head, a sceptre of gilt copper in his right hand, and a sceptre and dove of the same material in his left; and in this mimic semblance of state he is now lying. The chapel containing the remains of Henry V occupies the whole of the east end of the Confessor's, and is supposed to have been erected early in the reign of Henry VI. Several relics of the monarch's warlike achievements are preserved in this shrine, and the very helmet which it is said he wore in his boldest encounters with the enemy. In addition to the monuments, this chapel contains some other objects of curiosity. The principal of these is the ancient chair used at the coronation of the kings from the time of Edward I, and which, within its seat, has the 'prophetic or fatal stone of Scone,' – so called from the belief of the Scots, to whom it originally belonged, that whenever it was lost the power of the nation would decline. In the year 1296 was fought that dreadful battle between Edward I and John Baliol, which decided the fate of the latter; and this celebrated stone was then removed with the royal jewels to London, where it has ever since remained. The stone is twenty-six inches long, sixteen inches wide, and eleven inches thick, and is fixed in the bottom of the chair by cramps of iron. The more modern chair was fashioned for Mary, Queen of William III. The painted windows demand attention, both on account of their great age and their curiosity as works of art. The glass of which they are made is not less than the eighth of an inch thick, whilst the figures, which are nearly seven feet high, are formed out of an innumerable variety of small pieces, so cut as to compose, with proper shades of colour, the form and drapery of the characters described. In the legend of Edward the Confessor and the pilgrim, the deep and brilliant colours of the glass, the beautiful arrangement of the drapery, and the noble expression given to the countenances of the figures, well deserve the admiration with which they are viewed.

THE CHAPEL OF ST ERASMUS is the seventh, and by this we enter the eighth chapel, dedicated to ST JOHN THE BAPTIST. In the former must be noticed the elaborately wrought tomb of Henry Carey, Lord Hunsdon, first cousin to Queen Elizabeth; and the tomb of Cecil, Earl of Exeter, and his two countesses. In the ambulatory is a fine monument to General Wolfe (d. 1759), representing the death of the hero in his victorious expedition against Quebec. Screens formerly divided the east aisle of the north transept into the chapels of ST JOHN, ST MICHAEL, and ST ANDREW. Among the tombs especially demanding notice are Sir Humphrey Davy (d. 1829); Thomas Telford (d. 1834), a colossal figure by Bailey, in honour of the architect of the Menai Bridge; and a monument – one of Roubiliac's last and best works – to Joseph Gascoigne Nightingale and his lady. The lower portion appears throwing open its marble doors, and a shrouded skeleton as Death is seen launching his dart at the lady, who has sunk affrighted into her husband's arms. With this portion of the Abbey the guide usually ceases to attend, and the visitor pursues his way alone.

Entering the north transept, the magnificence of the interior at once strikes the beholder with reverential awe; grand masses of towering Gothic columns connect the pavement with the roof, and separate the nave from the side aisles. A screen divides the nave from the choir, which is surrounded by a noble organ. The walls are enriched with a great profusion of sepulchral monuments, and above the line of tombs there are chambers and galleries, looking dreary and solemn in their antiquity, and only relieved by the transient sunbeam glancing across the misty height of the nave. The northern window is richly ornamented with stained glass, representing the Holy Scriptures, surrounded by appropriate figures. From this window proceeds a calm ray of light, very advantageous to the display of the finely executed pieces of sculpture on which it falls, lighting up the interesting memorials of those whose exploits of exertions deserve the notice of posterity.

In the NORTH TRANSEPT are inscribed tombs covering the remains of the statesmen Pitt, Fox, Grattan, Canning, and Lord Londonderry. The latter has a fine statue of Carrara marble, placed there in June 1850. Bacon's noble monument to the Earl of Chatham, Flaxman's portrait-statue of Lord Mansfield, the fine statue of Sir William Follett by Behnes, and a statue without an inscription, representing John Philip Kemble the tragedian, will be noticed among the other memorials of the illustrious dead. Under the organ-screen are monuments to Sir Isaac Newton and Earl Stanhope. THE NORTH AISLE introduces us to tablets commemorative of the eminent musicians Dr Burney (d 1814), Dr Croft (d. 1727), Dr Blow (d. 1708), Dr Arnold (d. 1802), Dr Purcell (d. 1697), and a fine monument to the unfortunate Major Andre, executed by the Americans as a spy in 1780. We cannot quit this solemn scene without recalling the exquisite reflections made by Addison, and which are as appropriate now as when they were suggested by the associations of the place more than a century ago. 'When I look,' says our delightful essayist, 'upon the tombs of the great, every emotion of envy dies within me; when I read the epitaphs of the beautiful, every inordinate desire goes out; when I meet with the grief of parents upon a tombstone, my heart melts with compassion; when I see the tombs of the parents themselves, I consider the vanity of grieving for those whom we must quickly follow; when I see kings lying side by side, or the holy men that divided the world with their contests and disputes, I reflect with sorrow and astonishment on the little competitions, factions, and debates of mankind; when I read the several dates of the tombs, or some that died yesterday and some six hundred years ago, I consider that great day when we shall all of us be contemporaries, and make our appearance together.'

Leaving the interior of the Abbey, we next pass through the churchyard of St Margaret's, and enter DEAN'S YARD on the left, a small square enclosing a green, which serves as a playground for the scholars of Westminster School. Part of the north boundary of the square is formed by the outer wall of the JERUSALEM CHAMBER, in which King Henry IV died. The CLOISTERS are almost entire, and filled with monuments. In them may still be traced the signs of monastic life. The doorways are pointed out by which the monks proceeded to the refectory and other portions of the building set apart for their retreat; and one can hardly trace these winding passages, looking so cool and sombre in the summer's sunshine, without bringing to recollection the customs that prevailed, the mode of worship, the manners, habits, and opinions that existed when the venerable walls of those cloisters bore no sign of decay. They are built in a quadrangular form, with piazzas towards the court, in which several of the prebendaries have houses.

The entrance into the CHAPTER HOUSE, built in 1250, is on

one side of the cloisters, through a Gothic portal, the mouldings of which are exquisitely carved. By consent of the Abbot, in 1377, the Commons of Great Britain first held their parliaments in this place, until, in 1547, Edward VI granted them the Chapel of St Stephen. It is at present a repository of the public records, among which is the original Doomsday Book, now nearly 800 years old. It is comprised in two volumes; one a large folio, the other a quarto. The first, beginning with Kent and ending with Lincolnshire, is written on 382 double pages of vellum, in the same hand, in a small but plain character, each page having a double column. The quarto column in on 450 pages of vellum, in single columns, and contains the counties of Essex, Norfolk, and Suffolk. This singular record is in high preservation, the words being as legible as when first written, though the ink has been dry since 1086.

West of the Abbey stood the eleemosynary or ALMONERY, where the alms of the Abbey were distributed. It was here, in 1474, that William Caxton produced the first printed book. The house in which he is said to have lived fell down from decay in November, 1845; and, since then, the miserable dens and low lodging-houses by which it was surrounded have been all cleared away. The Sanctuary, where criminals successfully sought refuge from the consequences of their crimes, was close by. The open space in front of Westminster Hospital still perpetuates the name.

WESTMINSTER SCHOOL, in Dean's Yard, is certainly the first in point of antiquity in the metropolis, if not in rank. It is understood to have been founded towards the close of the eleventh century; but in 1569 Queen Elizabeth restored it, and provided for the education of forty boys, denominated the Queen's scholars. From this period it has been distinguished by the erudition of its masters and the shining talents of their scholars. When Camden, the renowned antiquary, was master, Ben Jonson was one of his pupils. Dryden not only studied within these monastic walls, but carved his name on one of the forms – a relic jealously preserved; and Cowley, Cowper, Southey, Wren, Locke, and Colman, may be enumerated as some few of the great men educated here, whose names the world will not willingly let die. Every

Christmas a play of Terence is performed by the Queen's scholars, according to an ancient custom; and in this many of the sons of our nobility and gentry display their elocutionary powers to advantage.

The WESTMINSTER HOSPITAL, built in 1834, in the Broad Sanctuary, at the north-west corner of the Abbey, was originally established in 1715, through the exertions of Mr Henry Hoare, the banker in Fleet Street and was the first hospital founded and supported by voluntary contributions. The present structure is from the designs of Mr Inwood, and is capable of containing 220 patients.

Retracing our steps to Old Palace Yard, we pass the place which was the site of the Houses of Lords and Commons from the reign of Henry III to the destruction of both by fire, October 16, 1834. In Bellamy's 'Kitchen,' a plain apartment, with an immense fire, meat screen, and a continuous relay of gridirons, the statesmen of England have often dined, and enjoyed an unpretending chop or steak with more apparent zest than in their own palatial residences, where luxury and splendour are visible in every part. The room latterly devoted to parliamentary proceedings was originally St Stephen's Chapel, founded by King Stephen, and a portion of the old Westminster Palace.

ABINGDON STREET brings us to that noble edifice, the New Houses of Parliament, or the 'New Palace at Westminster,' as it has been appropriately called, being the largest Gothic edifice in the world. The architect, the late Sir Chas. Barry (who died suddenly, May 12th, 1860, and was interred in the neighbouring old abbey, on the 22nd of the same month), incorporated the entire establishment of the Houses of Parliament, the Courts of Law, and Westminster Hall, in one edifice, as being most conducive to internal convenience and economy, and to the grandeur and importance of the exterior. The first stone was laid April 27, 1840. The building covers a space of nearly eight acres. The river frontage is 900 feet in length, and divided into five principal compartments, panelled with tracery, and decorated with rows of statues and shields, exhibiting the arms of the monarchs of England since the Conquest. The terrace is intended to be appropriated to the exclusive use of the Speaker and the members of both Houses for air and exercise. This terrace, built of Aberdeen granite, is 30 feet in breadth, and extends between the wings at the north and south ends of the front, a length of 680 feet. Behind, the building rises in three distinct stories; the first a basement, which is on the level of the street; the next is the story of the principal floor upon which the Houses of Lords and Commons, the state rooms, the division lobby, conference rooms, libraries, and other principal apartments and offices are placed: and the third contains committee rooms and other apartments for the officers of the House. The central portion of the river front and the towers at each wing run up another story. The three principal towers are called the Royal or Victoria Tower, the Central Tower, and the Clock Tower. The Victoria Tower, at the south-west angle, is a stupendous work, and contains the royal entrance, 75 feet square, and approaches an altitude of 340 feet, being only 64 feet less than the height of the cross of St Paul's. The Central Tower contains the grand central hall, and is 60 feet in diameter, and 300 feet to the top of the lantern surmounting it. The Clock Tower, nearest Westminster Bridge, is 40 feet square, and with its belfry spire, richly decorated, is 320 feet high. The smaller towers give a picturesque effect to the river front, which, with that portion of the structure, can be best seen to advantage from the opposite bank of the Thames. There are nearly 500 statues in and about the building, and the most eminent artists in every department have contributed to its embellishments.

The royal entrance is at the Victoria Tower, which communicates with the Norman porch, so designated from the fresco illustrations of the Norman kings and their historic exploits. On the right hand is the robbing-room, fitted up with much magnificence, and to this succeeds a spacious and sumptuously decorated apartment 110 feet in length, 45 in width, and 45 feet in height, called the Royal Gallery, ornamented with frescoes descriptive of events in English history, and having windows filled with stained glass, and a matchless ceiling emblazoned with heraldic insignia. The Princes' Chamber, an apartment equally splendid, leads into the HOUSE OF PEERS, a noble room 45 feet wide, 45 feet high, and nearly 100 feet long. The peers assembled here for the first time, April 15, 1847. At the southern end, on a dais of three steps, and surmounted by a superb Gothic canopy, is the royal throne. The body of the house is occupied by a large oak table and the red woolsack of the Chancellor. The carpet is blue, powdered profusely with stars, and the carpet of the throne is red, variegated with roses and heraldic lions. The chamber is lighted by twelve windows glazed with stained glass, representing the kings and queens of England, and at night it is illuminated by thirty branch lights and four elaborately wrought brass candelabra. The ornamental frescoes are in six compartments, three at each end, and are the first on a large scale executed in this country. The subjects are – the Baptism of Ethelbert, by Mr Dyce, R.A., Edward III conferring the Order of the Garter on the Black Prince, and Henry Prince of Wales committed to prison for assaulting Judge Gascoigne, by Mr Cope, R.A. In the central compartment, over the Strangers' Gallery, is the Spirit of Religion, by Mr Horsley, the Spirit of Chivalry, and the Spirit of Law, by Mr Maclise, R.A. Between the windows, niches, eighteen in number, sustain statues of the barons who enforced Magna Charta. The walls and ceilings are enriched, besides, with gorgeous decorations exhibiting the arms and escutcheons of the sovereigns and chancellors of England. The prevailing colour of the ceiling is rich clue, bordered with red and gold.

The House of Commons is 62 feet long by 45 broad, and is also 45 feet in height, being purposely as limited in dimensions as possible, that the speeches may be distinctly heard by all present. The House sat for the first time in this building May 30, 1850. It is in a direct line with the House of Lords, at the north end of the structure. The Speaker's chair is placed in such a position, that supposing all the doors open between them, the Chancellor on the woolsack and the Speaker in the chair would exactly face each other. Over the Speaker's chair is the Reporters' Gallery, and over that again is the Strangers' Gallery. It is calculated to accommodate 277 members on the floor, 133 in the side galleries, and 66 in the lower gallery over the bar; making 476 in all. The chamber is lighted by six windows of stained glass on each side, and the floor is of iron, perforated for the purposes of ventilation. The ceiling of brown oak is reticulated into a succession of quadrangles with richly carved borders, and the panel-fronts of the surrounding galleries are of the same characteristic national material. The centre window bears the emblazoned arms of the cities of London and Westminster ...

The public are admitted to view the House of Lords by an order from the Lord Chamberlain, or by the personal introduction of a peer when the House is not sitting. The orders are procurable on Wednesdays, between eleven and four. A peer's order will also admit to the Strangers' Gallery, to hear the debates. To the House of Commons a member's order will likewise procure admission. Though the stately Palace of the Parliament cannot for centuries rival in its associations the humbler structure of St Stephen's Chapel, let us hope that it will never forfeit its highest claim to our admiration as the classical sanctuary of Britain's intellectual greatness, the chosen palladium of her proudest attributes – freedom, eloquence, and power.

Continuing our way along MILBANK, we may mention that this, in the time of Elizabeth, was a mere marsh, and Milbank was the name of a large house belonging to the Grosvenor family, that derived its name from a mill once occupying its site.

The Church of ST JOHN THE EVANGELIST, seen on the right, was begun in 1721 and finished in 1728. To Sir John Vanbrugh this architectural eccentricity is ascribed, and its four belfries have not been inaptly compared to an inverted table with its legs in the air. Churchill, the satirist, was for some time the curate and lecturer here.

The PENITENTIARY, observed a little beyond, was designed by Jeremy Bentham, and is octagonal inform, enclosing a space of about eighteen acres. It was built in 1819, on ground bought in 1799 from the Marquis of Salisbury, and cost nearly half a million. It is devoted to the industrial reformation of prisoners, and as such is the largest prison in London. All convicts sentenced to transportation are here for three months prior to the sentence being carried into execution. On the Inspector's report to the Home Secretary, the place of transportation is then indicated. About 4,000 criminals are every year thus doomed to expiate their offences. Admission can only be obtained by an order from the Secretary of State for the Home department, or from the Resident Inspectors.

We next arrive at VAUXHALL BRIDGE, begun in 1811, and finished in June, 1816, at an expense of £300,000. It consists of nine cast-iron arches, each 78 feet in span, and is 810 feet long. The toll of one penny is demanded for each passenger; and a steamboat pier below materially contributes to increase the traffic. Vauxhall Bridge Road will conduct us to PIMLOCO and the opulent region of Belgravia, where a new town round Belgravia and Eaton Squares has arisen within the last ten years. The whole of this vast territory, now thickly inhabited by the wealthy and the titled, and having long lines of palace-like houses spreading forth in every direction, was within the memory of many living a spacious open tract, known as 'The Five Fields,' – a place infested by robbers, &c.

CHELSEA NEW BRIDGE, certainly one of the handsomest of the many bridges which now span the 'silent highway,' occupies a position near Chelsea Hospital, and leads to Battersea Park, to the formation of which the bridge is undoubtedly due. This convenient thoroughfare was opened to the public in March, 1858: its cost was £88,000.

Hence we can take an omnibus back to Charing Cross, or stroll leisurely through St James's Park, by way of varying our return.

Fifth Day's Route

DISTRICT III

From Charing Cross we make our way across Trafalgar Square to PALL MALL EAST, at the corner of which is the 'ROYAL COLLEGE OF PHYSICIANS,' built by Smirke at a cost of £30,000, and opened in 1835. The portico, supported by six Ionic columns, leads to a spacious hall and staircase. In the library are some fine portraits and busts of the most eminent physicians. Admission can be obtained by orders from the members. The UNION CLUB-HOUSE adjoining, in the square, was also built from the designs of Smirke. Wyatt's equestrian statue of George III was erected in 1836. The horse is considered a fine specimen of workmanship, and the likeness to the monarch admirable.

The HAYMARKET, so called form a market for hay having been kept here as late as 1830, introduces us to the Theatre bearing the same name, and which was built by Nash in 1821. It has a stately portico supported by six Corinthian columns, and an interior handsomely fitted up. It is one of the best conducted in the metropolis. HER MAJESTY'S THEATRE, on the opposite side, is the largest theatre in Europe, La Seala, at Milan, excepted, and is calculated to hold 3,000 persons. The present edifice was built from a design by Messrs. Nash and Repton, in 1818, and is surrounded on all sides by a covered colonnade, supported by Doric cast iron pillars. The interior has five tiers of boxes, which are each either private property or let to persons of rank and fashion for the season. Many of the double boxes on the grand tier have sold for as much as £8,000. Visitors to all parts of the theatre but the gallery are expected to appear in evening costume, frock-coats and coloured trousers and cravats not being admissible. The season usually begins in February and continues till August ...

The Club-Houses, those most magnificent buildings where the most distinguished members of the worlds of fashion, politics, and literature, meet for the purposes of lounging away their spare hours in conversation, reading, and refreshment, are now around us on every side, and merit a passing glance. For the convenience of the stranger, we group them together in that order which from this point seems most desirable for observation. There are thirty-seven principal clubs in the metropolis, comprising nearly 30,000 members. At the corner of Suffolk Street is the UNIVERSITY CLUB-HOUSE, built by Wilkins in 1824, for members of the Universities of Oxford and Cambridge. The TRAVELLERS' CLUB, 106 Pall Mall, was rebuilt by Barry in 1832. The club is limited to 700 members, and each pays thirty guineas on admission, besides his annual subscription. The ATHENAEUM CLUB, standing partly on the site of Carlton Palace, was built by Decimus Burton in 1829, and is an elegant edifice of Grecian architecture, with a statue of Minerva over the portico. The number of members is fixed at 1,200, and they must have attained distinguished eminence in science, literature, and the arts. The CARLTON CLUB, Pall Mall, has been lately rebuilt by Sydney Smirke, with three uniform facades in the Italian style. It is exclusively frequented by the Conservative party. The UNITED SERVICE CLUB was erected by John Nash in 1826, and is esteemed one of the most commodious. It is of the Doric order, with a noble portico of eight double columns, forming the entrance. The REFORM CLUB-HOUSE, on the south side of Pall Mall, was founded in 1832, and built from Barry's designs. The exterior is remarkably fine. In the interior are portraits of the leading Reformers. The entrance fee is twenty-six guineas, and each member pays ten guineas' annual subscription. The number of members is limited to 1,400. At the corner of St James' Square is the splendid new building of the ARMY AND NAVY CLUB, built in 1840, from the designs of Messrs Smith and Parnell. There are 1,450 members, who each pay an entrance fee of £30, and an annual subscription of six guineas.

Situated on the spot where Carlton House formerly stood, and at one of the entrances to St James' Park, is seen the Duke of York's column, erected by public subscription in 1833. The column, 124 feet high, was designed by Wyatt, is of Scotch granite, and is surmounted by a statue of the Duke, by Westmacott, fourteen feet high. A spiral staircase conducts the visitor, on payment of sixpence, to a gallery affording a fine view of the Surrey Hills and the West End; but since a lamentable suicide took place here in 1850, the railings have been enclosed in a manner similar to the Monument. It is open from 12 till 4.

PALL MALL, so called from a game of that name, introduced into England in the reigns of Charles I, is a thoroughfare full of historic interest, and the clubs, already mentioned, form a distinguishing feature of the liens of stately edifices that adorn this locality. In the height of the London season, brilliant and well-appointed equipages, and all the appliances of wealth and distinction, are to be here seen rolling along in every variety and in every direction. One might suppose that a succession of brilliant fetes was going forward, and that the rank, beauty, and fashion of the metropolis were wending their way to some scene of unusual gaiety. Few would imagine that the fair occupants of the carriages were intent merely on lunging in some emporium of taste, and that the bustle and excitement were things of everyday occurrence. Many stately mansions here have been gradually giving place to the warehouses and show-rooms of the trader. The large brick house where the Duke of Schomberg resided, is now devoted to trade. The late residence of the Duke of Buckingham, the saloons of which boasted the presence of a galaxy of rank and beauty unparalleled in any country, has been converted into a club-house, called 'The Park Club,' and a little higher up was the residence (No. 50) of Mr Vernon, in whose house, the home and haunt of art, was stored the magnificent collection of pictures which the owner bequeathed to the nation. It is now also a club-house. THE SOCIETY OF PAINTERS IN WATER COLOURS (No. 53), where many distinguished artists annually exhibit their pictures, and the BRITISH INSTITUTION next door, where two exhibitions are annually given of living artists in the spring, and the old masters in the summer, add the attractions of art to the associations of opulence. The latter exhibition, opened in 1806, was the celebrated Shakespeare Gallery of Alderman Boydell; on the front of the building may still be noticed a fine bas-relief of Shakespeare between Poetry and Painting, executed by Thomas Banks, at a cost of 500 guineas. MARLBOROUGH HOUSE, on the south side, was built in 1710, for the Duke of Marlborough, by Sir Christopher Wren, and became the property of the Crown by purchase in 1817, when it was appropriated as the residence of the Princess Charlotte and Prince Leopold, who will now have a royal successor in the Prince of Wales. The stupendous Car, which was used to convey the remains of the Duke of Wellington to St Paul's, on the occasion of his public funeral, is here shown. St James' Palace was originally a hospital, founded by some pious citizens even before the Conquest, and was seized by Henry VIII in 1531, when he converted it into a palace, enclosed the park, and made it an appurtenance to Whitehall. The ancient brick gateway, by which we enter, is the oldest portion of the building remaining. The palace is still used for the levees and drawing-rooms of the court, for which its arrangements are better adapted than for a royal residence. In the courtyard adjoining, the bands of the foot-guards play every morning at eleven, and their able performance of the most lively pieces of music should be heard. The apartments in the several courts are chiefly occupied by those attached to the court. The CHAPEL ROYAL is on the right, between the colour-court, where the bands perform, and the Ambassadors' court. The building is oblong, and is divided into compartments with armorial bearings. Among the memorable marriages that have taken place in this chapel may be mentioned, that of George IV and Queen Caroline, her present Majesty and Prince Albert, and the Prince Frederick William of Prussia and our Princess Royal, which took place in 1858. The Duke of Wellington, when in town, was a constant attendant of the morning service in this chapel, and the seats are nearly all appropriated to the nobility, who may here feel that the mightiest monarch and the meanest serf must bow at the same footstool. The service is performed at 8 a.m., and 12 noon; a fee of two shillings is usually paid for admission. The choral service is chanted by the boys of the Chapel Royal, who are maintained and taught out of the revenues. The Royal Family no longer attend, the Queen having had a chapel attached to Buckingham Palace.

ST JAMES' STREET, a direct thoroughfare, leading from the Palace into Piccadilly, has some buildings worthy of notice. WHITE'S CLUB-HOUSE (Nos. 37 and 38) was established as a chocolate house in 1699. The club is limited to 550 members, and in its bygone days has been famous for the immense amount of gaming here carried on. BOODLE'S, another club-house, is No. 28. BROOKES', a handsome building, and the former haunt of the Whig party, is No. 60; it was established in 1764. ARTHUR'S (No. 69) derived its name from the original proprietor, Mr Arthur, and is of equally long standing. THE NEW CONSERVATIVE CLUB-HOUSE, on the west side, occupies the site of the Old Thatched House Tavern, and was built in 1845, from the designs of Sydney Smirke. The interior is magnificently decorated, and the apartments at once convenient and surpassingly elegant in their arrangements. A little further towards Piccadilly is the MILITARY, NAVAL, AND COUNTY SERVICE CLUB, occupying the house that until 1849 was Crockford's celebrated club-house, where a man a day was ruined, according to the boast of that notorious gamester.

KING STREET, leading from the eastern side of St James' Street to ST JAMES' SQUARE, the most fashionable in London, contains the ST JAMES' THEATRE, built by Beazley for Braham, and chiefly used for French plays; and WILLIS' ROOMS, where the renowned assemblies take place, under the world-famous distinction of ALMACK'S.

Entering St James' Park by the old palace gateway, we pass on our right STAFFORD HOUSE, the town mansion of the Sutherland family. It was originally built for the Duke of York; but in 1841 it was sold to the present possessor for the sum of £72,000, and the Crown devoted the purchase money to the establishment of Victoria Park. The Sutherland Gallery contains a magnificent collection of pictures; and in size, taste, and decorations, the interior of the mansion is unequalled.

St James' Park covers an area of eighty-seven acres, and from its oblong form is about two miles in circuit. It was first formed and planted by Henry VIII, considerably improved by Charles II, and by a succession of judicious alterations and embellishments, made during the reigns of George IV and Queen Victoria, has reached the present highly ornamental condition in which we now view it. The fine gravelled avenue, planted with long rows of stately trees, is called the MALL. The south side of the Park, ranging from Storey's Gate to Buckingham Gate, is still known as the 'Bird-Cage Walk,' from the aviary established there by James I. the Wellington Barracks, occupying a large frontage on this side, were erected in 1834. The open space in front of the Horse Guards, is called the Parade, and here regiments are frequently reviewed. Here, also, are two curious pieces of ordnance; on a Turkish piece, brought by our troops from Alexandria in 1798, and the other a large mortar, taken in 1816 at the siege of Napoleon, and left behind on the retreat, by Soult. Its extreme range was said to be 6,220 yards, and its weight is recorded at 16 tons. The enclosure, with its serpentine walks through parterres and shrubberies, and its ornamental lake, with islands thickly planted in the midst, is a favourite promenade with all who can avail themselves of its privileges, and on a Sunday afternoon is crowded with the inhabitants of the dusty city, who are athirst for the sight of green leaves and opening blossoms. Owing to a recent admirable arrangement, by which the trees and shrubs are labelled with their respective English and botanical appellations, an attentive observer may gain a few agreeable lessons in botany during his stroll through the grounds. In the year 1837, the Ornithological Society was formed in the metropolis, having, as the original prospectus modestly averred, 'no privileges to claim or offer, excepting those of rendering services to science, and contributing to the amusement and information of the public.' Their object was, to include within their collection every species of hardy aquatic birds, waders, swimmers, and divers, and this idea has been most successfully carried out. The Society's cottage occupies the eastern extremity of the island in the park, nearly opposite to the State Paper Office and the Treasury. The design, by John Burgess Watson, Esq., presents a pleasing specimen of the Swiss style.

From different openings in the park some fine views may be gained of the surrounding buildings, and the massive towers of Westminster Abbey look nowhere so well as from the northern side of the enclosure. Seats are placed at convenient distances for the use of the public, and the time of closing the gates is notified at the several entrances.

The Green Park, which extends towards Piccadilly from St James' Park, has been much improved of late years, and now presents a delightful grassy surface, with undulating slopes, of more than fifty-six acres in extent. From the highest ground there is a pleasing prospect of St James' Park and Buckingham Palace, beyond which may be noticed the distant range of the Surrey hills. The eastern side is bounded by many of the finest mansions of the nobility, among which may be successively pointed out STAFFORD HOUSE, the residence of the Sutherland family BRIDGEWATER HOUSE, the residence of the Earl of Ellesmere, built in 1849 by Barry, and having a fine collection of pictures; SPENCER HOUSE, the residence of the Earl Spencer; and a fine old-fashioned house, distinguished by its bow window and pink blind, where Rogers, the poet and banker, resided, since 1808, up to the time of his death, and forming No. 22, St James' Place. The road leading from Buckingham Palace to Hyde Park Corner is called Constitution Hill.

Buckingham Palace, the town residence of Her Majesty, having cost millions of money, was finally completed by the architectural additions and alterations made in the year 1850. It was first built by Nash, on the site of Old Buckingham House, in the reign of George IV, and first occupied by her present Majesty in 1837. The marble arch, which cost £80,000, and gave rise to such a diversity of opinions as to where it should be placed, no longer forms the portal to the palace. The metal gates cost three thousand guineas. The state apartments look out upon the spacious and diversified gardens at the back; the throne-room is sixty-four feet in length, and elegantly hung with striped crimson satin. The ceiling is richly emblazoned, and beneath runs a frieze of white marble representing the wars of the Roses, designed by Stothard, and executed by Baily. The centre of the eastern front is occupied by the Green Drawing Room, and is fifty feet in length, and more than thirty in height, with hangings of green satin. The Grand Staircase, the Library, and the Sculpture Gallery, have been newly constructed and decorated, on a scale of great magnificence. In the State-rooms are pictures by ancient and modern masters, of the highest order of excellence. On the south side is the chapel, originally a conservatory; it was consecrated by the Archbishop of Canterbury in 1843. There is a small Pavilion in the Gardens which contains eight fresco paintings from Comus, exquisitely executed by Eastlake, Stanfield, Dyce, Landseer, Maclise, Ross, Ewins, and Leslie, with an ornamental border by Gruner. The Royal Mews has an entrance in Queen's Row; here are kept the state horses and carriages. The Royal Standard floating from the top of the palace indicates the presence of her Majesty within its walls. Admission to view the interior can only be gained in the absence of the royal family, and then only by special favour of the Lord Chamberlain.

By traversing the broad avenue of Constitution Hill, or, which is far preferable, taking an angular direction across the sloping uplands of the Green Park, we shall arrive at HYDE PARK CORNER, where the busy traffic of Piccadilly, streaming westward to the suburbs of Chelsea, Fulham, Brompton, Kensington and Hammersmith, gives a lively and animated aspect to the thoroughfare at this point. Before entering Hyde Park, we must pause to take cognizance of a few notable features that surround this locality.

The triumphal arch at the left of Piccadilly was designed by Decimus Burton, and erected in 1828. It is surmounted by Wyatt's equestrian statue of the Duke of Wellington, erected by a public subscription of £30,000 in 1846, and upwards of twenty-seven feet high. Opposite there is another archway with three avenues for carriages, two smaller ones for pedestrians, and a fine screen of fluted Ionic columns, extending 107 feet, and forming a grand entrance to Hyde Park. ST GEORGE'S HOSPITAL was built by Wilkins, and has a spacious frontage 180 feet in length, with a vestibule in the centre 30 feet high, and surmounted by lofty pilasters. There is a theatre for the delivery of lectures, a museum, and about 340 beds for patients, divided into 16 wards. The present building was erected about 20 years since; but the existence of the hospital dates from 1733. APSLEY HOUSE, the town residence of the Duke of Wellington since 1820, was considerably altered and improved by Wyatt in 1828, and now ranks as a fine addition to this part of the metropolis. The ornamental architecture of the building is of the Corinthian order, and the whole is enclosed by a rich bronze palisade. The interior is magnificently decorated, and there is a fine collection of paintings by old and modern masters, the latter chiefly referring to the memorable day of Waterloo and its associations.

Hyde Park was originally a manor belonging to Westminster Abbey; but in the reign of Henry VIII it was acquired by the Crown, and fenced in for the preservation of deer. The open iron railing was placed round it in the time of George IV. The park covers about 400 acres, and in the height of the season presents every fine afternoon a lively appearance, from the number of splendid equipages and fashionable visitors that throng the drives and promenades. At the south-east corner by the archway we have just described is a colossal statue of Achilles, cast by Westmacott from cannon taken in the victories of Salamancs, Vittoria, Toulouse, and Waterloo. It stands on a granite pedestal, is twenty feet high, thirty tons in weight, and the cost was defrayed by a subscription of £10,000 raised among the ladies. It is inscribed, 'By the Women of England to Arthur Duke of Wellington, and his brave Companions in Arms,' and was here erected 18th of June, 1822. From the extent and convenient situation of the park, it has often been chosen for reviews of troops; but its selection as the arena for the grand National Exposition of 1851 will not only show the dawning of a brighter era, but convince the world that it is still better adapted for exhibiting the blessings of peace than developing the arts of war. The scenery of the park is varied, and enriched by several fine plantations and a winding stream of water called the Serpentine, fifty acres in extent. It was formed in 1733 by Caroline, Queen of George II, who caused the bed of a stream to be enlarged that flowed through the park from Bayswater, and fell into the Thames at Ranelagh. This stream was cut off in 1834, and the Chelsea Water-works Company now supply the deficiency. The depth varies from two to forty feet. At the east end is a waterfall made in 1820, and at its western end is a neat stone bridge by Rennie, of five arches, and built in 1826. 12,000 persons have been known to bathe here of a Sunday, and in the winter the frozen surface is a favourite resort of skaters. On the northern bank is a small but appropriate edifice built by Decimus Burton, as the receiving-house for the Royal Humane Society, who have saved many thousand lives by their gallant exertions. The Society was founded by Dr Hawes in 1774, and is supported by the contributions of the benevolent. On the south side are the Knightsbridge Barracks. There are seven entrances open to the public from six in the morning till nine at night, viz – Hyde Park Corner; Cumberland Gate, Oxford Street end; Victoria Gate, Bayswater; Grosvenor Gate, Park Lane; Stanhope Gate, Kensington Gate, and the new Albert Gate at Knightsbridge. The park is only accessible to private vehicles; hackney carriages and cabs being rigidly excluded. According to the hour which the visitor selects for his stroll, he can enjoy either the delights of a purely sylvan solitude, or the gaiety of the fashionable world, in which he will here be certain to behold the regnant attractions.

Kensington Gardens, so closely connected with Hyde Park that we cannot dissever their descriptions, were originally the pleasure-grounds attached to Kensington Palace, and have been much enlarged by successive sovereigns. They are now about three miles

A high-society picnic in Kensington Gardens. Judging by the clothing this photograph was taken in Edwardian times, *c.* 1905. *(LoC)*

in circumference. The entrances are: near Victoria Gate; another at Kensington Gore, adjoining the palace; a third westward of the first milestone on the Kensington Road; and a fourth near the bridge over the Serpentine. Pedestrians only are admitted; and to those who can enjoy the pleasures of a saunter through the umbrageous avenues and agreeable vistas which this place affords, there can be no resort abounding with more facilities for enjoyment. Between 5 and 6 p.m., on every Tuesday and Friday in the summer months, the fashionable champetre concerts of the band of the First Life Guards may be heard in these grounds, and generally draw together a large concourse of visitors. The grounds were laid out by Kent, the renowned landscape gardener; but within the last ten years alterations, that have proved striking improvements, have been made with considerable advantage to the public KENSINGTON PALACE, where Her present Majesty was born, and the late Duke of Sussex died, is a large brick edifice, with no exterior beauty, but within possessing some handsome apartments. It was bought by William III from Heneage Finch, Earl of Nottingham, and Lord Chancellor, and has ever since belonged to the Crown. A small douceur will generally prevail upon the housekeeper to grant admission; but since the greater portion of the pictures has been removed, there is really very little to be seen. Those who like to emerge at the Kensington Gate, will be rewarded by extending their stroll to HOLLAND HOUSE, on the north side of the road, and about two miles from Hyde Park Corner. The mansion, which is one of the finest Elizabethan structures we have left, was erected by Thorpe, in 1607, for Sir Walter Cope. It afterwards came into the possession of Henry Rich, Earl of Holland, his son-in-law, and by whom it was first called Holland House. The earl, who was a political waverer in the troublous times of Charles I, was twice made a prisoner in this house, first by Charles, in 1633, upon the occasion of his challenging Lord Weston, and a second time, by command of the Parliament, after the unsuccessful issue of his attempt to restore the king in 1648. He lost his life upon the scaffold in the cause of monarchy in 1649, and, within four months from his death, Lambert, then general of the army, fixed his quarters at Holland House, which, however, was soon restored to the widowed countess. Its celebrity as the residence of Addison, who became possessed of it by his marriage, in 1716, with Charlotte, Countess Dowager of Warwick, and the impressive death of the illustrious essayist here in 1719, need not be detailed. About the year 1762, the property passed by sale to the Fox family, and here the statesman Charles James Fox, passed many of the earlier days of his life. His nephew, the late Lord Holland, distinguished for his varied proficiency in literature, and his warm patronage of a genius, afterwards became the owner. The stone gateway was designed by Inigo Jones; the raised terrace in front of the house was made in 1848;

and the mansion altogether, whether as a fine example of picturesque architecture, placed in a park-like domain, or as a place of historical fame and association with literature and art, is invested with the highest interest.

The South Kensington Museum has added largely to the attractions of this favourite portion of the metropolis. The School of Design, originally commenced in Somerset House, after gradually increasing in extent and usefulness, has now found a most appropriate and commodious home at South Kensington. A large collection of objects relating to education, architecture, and trade, of pictures, ornamental art, and models of patented inventions, is open to the public, daily, from 10 till 4, and from 7 till 10 in the evenings of Mondays and Thursdays, excepting holidays. The admission is perfectly free on Mondays, Tuesdays, and Saturdays; on Wednesdays, Thursdays, and Fridays, a charge of 6d is made for each person. Some choice pictures are here exhibited, including the Vernon and Turner Collection, removed from Marlbro' House. The Library of Art is open daily from 11 till 9 free to the regular students. Occasional students are admitted upon payment of 6d, which entitles to entrance for six days from the day of payment. The establishment of the Museum, which was brought about by the Commissioners for the Great Exhibition of 1851, bids fair to give additional interest and importance and importance to this already-attractive locality.

We may hence, by omnibus, return through Piccadilly to Charing Cross.

Piccadilly is shown in a map of London of the time of Queen Elizabeth as a rudely defined road out of the town, with one or two houses at the angle where the road, which afterwards became Regent Street, turned off, and a windmill a little to the east of this, the recollection of which is still preserved in Windmill Street. The origin of the name seems uncertain; but it was thought by some, at the commencement of the seventeenth century, to have been given to a noted house there as being the skirt or fringe of the town – a picardill having been a kind of stiff collar or fringe to the skirt of a garment. At the corner of DOWN STREET is the mansion, finished in 1850, of Henry Thomas Hope,

The hustle and bustle of Piccadilly Circus. The statue did not appear until 1893; referred to as Eros it is actually Anteros, the Greek god of requited love. *(LoC)*

Esq., and erected under the joint superintendence of M. Dusillion a French architect, and Professor Donaldson. It has a frontage of 70 feet in Piccadilly, and 64 feet in Down Street. The total height from the level of the street to the top of the balustrade is 63 feet. The building is enclosed with a handsome iron railing, cast in Paris for the purpose … The collection of pictures is extremely valuable. Clarges Street was built in 1717, and was so called after Sir Walter Clarges, the nephew of Anne, wife of General Monk. DEVONSHIRE HOUSE, by STRATTO STREET, is an old brick mansion built by Kent, in 1738, for William Cavendish, third duke of Devonshire, at a cost of £25,000. The old entrance, taken down in 1840, was by a flight of steps on each side. The gardens extended northward to those of Lansdowne House, in Berkeley Square. In Stratton Street, built 1695, and called after the

Baron Berkeley, of Stratton, in Cornwall, lived Mrs Coutts, afterwards Duchess of St Albans. The House (No. 1), is now the residence of Miss Angela Burdett Coutts, understood to be the wealthiest heiress in the kingdom. BERKELEY STREET leads to the aristocratic Berkeley Square, where is situated the noble mansion of the Marquis of Lansdowne. There is here a fine gallery 100 feet in length, filled with antique statues and busts. ARLINGTON STREET, on the opposite side, contains the mansions of the Duke of Beaufort (No. 22), the Marquis of Salisbury (no. 20), and the Earl of Yarborough (No. 17). Next door was the mansion (No. 16) of the Duke of Rutland, where the Duke of York died in 1827. In DOVER STREET is Ashburnham House (No. 80), the customary residence of the Russian Ambassador. ALBEMARLE STREET contains the ROYAL INSTITUTION, so famous for the weekly lectures on chemical science by Professors Faraday and Brande. It was established in 1799, and a handsome facade of fourteen fluted Corinthian columns, by Vulliamy, was added to the building in 1836. The cost of this tasteful embellishment was £1,853. An admission fee of five guineas, and an annual subscription of five guineas, entitle a member, who must be balloted for, to enjoy the privileges of the Institution. On the ground floor the principal apartments are, a newspaper room, a small library, and a cabinet of minerals. On the first floor is the apparatus room, communicating with the theatre, which will accommodate 900 persons. On the same floor is a spacious and valuable library. The laboratory on the basement story is fitted up on a scale of magnitude and completeness not before attempted in this country. In this apartment is the large galvanic apparatus with which Sir Humphrey Davy made his famous discovery of the composition of the fixed alkalies.

Burlington Arcade, a favourite lounge, and fitted up with some tasty shops, is upwards of 200 yards in length, and has a bazaar attached. It was originally built in 1819, sustained some few years back considerable injury by fire, and is now re-embellished. At night, when the shops are illuminated, the vista has a pretty effect. It is a thoroughfare into Cork Street. BURLINGTON HOUSE adjoining is almost screened from the sight of the passenger by a brick wall, behind which is a

Burlington Arcade, but alas that isn't Burlington Bertie of music hall fame. *(CMcC)*

spacious court-yard. The first house was built about 1650, and when Lord Burlington was asked why he built his house so far out of town, he replied, more like a peer than a prophet, 'because he was determined to have no building beyond him.' In 1785, when the title became extinct, the house became the property of the Dukes of Devonshire. THE ALBANY, a series of chambers on a superior, scale, deserves notice for the number of eminent literary men who have been its inhabitants, and amongst whom may be mentioned Monk Lewis, Canning, Byron, and Bulwer. The mansion in the centre was designed by Sir W. Chambers for the first Viscount Melbourne, who afterwards exchanged it with the Duke of York and Albany – whence its name – for Melbourne House, Whitehall. THE EGYPTIAN HALL, on the opposite side the way, owes its appellation to its style of architecture, and is celebrated as the spot where Albert Smith has, for nearly five years, ascended Mont Blanc daily, to the delight and amusement of thousands of visitors. The entertainment was certainly the most unique in London.

St James' Church was built by Wren in 1684, at the expense of Henry Jermyn, Earl of St Alban, from whom the adjacent street derives its appellation. The interior is of exquisite workmanship, and has a fine organ intended by James II for his popish chapel at Whitehall, and given to this church by his daughter Mary. At the east end of the chancel a new painted window, representing the crucifixion, was erected in 1846. In the churchyard adjoining lie Arbuthnot the wit, Akenside the poet, Dodsley the Bookseller, Gillray the caricaturist, and Vandervelde the painter. Here, and at St George's, Hanover Square, most of the fashionable marriages are solemnized. Hence we pass down the Haymarket, and again reach Charing Cross.

Sixth Day's Route

DISTRICT IV

From Charing Cross we now pursue the opposite direction of ST MARTIN'S LANE, noticing at the back of the National Gallery the new structure built and opened in 1849, called the ST MARTIN'S BATHS AND WASHHOUSES, and of which, in the first six months, no less than 106,760 persons availed themselves. At the end is CRANBOURNE STREET, that, in March 1844, was opened as a broad and commodious thoroughfare, communicating with Long Acre, and supplanting the former narrow outlet of Cranbourne Alley, which for so many years maintained a celebrity for straw bonnets and cheap millinery. We are thus introduced to LEICESTER SQUARE, so called from the stately mansion built by Robert Sidney, Earl of Leicester, that occupied its northern side, and which was frequently tenanted by branches of the royal family until the reign of George III. The square has a dingy, dreary aspect, and will soon disappear before the onward progress of improvement. In the centre is the large building erected by Mr Wyld for the exhibition of his gigantic model of the earth. Around the square are some popular exhibitions and taverns of repute.

BURFORD'S PANORAMA, and the WESTERN LITERARY AND SCIENTIFIC INSTITUTION, established in 1825, are here situated. On the south side, by St Martin's Street, lived Sir Isaac Newton; and Hogarth and Sir Joshua Reynolds were also inhabitants of houses on the eastern and western sides of the square.

Coventry Street, to which we are now brought, leads direct to Piccadilly. To give some idea of the immense cost involved in disturbing the old thoroughfares, we may mention that when the houses were taken down here in 1844, to form the present improved avenue, no less than £71,827 was paid to the Marquis of Salisbury for his claims upon the estate, and upwards of £100,000 was distributed among the shopkeepers, for the good-will of their respective establishments. In PRINCE'S STREET will be remarked the Church of ST ANNE'S, SOHO, the tower and spire of which, built in 1686 by Hakewell, enjoy the unenviable distinction of being the ugliest in London. The whole of this district is thickly crowded with foreigners, who, settling in this locality, have given quite a continental tone to the coffee-houses and dining-rooms of the neighbourhood.

Hence we continue along Coventry Street till we arrive at the REGENT CIRCUS, where a fine view of the splendid avenue of Regent Street becomes apparent, linking St James' Park with the Regent's Park by nearly two miles of mansion-like shops and palace-like mansions.

Regent Street was designed by Nash, and commenced under his direction in 1816. The houses in this magnificent thoroughfare are from the designs of Nash, Soane, Repton, Decimus Burton, and other architects, producing an extent and variety of architectural display unparalleled in Europe. The shops are of unequalled beauty, and unrivalled for the opulence of their contents. The quadrant was constructed for the purpose of avoiding the obliquity of the turning; but the shadow of the colonnade being found to interfere with the interests of the shopkeepers beneath, the 145 stately cast-iron columns that supported it were removed at the latter end of 1848, and the present architectural embellishments substituted. The building surmounted by the colossal figure of Britannia is the COUNTY FIRE OFFICE, founded by Barber Beaumont, and built in 1819. The attractions of the shop-windows, which, of course, are too varied to particularise, will be found amply sufficient to engage the attention of the stranger; but, to make our route more complete as well as more interesting, we shall notice as we proceed the places that abut on the thoroughfare, in addition to those that fall in the direct line of progress.

A new building called the LONDON CRYSTAL PALACE, to form a Bazaar, is just completed, close to the Regent Circus, mainly formed of iron and glass, for the exhibition and sale of choice specimens of manufacture. A large photographic establishment forms one of the principal features of this new lounge, and in addition to the display of wares, there is a conservatory, aquarium, and aviary attached. The principal entrance is in Oxford Street, two doors from Regent Street, the carriage entrance being in John Street, Oxford Street. The whole has been designed by the celebrated Owen Jones, the architect. ST JAMES' MUSIC HALL, erected for concerts, scientific meetings, public dinners, &c., has its main entrance at 27, Piccadilly, and 73, Regent Street. It is the third, in point of size, of the Halls used for these purposes in London, Exeter Hall, and the Surrey Gardens Music Hall being somewhat larger. This hall affords sitting accommodation for about 2,500 persons …

Golden Square is a small and not particularly verdant area on the same side as WARWICK STREET, where a fine Roman Catholic chapel is situated. In the centre of the square is a dismal looking statue of George I, brought from Canons at the Chandos sale.

On the right hand side of Regent Street is ARCHBISHOP TENNISON'S CHAPEL AND SCHOOL. On the opposite side is HANOVER CHAPEL, built in 1823 by Cockerell … The Ionic portico has been admired for its classic proportions, but the two square turrets on the top have been not inaptly compared to churchwardens' money boxes. HANOEVER SQUARE, to which HANOVER STREET leads, was built in 1718, and is one of the most fashionable of the squares of London. On the south side of the enclosure is a fine bronze statue of the statesman Pitt, executed by Chantrey at a cost of £7,000, and placed there in 1831. The statue is twelve feet high, and the granite pedestal on which it stands fifteen feet high. On the east side of the square are the HANOVER SQUARE ROOMS, where the concerts of the Philharmonic Society are held. The assembly room is capable of containing 800 persons, and is handsomely decorated. On the opposite side (No. 18) is the ORIENTAL CLUB, founded in 1824, for the friendly meeting of those gentlemen who have resided in the East. In Tenterden Street adjoining is the ROYAL ACADEMY OF MUSIC, founded in 1822 by the Earl of Westmoreland, and affording the first instruction that can be given to both resident and non-resident pupils. The terms of admission are proportionately high; the indoor pupils paying ten guineas entrance fee, and fifty guineas annually. ST GEORGE'S CHURCH, Hanover Square, was built by John James, and finished in 1724. It has a handsome portico of six Corinthian columns, and over the altar is a curious stained-glass window brought from a convent at Mechlin, and as old as the beginning of the sixteenth century. It is generally chosen by the fashionable world as the place of matrimonial solemnisation.

It will not be uninteresting to mention, that this large district, that for years has constituted the most fashionable haunt of the titled and the wealthy, was, not more than a century and a half ago, the most filthy and repulsive in the metropolis. In 1700, BOND STREET was built no further than the west end of Clifford Street, and took its name from the proprietor, a baronet of a family now extinct. NEW BOND STREET was at that time an open field, called Conduit Mead, from one of the conduits which supplied this part of the town with water, and CONDUIT STREET received its name for the same reason. Further west is GROSVENOR STREET, leading to GROSVENOR SQURE, formed in 1715, and occupying six acres of ground. The square and the adjoining streets are on the Grosvenor estate, from which they derive their name. An equestrian statue of George I formerly stood within the railings, but the pedestal is now vacant. It was at the Earl of Harrowby's (No. 39) where the Cato-street conspiracy was to have been carried out, and the massacre of the ministers consummated. Most of the squares about this neighbourhood, we may observe, seem to have the stamp of the last century indelibly impressed upon them.

As the eye catches a vestige of bygone days in the conical extinguishers on the railings, and the recollection of the old flambeaux is restored, with the accompanying adjuncts of linkboys and sedans, one may almost picture the old nobility in the court costume of the first and second Georges, dozing away their hundred years of somniferous captivity, and doomed some day to wake up, sword, bagwig, ruffles, and all, and take a wondering survey of this modern metropolis, with its perplexing growth of buildings, and puzzling magnitude of improvements.

Crossing Oxford Street – to which we shall presently return – a continuation of Regent Street brings us to the POLYTECHNIC INSTITUTION, one of the best and most instructive of our exhibitions, and first opened in the autumn of 1838. The premises of the institution are extremely well adapted for the purpose, and contain a lofty hall, 127 feet in length, a laboratory beneath, a commodious theatre for

Oxford Street – with 300 outlets it is the busiest shopping street in Europe. *(CMcC)*

optical effects, lecture room, and apartments devoted to the exhibition of mechanical and other models. The long canals in the centre of the great hall, with the reservoir or tank at the end, are said to contain ten thousand gallons of water, which, when requisite, can be emptied in a single minute. The Diving Bell is constructed of cast iron, and weighs three tons. It is impossible to indicate the precise nature of the exhibition for each day, as the details are constantly changing; but the philosophy of science being here always illustrated by brilliant experiments, rendered in the most popular manner, the visitor may go with a firm security of entertainment, and he cannot leave without having been instructed as well as amused. At the end of LANGHAM PLACE is ALL SOULS' Church, built by Nash, in 1823 ... The steeple, with its odd extinguisher-like shape, has been much criticised. A fine picture by Westall, R.A., is placed over the altar.

At the end of PORTLAND PLACE is a statue of the Duke of Kent, the father of her present Majesty. It was designed and cast by Gahagan. To the west are some of the finest and most aristocratically inhabited streets in the metropolis, but presenting nothing deserving especial mention. PORTMAN SQUARE, the residence of many of the nobility, was finished in 1784, on a spot of ground formerly known, from its proximity to Tyburn, as 'Great Gibbet Field.' At the north-west side of the square is the house occupied, till 1800, by the kind-hearted, but eccentric Mrs Montague, who, every May-day, used here to entertain the chimney-sweepers. In Baker Street, that extends from the square northward, is situated the celebrated.

Tussaud's Wax Exhibition – Amongst the almost endless attractions here, the most imposing are the magnificent combination of figures in the centre of the room, representing the Queen's coronation, with some of its principal actors, the Royal Family at Home, &c., &c. This exhibition should not be overlooked; and at the BAKER STREET BAZAAR is held the Christmas Cattle Show, that annually attracts a large concourse of visitors.

Returning to OXFORD STREET, and proceeding eastward, we have on our right hand, soon after passing ARGYLL STREET, the PANTHEON, converted in 1834 into a bazaar, having been closed for many years as a theatre. The alterations were designed by Sydney Smirke. The rooms above are for the exhibition and sale of pictures, and below is a well-arranged bazaar, with a conservatory, laid out in exquisite taste, and abundant in birds and flowers. There is an entrance to this portion of the building in GREAT MARLBOROUGH STREET.

The Princess' Theatre is on the opposite side the way, built on the site of what was formerly the Queen's Bazaar. The interior is elegantly decorated, and will contain about 1,800 to 2,000 persons. The late manager of this theatre, Mr Charles Kean, has done more for the advancement of the drama during his eight years' occupation than any man living. Inheriting a celebrated name, he has even added to its reputation by his unblemished character and conduct. His revivals of Shakespeare's plays were on a scale of grandeur never before thought of, and Mr Kean brought in the aid of almost every science to add to the attraction of the scene, so that the antiquary and the archaeologist were equally gratified with the mere dramatist, in witnessing the fidelity and attention to historical details in the various productions of Mr Kean, who has also had the honour of conducting the Court theatricals at Windsor Castle, &c. The last and best act of Mr Kean's managerial career was to preside at a public meeting of the poor players' friends (in July, 1858), for the purpose of establishing a Dramatic College, for providing homes for the poor and distressed members of the profession – the first stone of which was laid by His Royal Highness the Prince Consort, on the 1st of June, 1860, at Woking, in Surrey. During the last 30 years Mr Charles Kean has elevated the profession of the stage, and placed himself as the first tragedian of the day. Mr Kean is still in the prime of life, having been born in Waterford, Ireland, in 1811.

Soho Square, on the right hand side of Oxford Street, and to which the short thoroughfare of CHARLES STREET will conduct us, is chiefly tenanted by music publishers and those connected with the musical profession. In the centre is a statue of Charles II, in whose reign the ground was principally built upon. The large building on the north-west side is the SOHO BAZAAR, the largest in London, and still much frequented for the purchase of fancy articles, and as a fashionable lounge for ladies. It was established in 1815.

At the eastern extremity of Oxford Street, turning a little to the right, we enter Broad Street, a continuation of Holborn, and have before us the parish church of ST GILES'-IN-THE-FIELDS, a name that has long since lost its rural significance. The church was built by Henry Flitcroft on the site of an older one, in 1784, and has a tower at the west end. Over the street-entrance to the churchyard is the Lich-gate, having an elaborate and curious specimen of bronze sculpture, representing the Last Judgment, brought from Florence, and placed on the gate of the old church in 1686. The church itself contains little to demand attention on the exterior, and within, the chief monuments of interest is a recumbent figure of Alice, Duchess Dudley, who died at her residence, in this parish, 1669, aged 90; she was the widow of Sir Robert Dudley, the son of Robert, Earl of Leicester. On the eastern side, is a monument erected by Inigo Jones, at his own expense, to George Chapman, the first metrical translator of Homer (d. 1634); and here, too, lies Shirley, the dramatist (d. 1666), Sir Roger l'Estrange, the journalist (d. 1704), and Andrew Marvel (d. 1678), the stench-hearted poet and patriot. An altar-tomb records the interment here of Richard Penderell (d. 1671), 'preserver and conduct to his sacred majesty, King Charles II, after his escape from Worcester fight.' The epitaph inscribed upon his tomb is such a solemn specimen of bombastic absurdity, that it will repay for being transcribed:

Hold, passenger, here's shrouded in this hearse
Unparallel'dPendrill, through the universe,
Like when the eastern star from heaven gave light
To three lost kings, so he in such dark nigh
To Britain's monarch, tost by adverse war,
On earth appear'd a second eastern star;
A pole, a stern in her rebellious main,
A pilot to her royal sovereign.
Now to triumph in heaven's eternal sphere
He's hence advanced for his just steerage here;

Whilst Albion's chronicles with matchless fame
Embalms the story of great Pendrill's name

On the very verge of the churchyard, overlooking the busy traffic of
Broad Street, lies a flat stone, having upon it some faint vestiges of
what was once a coat-of-arms and some appearance of an inscription;
but the most expert of heralds would fail to describe the one, and,
eyes, however penetrating, may be baffled to decipher the other. Yet
this is a grave without its dead – a mockery of the tomb – a cheating
of the sexton; for hither were brought the decapitated remains of one
who was among the brightest and most popular young noblemen of
his time, and hence were they afterwards disinterred and privately
conveyed to Dilston, in Northumberland, where they moulder in the
family vault, amid the ashes of his forefathers. Here, in fact, was first
deposited the body of the amiable and unfortunate James Radcliffe,
Earl of Derwentwater, who fatal connection with the fortunes of the
pretender, and untimely death on Tower Hill, are matters of history,
and reveal a sad tragedy, in which he was at once the hero and the
victim. The burial-ground of the parish, until the closing of all such
places by a recent act of parliament, was in the Pancras Road, near
the old church of St Pancras. The ground was laid out and a chapel
built in 1804, and there rest the remains of Flaxman, the eminent
sculptor, and Sir John Soane, the architect. The central point in this
neighbourhood, called SEVEN DIALS, and whence seven streets
radiate, derived its name from a column, on the summit of which
were seven dials occupying the centre. It was removed in 1773, under
the absurd and erroneous impression that a large sum of money had
been buried beneath. The angular direction of each street renders the
spot rather embarrassing to a pedestrian who crosses this maze of
buildings unexpectedly, and frequently causes him to diverge from
the road that would lead him to his destination.

Drury Lane, now the most uninviting street in London for a residence,
was, up to the reign of William III rather a genteel and fashionable
locality. It derived its name from Drury House, the mansion of Sir
William Drury, and which afterwards passed into the possession of

the Craven family. They Olympic Theatre partly occupies its site. The Marquis of Argyll and Alexander Earl of Stirling both had houses in this street between 1634 and 1637; and here, likewise, lodged Nell Gwynne. GREAT QUEEN STREET, leading to Lincoln's Inn Fields, was built in 1629, and was so called after Henrietta Maria, Queen of Charles I. the house in which Sir Godfrey Kneller lived was lately sold; the original houses on the south side were built by Inigo Jones. In the Baptist Chapel, in Little Wild Street, a sermon commemorative of the great storm of November, 1703, is still annually preached. The street was so called from Weld House and gardens that once occupied its site.

Long Acre, for nearly two centuries the chosen abode of coach-makers, contains a spacious building, erected in 1850 from the designs of W. Westmacott, and appropriated for lectures, concerts, &c., under the title of 'ST MARTIN'S MUSIC HALL.'

Bow Street, in which the celebrated police office is situated, rife with the associations of the drama and its votaries, is said to have been built in 1637, and to have been so called from 'its running in shape of a bent bow.' Waller the poet, Wycherley the dramatist, and Fielding the novelist, who here wrote 'Tom Jones,' were all inhabitants of this street. The corner house on the western side, abutting on Russel Street, was the celebrated 'Will's Coffee House,' the famous resort of all the wits in the days of Dryden, and so called from one William Urwin, who first established it.

In RUSSELL STREET were two other celebrated coffee-houses, Tom's (No. 17) on the north side, and Button's on the south side exactly opposite. TOM'S COFFEE HOUSE, so memorable for its frequenters in the reign of Queen Anne, and for half a century afterwards, became in 1768 the focus of the conversational talent of Dr Johnson, Garrick, Murphy, Dr Dodd, Goldsmith, Sir Joshua Reynolds, Foote, Sir Philip Francis, George Colman the elder, and others of rank and eminence, being then converted into a suite of rooms for the friendly reunions of the distinguished subscribers. Button's, so called after Daniel Button, servant to Lady Warwick, whom Addison married, was established in 1712, and is well remembered by all readers of the 'Guardian,' for the lion's head that was here set up as a letter-box to

A fine bunch – flower ladies at Covent Garden. *(LoC)*

receive the correspondence. This ingenious piece of workmanship, 'a proper emblem of knowledge and action, being all head and paws,' after undergoing various changes of ownership, was finally purchased by the Duke of Bedford, for his mansion at Woburn, where it is still carefully preserved. Addison avowedly derived the idea from the use of the lion erected near the Doge's palace, at Venice, into the wide gaping mouth of which public and private accusations were conveyed by anonymous informers. Addison, Pope, Steele, Swift, Arbuthnot, and many others bearing great and distinguished names, were regular visitors to Button's.

We now approach COVENT GARDEN MARKET, the great metropolitan fruit and flower market, and so called from the ground on which it stands being originally the convent garden of the Abbey at Westminster. The open quadrangle was formed in 1631, at the expense of Francis, fourth Earl of Bedford; and the piazza was chiefly constructed from the designs of Inigo Jones. The original market stood in the space on which Southampton and Tavistock Streets are now built, and thence was removed further into the square, the sides of which were then surrounded with mansions of the nobility and gentry, who have long since been displaced by tavern and hotel keepers. The present market was erected at the cost of John, Duke of Bedford, in 1830, and from the design and under the direction of Mr Fowler. The market is placed under the control of an officer called clerk of the market, and three beadles or toll collectors; and the revenue derived therefrom by the Bedford family is very considerable. The toll for potatoes, the market for which fronts Tavistock Row, is 1s 2d per ton; on vegetables, 1s per wagon; the latter are pitched in the spaces, and still sold in open market, to the higglers and retail dealers who principally supply the shops of the outskirts. The fruit, flower, and herb markets occupy the centre and north avenues of the market, and the central avenue, on a market day as you enter from the church, presents, in the spring and summer, a flower show of surpassing beauty. 'Few places,' observes a well-known writer, 'surprise a stranger more than when he emerges suddenly from that great, crowded, and noisy thoroughfare, the Strand, and finds himself all at once in this little world of flowers. In this spot are to be found the first offerings of spring; the snowdrop, that comes like an unbidden guest, violets and primroses, which have been gathered in many a far-off dell and sunny dingle, come to tell us the progress that nature is making in the green and out-of-door world. Many a sad and many a pleasing thought must have been awakened in the bosoms of thousands who have long been indwellers in this mighty city, by walking through the ranks of flowers which are here placed. They must have recalled the image of some old home far away, and probably never again to be visited by them – the porch over which the woodbine or jasmine trailed, and the garden fence along which the clustering moss roses hung many a flower is thus borne away and treasured for the old memories it awakens, and for the tender recollections it recalls. Here are purchased the cut flowers that decorate the banquet and the ball-room – the posy which the blushing bride bears with downcast look in her hand – the bouquet, which is rained down at the feet of our favourite actresses; and here also affection comes for its last tribute to place beside the pale face of the beloved dead, or plant around the grave in the cemetery. The house of mirth and the house of mourning are both supplied from the same common store, and pride, love, interest, fame, and vanity, come hither to select their garlands.' From each corner of the wings, facing Russell Street, are flights of steps leading to conservatories above, ornamented with a fountain, and affording a good view of the general appearance of the market and the arcade beneath. The market days are Tuesday, Thursday, and Saturday, but the latter is the principal. At a very early hour in the morning, generally by 8 o'clock, the whole of the streets which open into Covent Garden are thronged with vehicles, and buyers and sellers are astir with the dawn to effect the sales and purchases which are to supply the dinner-tables of London with vegetables. From 5 till 7, the market is one busy scene of animation, and the stranger should on no account miss an opportunity of being present. It is not generally known that this district was separated from the adjoining parish of St Martin's-in-the-Fields, and formed into a parish during the Commonwealth, which act being considered illegal, was obliged to be confirmed by another passed in 1660 ...

St Paul's Church, at the western end, was rebuilt by Hardwick, on the plan and in the proportions of the old church by InigoJones, that was built in 1633, and destroyed by fire September 17th, 1795. The original clock was the first with a long pendulum made in Europe; the present has an illuminated dial. In the churchyard are buried, among other eminent personages, Samuel Butler, the witty author of Hudibras, and who died in Rose Street, Long Acre (1680), of consumption accelerated by poverty. Wycherley, the dramatist (d. 1715); Grinling Gibbons, the sculptor (d. 1721); Susannah Centlivre, the lively authoress of some of our best comedies (d. 1723); Macklin, the actor, who died in 1797, at the great age of 107; and Dr Walcot (d. 1819), the Peter Pindar of satirical memory. The hustings for the old Westminster elections were always erected on the east side of the church, and the space being then entirely open, formed the battle-field for the supporters of the different candidates. In King Street is the GARRICK CLUB, instituted in 1831 as a club for those connected with the drama, and having the finest collection of theatrical portraits extant.

The New Royal Italian Opera, Bow Street, is built on the site of the late Theatre Royal, Covent Garden, which, at the period of its destruction by fire, in March, 1856, was decidedly the most splendid theatre in Europe. The present structure is in every respect worthy of its predecessor, and is really a beautiful building, particularly well adapted for the purpose for which it was constructed, its acoustic properties being very remarkable. It was completed in a most incredibly brief period, from the design of Charles Barry, Esq., and was opened within six months from the laying the foundation stone by the proprietor, Mr Gye, to the astonishment of all who had watched its progress – the interior being completed in a sufficient state for opening to the public within that time, and the entire design, which embraced a concert and floral hall, has since been finished in all its detail.

Drury Lane Theatre was built by Wyatt in 1812, on the site of a former one burned down in February, 1809. The present portico and colonnade were subsequent additions. The interior is light, elegant, and capacious, and will contain about 2,500 persons. The heavy expenditure of these establishments seems latterly to have been a fatal impediment in the way of their success. Nineteen out of Dryden's twenty-seven plays were produced at the old theatre that formerly occupied this spot; seven out of Nathaniel Lee's eleven; all the good ones of Wycherley; two of Congreve's; and all Farquhar's except the 'Beaux Stratagem,' whilst in the building that immediately preceded the present one, Sheridan produced four of his finest plays. The recollections of the past should serve as a stimulus to the dramatic enterprise of the present; but we are afraid 'Old Drury' can never be again so famous a theatre as it has been.

At the back of Drury Lane is Princes Street, leading to DUKE STREET, where there is a Roman Catholic chapel much frequented by the humbler class of foreigners and Irish who live about the neighbourhood. The first chapel on this site was destroyed during the riots of 1780. The streets leading to CLARE MARKET indicate the name of William Holles, created Baron Houghton, Earl of Clare, who had a mansion here. The market is surrounded by slaughter-houses, and of a Saturday night presents a noisy indication of the marvellous extent to which street traffic is carried on in this vicinity. PORTUGAL STREET was once famous for the LINCOLN'S INN THEATRE, afterwards converted into Copeland's china repository, and within the last seven years pulled down to enlarge the museum of the Royal College of Surgeons. Here was the 'Beggar's Opera' originally produced in 1728, and hence did Lavinia Fenton, the original Polly go to be made Duchess of Bolton. In the churchyard, which is the burying-ground to St Clement's Danes, Joe Miller, of Jest-book celebrity, has a headstone to his memory. KING'S COLLEGE HOSPITAL was instituted 1839. In the ten years succeeding, no less than 11,747 cases have been relieved within its walls, and medical assistance given to 138,448 out-patients, making in all a sum of 150,195 cases in which human suffering has been removed or mitigated. The Hospital makes up 120 beds. In Portugal Street is the INSOLVENT DEBTOR'S COURT.

Lincoln's Inn Fields form a fine open square, said to be the dimensions of the base of one of the pyramids of Egypt. The western side was built by Inigo Jones. Here, on the 21st of July, 1683, was beheaded Lord William Russell; he had been tried and condemned to death in Hicks' Hall. On the north side (No. 13) is SIR JOHN SIANE'S MUSEUM, open to the public gratis, on Thursdays and Fridays, during the months of April, May, and June. Foreigners, and those unable to attend at these stated periods, are admitted by special application, on Tuesdays, from February till August. It is usual to call a few days before, and leave the name and address of the party desiring admission with the curator, when the ticket of admission will be granted upon personal application, or forwarded by post. The collection is one of great value and interest, and is contained in no less than twenty-four rooms, many of them, however, being of exceedingly limited dimensions. Architectural antiquities, curious relics, and some fine paintings by the most eminent masters, render a visit extremely gratifying; and the manner in which so miscellaneous an assortment is arranged within so limited a space, deserves notice. Here is a fine Egyptian sarcophagus formed of alabaster, and, though nearly three inches thick, perfectly transparent. It was discovered by Belzoni in 1816, and purchased by Soane for £2,000. It is said to be the tomb of Osirei, father of the Great Rameses, but it has an antiquity to boast of full three thousand years. Among other interesting objects, will be found the Napoleon medals, Sir Christopher Wren's watch, Peter the Great's pistol, formerly in Napoleon's possession, TippooSaib's ivory table and chairs, from the Seringapatam palace, Hogarth's original paintings of the 'RAKE'S PROGRESS,' and 'The Election,' paintings by Canaletti, Sir Joshua Reynolds, Turner, Sir Thomas Lawrence, with some curious manuscripts, among which is Tasso's original copy of the 'Gerusalemme,' and some rare books, including the first folio editions of Shakespeare, bought from the Kemble collection. The mansion was built bySoane in 1812. LINDSEY HOUSE (No. 59) was originally built by Inigo Jones for the Earl of Lindsey, who was General of the King's forces for Charles I, and fell at the battle of Edgehill. A fine mantelpiece of the period is still to be seen in part of the chambers.

Those much frequented thoroughfares, GREAT and LITTLE TURNSTILE, derived their names from the turning-stiles which two centuries ago stood at their respective ends, and were so placed both for the convenience of foot passengers, and to prevent the straying of cattle, the fields being at that period used for pasturage. On the eastern side of the square, occupying a portion of what was, till very recently, Lincoln's Inn gardens, is the new LINCOLN'S INN HALL and Library, built by Hardwick in the Tudor style, and publicly opened by her Majesty with great ceremony in October, 1845. The hall, which has a roof of oak finely carved, is 62 feet high, 45 feet wide, and 120 feet in length. The library is 80 feet long, 40 feet wide, and 44 feet high, and contains some valuable records, and a fine collection of law books. The CHAPEL, built by Inigo Jones, and consecrated in 1623, is at the back of these buildings, and is chiefly noticeable for some richly stained glass windows. It is reared on huge pillars and arches, leaving an open walk beneath the chapel, which was formerly much frequented.

On the south side of Lincoln's Inn Fields is the ROYAL COLLEGE OF SURGEONS, a massive building erected from the designs of Barry, and presenting a noble colonnade and portico of the Ionic order ... The magnificent MUSEUM attached to the College – the first of its kind in the world – owes its foundation to the untiring industry and well-directed talents of John Hunter, the great anatomist and physiologist. It was originally arranged by him in 1787, and having left directions in his will that the collection should be offered to government, Parliament, six years afterwards, voted £15,000 for the museum, and a building being erected here for its reception, it was first opened in 1813. This proving too small for the display and arrangement of the specimens that were afterwards added, the present noble structure was built in 1836, at the expense of the College, and at the cost of £40,000. At present the total number of specimens is about twenty-three thousand, and of these ten thousand belonged to Hunter's original collection. It would be manifestly impossible to give even a synopsis of those specimens in the prescribed limits of this work, and indeed the majority of them would be of little interest to the general reader. We shall therefore confine ourselves to those that usually invite the curiosity of the non-professional visitor, and refer others desirous of becoming more intimately acquainted with the preparations, to the elaborate catalogues of the Museum. The view that meets the eye on entering at the chief door from the hall of the College, is particularly striking and impressive. The first large object seen on the right, is the fossil shell of a gigantic extinct armadillo from Buenos Ayres. A shell of the common armadillo is placed on this enormous specimen, to show by comparison its vast size, which was its only protection, as it had no joints to roll itself up with, like the animal of the present day. On the left is the fossil skeleton of the mylodon, a large extinct quadruped of the sloth family, also found at Buenos Ayres. It is disposed as if climbing up a tree to feed on the branches, such being the manner in which it is conjectured its subsistence was procured. Beyond this, to the left, is the skeleton of the hippopotamus, and on the extreme right, over the shell of the armadillo, are the bones of the pelvis, tail, and left hind leg of the mighty megatherium, an animal of antediluvian associations. It seems to have been a sort of stupendous sloth, with haunches more than five feet wide, a body twelve feet long, and eight feet high, feet a yard in length, and terminated by most gigantic claws. Its tail was clad in a kind of armadillo-like armour, and was much larger than the tail of any other beast. The entire frame was an apparatus of colossal mechanism, calculated to be the vehicle of life and enjoyment to a gigantic race of quadrupeds, which, though they have ceased to be counted among the living inhabitants of our planet, have in their fossil bones left behind them imperishable monuments of the consummate skill with which they were constructed.

The cabinets on each side the centre avenue, contain various anatomical preparations of parts of the human subject, fishes, and reptiles. The large skeleton to the right of the centre is that of Charles Byrne or O'Bryan, the Irish giant, and is eight feet in height. He died in Cockspur Street in 1783, at the age of twenty-two, his death being accelerated by excessive drinking. Two ordinary skeletons, male and female, are placed on his left side, and on his right is that of Caroline Crachami, the Sicilian dwarf, who died in Bond Street in 1824, at the age of ten years. The skeleton, which is only twenty inches in height, is placed under a glass case. On the pedestal there are two plaster casts of hands – one of Mons. Louis, the French giant, who measured seven feet four inches, and the other the right hand of Patrick Cotter, whose height in 1802 was eight feet eight inches. In the glass case adjoining is preserved the glove of O'Bryan. His shoes are in the possession of a gentleman at Chertsey, and are more like huge coal-scuttles than the ordinary coverings of any human feet. Proceeding along the museum on the left, are casts in plaster of the bones of an extinct and huge bird, which must have stood at least ten feet high, and was a native of New Zealand. It is called the Dinornisgiganteus, and is placed, by way of contrast, at the side of a full-grown ostrich. Still further is the skeleton of an American elk, and under it that of the great penguin, from the extreme southern point that Ross touched at. This is the only specimen of the kind in England. Behind this is a specimen of the giraffe, and on the right is seen the skeleton of the gigantic extinct deer, the MigacerosHibernicus, very commonly but erroneously called 'the Irish elk.' It was exhumed from a peat-bog near Limerick. The span of the antlers, measured in a straight line between the extreme tips, is eight feet; the length of a single antler, following the curve, seven feet three inches; height of the skeleton to the top of the skull, seven feet six inches; weight of the skill and antlers, seventy-six pounds. The large skeleton in the centre will be looked at with interest; it is that of the Elephant Chunee brought to England in 1810. After being exhibited on the stage of Covent Garden Theatre, it was purchased by Mr Cross for his menagerie at Exeter Change, and in consequence of an inflammation of one of the tusks, which rendered the poor animal ungovernably violent, it was shot in 1826. The company of soldiers employed to shoot him discharge upwards of one hundred bullets and musket balls at him without effect; and it was only when the familiar voice of the keeper called him by name that the animal turned round, presented a vulnerable point and was short dead at the feet of his well-known attendant …

Passing through a doorway on the left hand, we enter the small museum, which contains many objects of popular interest. Immediately before us is the skeleton of a man who died at the age of twenty-five, from hydrocephalus, or water on the brain. The skull is enormous, measuring forty-eight inches in circumference, and the entire skeleton displays many peculiarities highly interesting to the anatomist. It was presented by the late Mr Liston, the surgeon. In the next case are the two skulls of a double-headed child, born in Bengal, and who lived to be four years old, when it was killed by the bite of a cobra di capello. The skulls are united by the crowns, and the upper head is consequently inverted. It had four eyes, which moved in different directions at the same time, and the upper eyelids were never thoroughly closed, even when the child was asleep. In the same case is a portion of the intestines of Napoleon, showing the progress of the disease which carried him off. Adjoining this singular relic of the exiled Emperor, is a very remarkable skeleton, the joints of which are anchylosed, or rendered immoveable by unnatural splints of bone growing out in all directions. Here, too, is preserved a female monstrous embryo, found in the abdomen of a boy sixteen years of age, at Sherborne, in Dorsetshire, June 16, 1814. But, perhaps, the object of the greatest interest is the preparation known as the shaft case, between the wall cabinets on the left hand. On the 13th of June, 1812, Mr Thomas Tipplo was impaled by the shaft of a chaise, near Stratford, in Essex. The shaft entered his chest under the left arm, and came out under the right arm, being thrust through by the violence of an unruly horse, as far as the first tug hook, which also penetrated the chest, and wounded the left lung. Two veterinary surgeons, Messrs. E. and H. Lawrence, who were passing at the time, extracted the shaft; and, wonderful to relate, the patient recovered, surviving the injury eleven years. As a companion to this, is the iron pivot of a try-sail mast which was driven right through the body of a seaman, John Toyler, a Prussian by birth, of the brig Jane of Scarborough. The accident occurred in the London Docks, February 26, 1831. Whilst guiding the pivot of the try-sail mast into the main boom, the tackle gave way, and the pivot passed obliquely through Toyler's body between the heart and the left lung, and pinned him to the deck. The try-sail mast was 39 feet long, and weighed about 600 pounds. He was conveyed, apparently dead, to the London Hospital, where, under the care of Mr J. G. Andrews, he recovered so entirely in five months as to be able to walk from the hospital to the college and back again. He at the same time sustained various other injuries; his scalp was laid open, and his lower jaw and four ribs fractured; but he ultimately returned to his duties as a seaman, and not very long ago revisited the college in a robust state of health. Here, also, is the cast in wax of the band that united the Siamese twins. There are several mummies in this room, amongst which may be observed the wife of the eccentric Martin van Butchell, and a female who died of consumption in 1775. The plan pursued, was that of injecting all the vessels with camphor and turpentine. A mummy in a sitting position, with its cheeks resting on the hands, deserves attention. It is supposed to be that of a Peruvian nobleman who immolated himself with his wife and child some centuries ago. The expression of the figure is painful. The portrait of

Hunter is by Sir Joshua Reynolds. We have thus sketched the principal points of the collection, feeling that from what has been here only superficially described, there is amply sufficient to interest the non-professional visitor, as well as those for whose anatomical pursuits the specimens were originally accumulated. But unrivalled as this collection certainly is, scarcely a day passes without some addition to its stores. 'Doctors on shipboard, doctors with armies, doctors in Arctic ships, or on Niger expeditions; in the far regions of Hindustan, and in the fogs and storms of Labrador, think now and then of their 'dissecting days,' and of the noble collection in Lincoln's Inn Fields, which every true student feels bound to honour, and to help to make complete. Many, when going forth into distant countries, are supplied from this place with bottles especially adapted to receive objects in request, and receive also a volume of instructions how the specimens may be best preserved. Never a week passes but something rare or curious makes its appearance in Lincoln's Inn Fields; sometimes from one quarter, sometimes from another, but there is always something coming, either by messenger or parcel-cart ... When the elephant died at the Regent's Park Gardens, a College student and an assistant were busily occupied for days dissecting the huge animal. When the rhinoceros expired at the same place, a portion of its viscera was hailed as a prize; and when the whale was cast, not long ago, upon the shores of the Thames, the watermen who claimed it as their booty, steamed off to the College to find a customer for portions of the unwieldy monster; nor were they disappointed.'

Crossing Holborn, through Great Turnstile, or by the upper end of Chancery Lane, we may penetrate the shady avenues of GRAY'S INN, another inn of court, with two inns of Chancery attached (Staple Inn and Barnard's Inn), which has sufficient antiquity to date back its records to the time of Edward III. It was originally the residence of Lord Gray; the hall was built about 1560, and the gardens, to which it is said the great Lord Bacon contributed a few trees, planted about 1600. Among its more eminent students may be mentioned Hall the chronicler, the great Lord Burleigh, Bacon, Bradshaw, who sat as president at the trial of Charles I, and Robert Southey.

Within Gray's Inn Gate was the shop in which Jacob Tonson, the bookseller, began his publishing career. Gray's In Walks used to be a favourite promenade in the time of Charles II, and in the days of the Tatler and Spectator. BEDFORD ROW, adjoining, is a fine specimen of the broad thoroughfares of a century back, when all beyond this point was nearly open country to the very margin of Hampstead and Highgate. The name is derived from the benevolent purposes to which those lands and others adjacent were devoted by Sir William Harpur (Lord Mayor of London in 1561, died in 1573), who bequeathed the revenues to Bedford, his native place, there to found a free and perpetual school, and endow other charities. In this row lived Bishop Warburton, and here in 1731, in the eighty-second year of her age, died Mrs Elizabeth Cromwell, granddaughter of Oliver Cromwell. At No. 14, John Abernethy, the celebrated surgeon, breathed his last. In RED LION SQUARE is situated the office of the MENDICITY SOCIETY, an excellent institution, and as serviceable for assisting the really necessitous poor as for the invaluable aid which it furnishes to the public in detesting the extensively ramified system of the begging letter imposter. In this square lived and died the benevolent Joseph Hanway the traveller, who was the first to venture to carry an umbrella in the streets of London, and who, after carrying one for thirty years, saw them come into general use.

Returning to Holborn, we can hence pass either to Charing Cross or Temple Bar, and having thus completed our walks through the West-end of London, prepare to take an equally interesting, and perhaps even a more excursive, ramble in a northerly direction.

The British Museum in Bloomsbury. Bradshaw informs us that the domed reading room could accommodate 80,000 books of 'average thickness'. He was also much taken with the Egyptian collection and by the Elgin marbles *(LoC)*

PART FOUR

The North

Seventh Day's Route

DISTRICT I

Commencing our progress northward from TOTTENHAM COURT ROAD, so called from it leading to the ancient manor of 'Tottenham Court' belonging to St Paul's, we deviate into GREAT RUSSELL STREET for the purpose of introducing the visitor to that noble institution, the BRITISH MUSEUM. This may truly be described as a spot where British enterprise has brought from every country something to attract the eye and interest the mind; where the rudest indications of barbaric skill and the highest manifestations of civilised ingenuity are alike preserved; and for which nature has surrendered its stores, art contributed its fairest creations, discovery yielded its richest treasures, and antiquity displayed its choicest relics, to bring the triumphs of the present into startling contrast with the glories of the past.

The British Museum stands upon the site of Montague House, where the collection was exhibited until the new building was completed for its reception in 1850, until which time, part of the old mansion of the Dukes of Montague was visible; but the gateway being then finally demolished, the last vestige of the ancient structure disappeared, and now the Museum, with its majestic portico, forms a striking architectural ornament to the street in which it stands.

The present building was commenced in 1823 from the designs of Sir Robert Smirke, and has been completed at an expenditure of

£753,495. It is of the Grecian Ionic order of architecture. The principal entrance has a magnificent portico, supported by eight columns, and with the wings on each side forms a frontage of 370 feet. Passing under this portico by a massive and finely carved oaken doorway, we enter the new hall, 30 feet high, and 62 feet by 51 broad. A grand staircase, 17 feet in width, and enclosed by walls of highly polished red granite, leads to the suite of rooms appropriated to the NATURAL HISTORY DEPARTMENT, and to the left is the GALLERY OF ANTIQUITIES. For the convenience of those who can only take a rapid glance at the contents, we shall proceed to give a general indication of the most popularly interesting objects; but those who contemplate – as it deserves – devoting several days to an examination of this interesting building, should purchase the catalogues that are to be obtained about the Museum.

In the HALL will be noticed Chantrey's statue of Sir Joseph Banks, and Roubiliac's statue of Shakespeare, the latter sculptured with all the skill of that celebrated artist, but, at the same time, possessing all the faults of an unnatural school. Near it is the statue of the Hon. Anne Seymour Damer, a liberal patroness of sculpture, in which she had some skill herself, as her own miniature figure of the genius of the Thames, which she holds in her arms, will testify. Passing on to the MAMMALIA SALOON, we find ourselves in a spacious lofty apartment, around the walls of which are arranged the specimens of rapacious and hoofed beasts; whilst on the floor are placed the larger animals, among which will be observed the wild ox, from Chillingham Park, Northumberland. A miscellaneous collection of animals of the monkey tribe will be seen in a number of the cases; among these is a fine specimen of the black ourang, a native of Africa. Passing onwards will be noticed the species that have prehensile tails, with which they lay hold of branches, and thus in climbing have all the advantages of a fifth arm. The monkeys that are natives of America differ from those found in the other quarters of the globe, in having longer tails and no pouches in their cheeks. Case 18, especially, presents some beautiful varieties, amongst which the bearded ape is conspicuous, and close to it is the rib-nosed baboon, that once was a great favourite at Exeter

Change, where he had been taught the questionable accomplishments of drinking grog and smoking tobacco.

The Eastern Zoological Gallery introduces us to a varied collection of birds, that are alike distinguished by the richness and brilliancy of their colours, and the beauty and elegance of their forms. The first section contains the Rapsorial and Passerine birds (birds of prey), which generally build on trees or high places, and have their young hatched blind and nearly naked, so that for a time it is necessary for them to be fed by their parents, and remain in the nest. The first family is that of the condors, chiefly inhabitants of America. The muscles in the wings of these giants of the feathered race are so powerful, that a blow from one of them has destroyed life. A magnificent of the golden eagle, with the wings extended, shows the rapacity with which it devours its prey. The family of falcons (Falconidae), which occupy the next cases, have their heads covered with feathers, and the eyebrows prominent, giving the eye the appearance of being deeply set in the head, and imparting a character very different from that of the vultures. The beak exhibits a remarkable conformation, having a deep notch near its roof, which enables them to wound or tear their prey with greater facility. The other varieties here are the ignoble falcons with simple, and the hawks with rather longitudinal nostrils; whilst the honey buzzard, osprey, and kites, have and oblique slit covered with a valve behind. These distinctions will readily enable the visitor to distinguish the several kinds. Amongst the hawks, the most remarkable bird is the secretary, brought from the Cape of Good Hope, where it is called the serpent-eater, from those reptiles being its prey. Next are the eagles, to describe the different varieties of which a volume might be devoted. We now approach the numerous and most solemn family of the owls (Strigidae) most of which are remarkable for the radiated circles of feathers surrounding their eyes, and for their large ears, which, as they hunt in the dark, may enable them to discover their prey by the sense of hearing when not within the range of their imperfect vision…

The ostrich – among birds what the camelopard is among animals – is so incapacitated by its heaviness for flight, that it has recourse to its legs instead of wings for safety, and in this manner it has been known to outstrip the fleetest horse. In the same case (109) is the bustard, the largest of European birds, and the rarest with us; the peculiar conformation of the breast deserves notice. In Case 114 is the singular bird called the trumpeter, of which there are only two species, found in South America and the Brazils. It is of use there to the natives when domesticated, by its quality of making a peculiarly shrill noise, or 'trumpeting,' when danger is near; for this purpose it is often set to guard poultry, and feeding chiefly on serpents, its presence is much sought after … Here (Case 108) is the foot of the Dodo, a bird now supposed to be extinct, and only known by a few scanty remains, and a painting here exhibited, sketched from a living bird brought from the Mauritius …

The collection of fossils, insects, reptiles and crustacean, is very complete and interesting; but as the inscriptions speak for themselves, it is unnecessary to occupy the time of the reader with a bare enumeration of names. We must, however, direct the visitor's attention to the mineralogical and geological collections in the northern gallery, and especially to the meteoric stones, enormous masses of iron that have fallen from the sky at different times and places. Here, also, is exhibited the famous 'Show-stone' of Dr Dee, in Case 20. In the Medal Room is a valuable assortment of ancient Greek, Roman, and British coins, chronologically and geographically arranged.

THE EGYPTIAN ROOM, that lies to the left at the extremity of the eastern gallery, contains various Egyptian curiosities, of which the most important are the mummies. The Case RR, contains the mummy of Harsontioff, priest of Ammon. The upper part is enveloped by a linen covering of blue, with figures and subjects embossed and gilded. On the head is the scarabaeus or sacred beetle; round the fillets of the head are embossed lines of hieroglyphics, and on the soles of the sandal are two bearded male figures, with their hands and arms tied, short garments round the loins, and the chlamys on their shoulders emblematical of the enemies of Egypt. Its dimensions are about five feet eight inches. Case UU, is the coffin of Penamoun, the incense-bearer of Thebes. The face is of dark-polished wood, ornamented with a small square beard. The head is in a rich claft, representing the wings and body of a bird, with two side ornaments; round the neck is a pectoral plate representing a disked face in a boat. The hands are crossed on the breast, each holding a roll of papyrus, and below is the good demon. Round the sides of the chest, traced in yellow upon a black ground, is a cat grasping a snake; the mummy on its bier with the soul soaring above, an indubitable proof that the Egyptians believed in the immortality of the soul; and in addition to these, we find a temple on a mountain, above which are the symbols of east and west, a lion-headed mummied deity holding two swords, a man walking holding in each hand a star, the judgment-scene, a deity with two snaked heads, and the disc of the sun descending below the solar mountain. Next in interest may be considered the Case Z Z, containing the mummy of Mautemmen, a female attendant on the worship of Ammon, and most probably a priestess. The body is swathed in such a manner as to exhibit the whole of the form, and it is impossible to look upon the perfect preservation of this figure without emotion. Round the body, ankles, and upper parts of the arms, are broad bands similarly ornamented, others are narrower and cross from the shoulder to the belt, whilst the arms are swathed with narrow strips like the animal mummies. The back part of the head, and the extremities of the head and feet are bared, representing the hair and bones. In the centre of the room (Case AAA) is the wooden sarcophagus of Cleopatra, daughter of Candace. On the arched part of the cover are judgment-scenes before Ra and Osiris, a train of inferior deities seated in porches and holding swords in their hands; two rows of hawks with human and animals' heads, on one side a boat with a disc attached to a snake drawn by four deities; on the other a boat with a disc of the symbolic eye attached to a snake drawn by three jackals; the good demon; the scarabaeus with extended wings, and Isis and another deity paying it homage. The interior represents heaven surrounded by zodiacal signs, and at the sides of the head are four tortoises. The upper and has the hawk, and the lower the sacred cow, seated on a pedestal. On the sides are the twenty-four hours as female figures, twelve on each side, and each procession being closed by a thirteenth female and personifications of the morning and evening star. It is nearly 6 feet in length, 2 in breadth, and 2 feet in height. In Case DD, we find the mummy of part of a bull, remarkable for its perfect preservation, after a lapse of three thousand years. On the forehead is the triangular mark of Apis, to whom all cattle were sacred. In Case BB, we meet with a small coffin in a vaulted cover, containing the mummy of a Greco-Egyptian child. The body is covered with an external wrapper, having a representation of the deceased in a toga. The hair is crowned with a wreath, the feet are in shoes, and the left hand is holding a branch of laurel, whilst the other is raised. On the top of the cover is a viper between two wreaths. In Case EE are mummies of the ibis and the crocodile, embalming being as much practiced by the Egyptians on animals as it was upon mankind; and, as these specimens show, even vegetables have been embalmed in a similar manner. The small bronze Egyptian deities in Case A cannot fail to repay inspection, from their singularity of design and beauty of execution. In Case F are some specimens of Coptic carving, that make it difficult to say whether the grotesque or the beautiful most predominate. Here is a small figure that seems formerly to have had a spear in its hand. The arms are jointed as if once moveable, and the cap which surmounts the head is remarkable for the singular form which it exhibits …

The rooms leading from this are filled with vases and terra cotta, chiefly of Etruscan workmanship. The Bronze Room contains the Barberini, or Portland Vase, that in February, 1845, was wantonly injured by a supposed lunatic, who mischievously smashed it into pieces; but it has since been so cleverly restored, that the union of the fragments is scarcely perceptible. It was discovered in a sepulchral chamber about three miles from Rome, in 1643, and bought by Sir William Hamilton at the sale of the Barberini Library, where it was deposited. Though placed in the British Museum since 1810, the vase is still the property of the Duke of Portland, into whose possession it came by purchase, having been bought by the Portland family for £1,029.

We now descend to that magnificent hall on the ground floor called the EGYPTIAN SALOON, containing the most valuable collection of ancient colossal sculpture in the world, and the perspective at once impresses upon the mind an idea of extraordinary grandeur. The general characteristics of these specimens of Egyptian sculpture are extreme simplicity or uniformity in the composition of the lines, want of variety of action, and the absence of any sentiment or expression in the heads. Their statues are either standing quite upright, sitting with all their limbs at right angles to the body, or kneeling on both knees. The backs are uniformly supported by a kind of block or pilaster, which is generally covered with hieroglyphics, and the heads, when they are human, are sometimes uncovered, but more frequently they are surmounted by an emblematical head-dress, in which is distinguished the lotos, a globe, a serpent or some sacred symbol, or else the covering consists of a kind of close cap, entirely concealing the hair, and falling in broad flaps upon the shoulders. For the light or majestic drapery of the Grecians, possessing all that is beautiful in outline, admirable in effect, noble in design, and perfect in execution, we are here presented with enormous masses of granite and porphyry, with colossal fragments of gigantic statues, whose enormous dimensions, overwhelmed by the shocks of nature or the fury of the elements, have been scattered in ages past over regions at present inaccessible, or buried beneath those arid and burning sands, which have at once been their tomb and their protection. That stately figure, resting his hands upon his knees and having a grave monarchical aspect, is the statue of Bubastes (No. 63) and of which Nos 62 and 37 are counterparts. The pillar (No. 64) is a granite column, with six rows of shields containing hieroglyphics, among which the names of Rameses and Amenoph III have been identified. No. 67 is the fragment of a statue belonging to the pedestal of the great Sphinx, and is presumed to be emblematical of a shepherdess of protectress of the fields. No. 70 is a broken fragment of what was once a seated male statue, holding in front of its knees a child, standing with a label on his breast, inscribed with hieroglyphics, indicative of the royal name Amyrteus. On each side are two most curiously carved figures, one representing an agricultural labourer, with an implement resembling a pickaxe in his left hand; the other being a statue of a prince of Ethiopia, holding in his hands an altar, inscribed with hieroglyphics, and having on it a ram's head to be offered as a sacrifice. We now come to a beautiful fragment of a colossal statue (No. 19), which is sure to attract attention. This is called the head of the young Memnon, but in reality it is the upper portion of a statue of Rameses the Great, brought by Belzoni in 1817 from the ruins of the Memnonium, a building dedicated to Memnon, at Thebes. This fragment is composed of one piece of granite of two colours, and the face, which is in remarkably fine preservation, is executed in a very admirable manner. It will be observed that there is a hold in the right breast, drilled, it is supposed, by the French for the purpose of blowing off with gunpowder the right shoulder, and rendering the transport of the head more easy ...

We now proceed to the ELGIN SALOON, where the Elgin marbles are deposited, and which are universally acknowledged to be the most valuable extant. They are mostly basso-relievos, and fragments of statuary that adorned the Parthenon at Athens, and were so called from the Earl of Elgin, who obtained permission to bring them from Greece, in 1801. The collection was purchased for £35,000, and thus these sculptures were rescued from destruction, and preserved among our choicest national treasures. To better understand these, the visitor should first examine the two models in the PHIGALIAN SALOON, one the restored model of the Parthenon, the other a model of the Parthenon after the Venetian bombardment in 1687. The building of the Parthenon is recorded by Plutarch, in his life of Pericles, who also informs us that Phidias was entrusted with the control and superintendence of all the great works undertaken during his administration; and it may reasonably be inferred, that the sculpture which adorned this noble temple, was designed by that great master, and executed by the disciples of his school under his immediate direction. Particular attention should be bestowed on (98) the head of a horse from the car of night, full of vivacity and strength of expression. The red numbers are to facilitate a reference from the Museum synopsis to the marbles, and are those now in use. Two of the most celebrated features of the room are the Ilyssus (99), and the Theseus (93). The first is the personification of the small stream that ran through Athens, and although mutilated, is the very triumph of art; whilst the other presents a striking effect, from the regularity and precision with which the lineaments of the human form have been transferred to stone. Though more than two thousand years have passed away since the gifted hands which gave them being have crumbled into dust, they are still acknowledged the types of abstract beauty, and artists bow before them as the idols of artistic worship. The Metopes, or groups which adorn the frieze, are remarkably fine, but our limits forbid us dwelling upon them. The other rooms contain the Xanthian marbles, brought from the ruined city of Xanthus, and of an earlier date even than those of the Parthenon; the Bodroum marbles, brought to England in 1846, from Asia Minor; the Nimroud marbles, which we owe to Dr Layard's recent researches on the site of the ancient Nineveh; and the Townley Collection, bequeathed by their collector, Charles Townley. All these have objects of rare and enduring interest; but as a cheap catalogue gives the enumeration of their names – and we could here d little more – we shall employ the space at our disposal for the description of the remaining portions of the Museum.

LIBRARY – For this purpose a new building on a most magnificent scale, peculiarly adapted for the literary requirements of the age, has just been completed. The building occupies the inner quadrangle of the Museum. The details of the plan were suggested by Mr Panizzi to the trustees; the plan was approved of, and Mr Sydney Smirke appointed as the architect of the undertaking. The sum of £61,000 was set apart to defray the cost of the building.

THE READING-ROOM contains ample and comfortable accommodation for 300 readers. Each person has a separate table 4 feet 3 inches long. He is screened from the opposite occupant by a longitudinal division, which is fitted with a hinged desk graduated on sloping racks, and a folding shelf for spare books. The framework of each table is of iron, forming air-distributing channels, which are contrived so that the air may be delivered at the top of the longitudinal screen division, above the level of the heads of the readers, or, if desired, only at each end pedestal of the tables, all the outlets being under the control of valves. A tubular foot-rail also passes from end to end of each table, which may have a current of warm water passed through at pleasure, and be used as a foot-warmer.

The Catalogue tables, with shelves under, and air-distributing tubes between, are ranged in two concentric circles around the central superintendent's enclosure or rostrum, the latter being fitted with tables, ticket boxes, with dwarf partitions surmounted by glass screens, dividing a passage leading to the surrounding libraries. Altogether, the building is remarkable, not only for its immensity, but for the ingenuity displayed in its interior arrangements. It is calculated that the inner library shelves in galleries within the dome-room will contain 80,000 volumes. Two lifts are placed at convenient stations, for the purpose of raising the books to the level of the several gallery floors. The building contains three miles lineal of bookcases, and which in all the cases are eight feet high; assuming them all to be spaced for the averaged octavo book size, the entire ranges form twenty-five miles of shelves; assuming the shelves to be filled with books, of paper of average thickness, the leaves placed edge to edge would extend about 25,000 miles, or more than three times the diameter of the globe …

We are again in the midst of the squares. BLOOMSBURY SQUARE, first laid out by the Earl of Southampton, about 1670, has a fine bronze statue, by Westmacott, of Charles James Fox, opposite Bedford Place. The church, with the peculiar steeple seen towering above the surrounding buildings, is the parish church of St George's, Bloomsbury, built by Nicholas Hawksmoor in 1730. A statue of King George I crowns the steeple. RUSSELL SQUARE, containing a statue, by Westmacott, of Francis, Duke of Bedford, was built in 1803. In Great Coram Street is the RUSSELL INSTITUTION, founded in 1808 as a lecture-hall and library, and possessing Haydon's celebrated picture Retreat of the Ten Thousand, presented in 1836 by the Duke of Bedford. QUEEN'S SQUARE, adjacent, was planted in the reign of Queen Anne, and contains a statue of that Queen. TORRINGTON and WOBURN SQUARES are also great ornaments to the neighbourhood.

In Gower Street is UNIVERSITY COLLEGE HOSPITAL, founded in 1833. The first stone of the north wing was laid by Lord Brougham in 1846. Nearly opposite is the LONDON UNIVERSITY COLLEGE, founded in 1828, and built by Wilkins, the architect of the National Gallery. It is furnished with every professional capability for prosecuting studies in science and the classics, and for the benefit of persons who, by their religious opinions, were precluded from taking degrees in the Universities of Oxford and Cambridge. In 1850, the University had on its books 546 graduates, and 810 matriculated under-graduates. The building extends a length of 420 feet, and has a richly ornamented Corinthian portico, ascended by a flight of steps.

Regent's Park – Entering the NEW ROAD [Euston Road], and turning to the left, we reach the REGENT'S PARK, consisting of about 400 acres, occupying the site of Old Marylebone Fields. The park and the surrounding crescents were laid out in 1812, from a plan by Nash, and the ornamental plantations, and the broad sweeping avenues that intersect the greensward in all directions, were further improved and extended in 1833 and 1838. Around the terraces of striking architectural magnificence, and the outer road forms an agreeable drive of nearly three miles in length; whilst the enclosure, with its broad and shaded avenues, its smoothly gravelled walks, its soft green turf, its rows of stately trees, its pleasant vistas, and the zone of noble mansions by which it is engirdled, is a rare boon to the pedestrian, and of which the Londoner may well be proud. At the south end of the park is the COLOSSEUM, one to the most popular exhibitions in the metropolis, and built by Decimus Burton in 1824. From the moment the visitor enters the building, until he retires, the scene presented is the most varied and pleasing that can be imagined. The celebrated picture of London (taken from the bell of St Paul's), and a view of Paris by moonlight, are among the chief attractions, which consist of entertainments and lectures upon the model of the Polytechnic Institution. A little further on, at the north-east corner of the park, is the Gothic structure of St KATHERINE'S HOSPITAL, built in 1827, and containing a chapel, six residences for pensioners, and a detached residence for the master. It was originally founded near the Tower by Maude of Boulogne, the wife of King Stephen, and for centuries did the lowly turrets of St Katharine attract the gaze and inspire the prayer of the outward-bound mariner, and through many generations was the top-sail lowered in reverence to its tutelar saint, as the well-manned vessel, laden with the precious freights of early commerce, slowly passed along. But now in St Katharine's docks the merchant ships of London ride over the spot where the convent once stood, and, transplanted here, it affords to this day a comfortable subsistence to its lay sisters and brethren, at the nomination of the

An elephant in central London: This overloaded pachyderm – more correctly classified as a proboscidea nowadays – takes visitors for a ride at the Zoological Gardens in Regent's Park. From the size of its ears this is an Asian elephant. *(LoC)*

The Monument

Constructed between 1671 and 1677, the Monument stands as a permanent memorial to the Great Fire of London. The column is hollow and a cantilevered staircase of 311 breath-stealing steps leads visitors to a viewing balcony at the top. It was designed by Christopher Wren and Robert Hooke with a dual purpose in mind, as they utilised the hollow shaft as a zenith telescope – a fixed one looking straight up. It was also used for gravitational, barometric and pendulum experiments with an underground laboratory at its base. *(LoC)*

Below: Looking upwards through the centre of the spiral staircase. *(JC)*

The Tower of London

It's a castle really, founded in 1066 by the Norman conquerors to oppress the locals rather than keep hostile armies out. Home of the Royal Mint and the Crown Jewels, it has seen a procession of high-profile prisoners lose their heads. *Below*, figures of authority: In 1839 Parliament formalised London's assorted police forces into one. The Beefeater is wearing the Tudor state dress, *c.* 1895. *(CMcC & LoC)*

The Port of London

By the latter part of the nineteenth century the wharves and warehouses of the Pool of London were at bursting point, due largely to the system of Legal Quays instigated during the reign of Elizabeth I and by a rapid growth in trade with the Empire. It is said that by 1800 there were nearly 2,000 vessels vying for space and when the congestion was at its worse, a man could walk from one bank of the river to the other on their decks. New commercial docks created on the eastern side of London brought some relief to the overcrowding. *(CMcC)*

Thames steamers
These vessels were not just for the tourists, and in Victorian times they provided an important means of transportation. *Above,* passing Lambeth Palace. *(LoC)*

London Bridge
It didn't fall down, not quite, but the nineteenth century bridge, *above,* was sinking. It was sold in 1968 and then shipped, piece by piece, to be re-assembled in the USA. This view from *c.* 1900 shows the Monument and St Magnus-the-Martyr on the northern side. *(LoC)*

London's other bridges

There are thirty-four crossings over the River Thames within the Greater London area, if you include all the road, rail and pedestrian bridges. However, there were considerably fewer in Bradshaw's time as many of the rail bridges came later in the nineteenth century, and a number of road bridges were rebuilt during the twentieth. The most prominent post-Bradshaw bridge is Tower Bridge which was completed in 1894. The Millennium pedestrian bridge of 2002 is the most recent. *Top*, the latest version of the Vauxhall Bridge dates from 1906. *(Clickos/ Dreamstime) Bottom*, Claude Monet's painting of the old Waterloo road bridge which was replaced by the present concrete structure in the 1940s.

Greenwich

Famous for the magnificent Royal Hospital and Naval College, the Park and the Royal Observatory which gives us the Greenwich Meridian and Greenwich Mean Time (GMT), this is also home to the National Maritime Museum. *(CMcC)*

Above: Bradshaw says, 'Greenwich presents a striking appearance from the river, its Hospital forming one of the most prominent attractions of the place'. *Above,* this postcard shows the less familiar side of Greenwich, the Town Hall. *(CMcC)*

Richmond
Above, Hill Street and Town Hall at Richmond. Whether reached by train or steamboat, Bradshaw assures us that the walks by the river and the leafy luxuriance of the park make this a 'region of loveliness'.

Hampton Court Palace
The 'Wrenovated' east side of Hampton Court was remodelled in a Versailles-inspired style, but following Queen Mary's death in 1694 King William lost interest in the Palace. It was here, in 1702, that he fell from his horse and died shortly afterwards. *(Man vyi)*

Bacon's Map
of London

Published in 1890

BACON'S
NEW MAP OF
LONDON,
DIVIDED INTO HALF MILE SQUARES & CIRCLES
SCALE FOUR INCHES TO THE MILE.

Squares & Gardens
Cemeteries
Railways & Stations thus
Tramways
Omnibus Routes
Public Buildings
Churches & Chapels
Theatres
Board Schools
County Courts
Police Courts
Boundaries Postal Districts
Par¹ Boroughs
School Br⁴ Dis¹

Balloons over and in London

Above: An impromptu landing by a gas balloon brings this busy London Street to a standstill, *c.* 1910 The location is thought to be High Holborn. *(CMcC)*

Left: In the latter half of the nineteenth century, these large tethered balloons became popular attractions in a number of European cities. This poster, from the late-1860s or early-1870s, advertises ascents from the Ashburnham Park in King's Road, Chelsea. According to the caption, ascents took place from 'May 1st and every day (weather permitting) from 1 till 7, with the immense steam captive balloon, constructed on the same system as that which acted with such success at the Universal Exhibition of 1867, in Paris.' The reference to steam comes from the steam-driven winch which hauled the balloon back down to earth. Tethered balloons have enjoyed a limited revival in recent years. *(LoC)*

Queen's Consort of England. There are some extensive barracks in Albany Street, at the back of this portion of the Park, under the title of the Horse Guards Barracks.

The Botanic Gardens, covering twenty acres, form an interesting feature of the inner circle. They belong to the Royal Botanical Society, founded in 1839, and in the handsome conservatory frequently attract 2,000 visitors to behold the collection of rare plants. ST JOHN'S LODGE, in the immediate vicinity, is the seat of Sir Isaac Lionel Goldsmid. The mansion overlooks a beautiful lake, overhung by graceful trees, and margined by the garden and archery grounds of the Toxopholite Society. On the line of the outer road is Holford Villa; and a little to the south the villa of the Marquis of Hertford. Altogether, the mansions of this district are among the most pleasing of all the architectural creations that serve to increase its picturesque beauty. Their structure is light and elegant, and very different from the brick and mortar monstrosities that line the southern outlets of London. They have all the freshness and quietude of rural retreats, though the wealth and fashion of the metropolis congregate in the same parish; and their gay equipages are constantly whirling along the adjacent road. The south side of the park, parallel to the New Road, is about half a mile in length; the east side, extending northward to Gloucester Gate, is nearly three-quarters of a mile.

The Zoological Gardens, on the north-eastern slope of the REGENT'S PARK, were instituted in 1826, the principal founders being Sir Stamford Raffles and Sir Humphrey Davy. On Mondays the admission is sixpence, on other days one shilling each. There are about 1,500 living specimens, and of these 152 species belong to the mammalian alone; among which, the last attractive feature is the young Hippopotamus, captured in August, 1849, at the island of Obaysch, about 1,350 miles above Cairo, and transmitted to this country as the gift of the Pasha of Egypt, in June 1850. There have been several recent improvements in the gardens, and additions to the buildings. A new entrance has been formed at the termination of the broad walk in the Regent's Park, which saves the foot visitor the trouble of going round by the road. The latest improvement has been the conversation of the building which was formerly occupied by the carnivore, into a Reptile House. This place adjoins the Museum, and externally it is fitted up in the style of a Swiss cottage ... In 1849, the number of visitors was 168,895. The view of Primrose Hill from this part is extremely pleasing, and the hill itself, which is now almost belted with buildings, affords in return a good opportunity for surveying to advantage the western portions of the metropolis.

West and north-west of the park is a picturesque and fashionably inhabited locality, of considerable extent, and called ST JOHN'S WOOD, from the ground having formerly belonged to the priors of St John of Jerusalem. The villas are of the first class; and the roads, laid out within the last ten years, are lined with the prettiest ornamental cottages and gardens imaginable. In Hamilton Terrace is

Opened in 1854, Brunel's design for the 'New' Paddington station was influenced by Joseph Paxton's Crystal Palace of iron and glass for the Great Exhibition of 1851.

ST MARK'S CHURCH, built in 1847 at a cost of £9,830. ST JOHN'S WOOD CHAPEL is of little architectural merit; but in the burial-ground adjoining lie not a few whose names are familiar to the ear, and among which we may make mention of JOANNA SOUTHCOTT (d. 1814), whose claims to the character of a prophetess have been long since satisfactorily examined and decided; Richard Brothers (d. 1824), another wild claimant to the inspiration of prophecy; and the clever performer Daniel Terry (d. 1829), who, as actor and dramatist, alike merited the favour of the public, and the friendship of Sir Walter Scott.

Lord's Cricket Ground, a famous spot for the gentlemen of the bat and ball, is near the Eyre Arms Tavern, and abutting on the St John's Wood Road; a great match, frequently recurring through the season, is a sight worth witnessing.

In the rear of this district, stretching away to the very verge of Hyde Park and Bayswater, lies a town, or rather city, of squares, crescents, terraces, and noble streets, comprising stately mansions, and two spacious churches, all built within the last dozen years. The erection of an entire district, Portland New Town, and apparently interminable lines of Grecianized villas, extending from the Edgeware Road, have arisen with almost magical celerity, on what was, till very recently, mere waste and neglected ground. The increased value of this property may be estimated by the fact, that a plot of land which, in the early part of the last century, was let for £12,000, and the manors of Paddington and Westbourne, which, at the dissolution, produced but a trifling sum, now return to the Bishop of London a rental of £75,000 per annum. Three guineas a foot for building-ground has been frequently paid, when a good situation was wanted by a speculator.

PADDINGTON was, but a few years back, a rural village, with a few old houses on each side of the Edgeware Road, and some rustic taverns of picturesque appearance, screened by high elms, with long troughs for horses, and straggling sign-posts. The green was a complete country retreat, and the group of elms was a study for all the landscape painters in the metropolis. The diagonal path led to the church, then a little Gothic building overspread with ivy, and as completely sequestered as any village church a hundred miles from London. It was pulled down in 1791, and the present one erected in its stead. Nollekens the sculptor, Mrs Siddons the actress, and W. Collins the marine landscape painter, are buried in the churchyard. There are four new churches recently built in the parish – ST JAMES', ST JOHN'S, HOLY TRINITY, and ALL SOUL'S; and it is now one of the busiest and most thickly populated of the London suburbs. In Praed Street is the terminus of the GREAT WESTERN RAILWAY, opened for short distances in June 1838, and to Bristol in June 1841. The basin of the Paddington Canal is in convenient proximity. The whole of this newly created district is a wonder of architectural magnificence. All the way westward from Hyde Park Terrace, through Bayswater to Notting Hill, the road is flanked with elegant and massive mansions, and on the western verge of Kensington Gardens is a new thoroughfare to Kensington itself, on which are built several detached villas in the striking Italian style, with ornamental parapets and prospect towers. The now happily forgotten, but once famous, agent of capital punishment, the 'leafless tree' of Tyburn, stood on the spot of ground occupied by No. 49, Connaught Square. The last execution there took place in 1783.

Re-entering the New Road by Lisson Grove, we pass the MARYLEBONE BATHS AND WASH-HOUSE, erected January 1850, adjoining the District County Court. The design is in the Italian style, and the building has a frontage of 160 feet, with a depth of 230 feet. There are 107 separate baths, besides two large swimming baths, with a constant supply of tepid water. The cost was about £20,000, including the freehold site. MARYLEBONE NEW CHURCH, opposite York Gate, one of the entrances to the Regent's Park, was built in 1817, at a cost of £60,000. FITXROY SQUARE, completed 1793, and EUSTON SQUARE, of much later erection, derive their names from the FITZROYS, Dukes of Grafton, and Earls of Euston, who are the ground landlords. An opening at the northern end leads to the stately terminus of the NORTH WESTERN RAILWAY, which was first opened to Birmingham September 17, 1838. The massive, but elegant, entrance is in the Grecian Doric style of architecture, and is

164

70 feet high. The great hall, opened in May 1849, is of immense size, and magnificently embellished. It is said to have cost £150,000. On the other side of Euston Square, in the New Road, is ST PANCRAS NEW CHURCH, finished in 1822 ... The exterior is adapted from Greek models, and the entablatures of the side porticoes are supported by Caryatides, holding ewers and inverted torches. The pulpit and reading-desk are formed from the celebrated Fairlop Oak, that was blown down in 1820, after having, for some seven centuries, graced the avenues of Hainault forest. The interior of the church is elegantly constructed, and greater light and elevation are only wanted to render it faultless.

Passing at the back of the church through BURTON CRESCENT, so called after the builder, and entering HUNTER STREET, we may point out the NATIONAL SCOTTISH CHURHC in REGENT SQUARE, originally built for Irving of 'unknown tongue' celebrity. It is a large Gothic structure of little architectural merit. Crossing BRUNSWICK SQUARE into Guildford Street, the FOUNDLING HOSPITAL is seen to the left, founded in 1739 by Captain Thomas Coram, as a hospital for poor illegitimate children whose mothers are known, and whose reception is regulated by a committee, who examining whether the case is such as to require the relief afforded by the institution or not. It is a handsome structure, with a good garden and commodious playground for the children. The chapel is in the centre, and the east wing is appropriated to the girls, and the west to the boys. The annual income is averaged at £10,000, and about 460 children are maintained and educated. In the interior are some excellent paintings by Hogarth and others. A visit during Divine service on a Sunday to the chapel, is a great treat to the lovers of sacred music, and the interesting and impressive scene to be there witnessed will not be readily forgotten.

LAMB'S CONDUIT STREET, deriving its name from a conduit that stood in the fields near Holborn, and which was erected, in 1577, at the expense of a benevolent clothworker of that name, will bring us to RED LION STREET, whence retracing our steps through a district already made familiar to the reader, we can regain the point of our departure.

Eighth Day's Route

DISTRICT II

Taking again a northerly course, we pursue our way from Holborn up GRAY'S INN LANE, in which stands the ROYAL FREE HOSPITAL, founded in 1828, and affording, as its name implies, immediate assistance to all destitute persons requiring medical relief. From the period of its foundation till 1849, 310,547 persons have been gratuitously relieved, and of these 28,190 belonged to 1849 alone. The road leads to KING'S CROSS, so called from an execrable statue of George IV, that stood there till 1842, and which has also derived the name of Battle Bridge from a sanguinary battle fought at this spot between King Alfred and the Danes. Here is the terminus of the GREAT NORTHERN RAILWAY, for which the site was cleared in 1850. The road, close by, branches off in a north-westerly direction to CAMDEN TOWN and KENTISH TOWN, leading past the old Church of ST PANC RAS, originally erected in 1180, and repaired and enlarged in 1848. Nearly opposite to the church is a neat and commodious range of residences known as THE MODEL BULDINGS, and supplying all the conveniences of a metropolitan lodging-house on a better and more economical principle.

For the sake of visiting localities of greater interest, we shall, however, turn aside from Gray's Inn Lane, nearly opposite Theobald's Road, and enter COLDBATH FIELDS, a district long built over, but once famous for a cold spring that still exists in Bath Street. Here is the MIDDLESEX HOUSE OF CORRECTION, opened in 1794. There are 530 cells, and the average number of prisoners daily within the walls, and subject to penal discipline, is 1,000. Workshops on a large scale have been recently added, to furnish employment to the prisoners.

The eastern wall of the House of Correction runs parallel with the Bagnigge Wells Road, where stood Bagnigge Wells, a king of minor Vauxhall of the day, and existing within the last half century; but of late it has been built over by the Messrs.Cubbitt, who have extensive premises at the back, forming quite a little town of itself. In Exmouth Street is the SPA FIELDS CHAPEL, once a theatre, and purchased for its present purpose by the Countess of Huntingdon.

SADLER'S WELL'S THEATRE is in the immediate vicinity, its western side, till very lately, having a fine grove of trees forming an avenue to the St John Street Road. The name originates from the discovery, in 1683, of a well on this spot, by Mr Sadler, one of the surveyors of the highways, and who built a Music House to divert the company attracted by the mineral spring. Latterly, having enjoyed the advantages of more creditable management, it has become one of the most favourite establishments in the metropolis. A neighbouring tavern reminds us our proximity to the NEW RIVER head and reservoir, which, after having originated with the enterprise of Sir Hugh Myddelton, who was ruined by the scheme, now brings a fortune to every shareholder. Its length from Chadwell, in Hertfordshire, where it rises, to this point, where it supplies the greater part of the metropolis on the north side the Thames, is nearly forty miles.

In 1862 London had a prison population of over 12,000. This is Pentonville. *(CMcC)*

PENTONVILLE, a large district on the north side of the New Road, was unbuilt upon till 1773, when the fields of Mr Henry Penton were appropriated to receive the increasing population. Of late years it has extended rapidly. Barnsbury Road and Barnsbury Park, a new and daily improving district, derive their names from Lady Juliana Berners, Abbess of St Albans, who had a large manor in this neighbourhood. WHITE CONDUIT HOUSE, a once favourite place of entertainment, and much resorted to in the days of Oliver Goldsmith, who was one of its frequent visitors, was demolished in 1849, and a street and a similar tavern were erected on its grounds. THE PENTONVILLE or MODEL PRISON, in the Caledonian Road, was built in 1842 at the cost of £84,169. It occupies about seven acres of ground, and contains 1,000 separate cells, which are well lit, warmed, and ventilated on an improved plan. In 1849, the total number of prisoners was 1,106; the total expenses for the same year £15,675; but from this a deduction is to be made of £2,425, earned by the prisoners, who are either taught useful trades, or pursue their original vocation within its walls. The West India Docks and Birmingham Junction Railway runs close by; and a little further on is the CALEDONIAN ASYLUM, built in 1828, 'for the purpose of supporting and educating the children of soldiers, sailors, and marines, natives of Scotland, who have died or been disabled in the service of their country, and or indigent Scotch parents resident in London, not entitled to parochial relief.' From Copenhagen Fields opposite, now the site of the great cattle market formerly held in Smithfield, there is a good view of northern London and the country towards Highgate, Hornsey, and Essex.

The NEW ROAD at 'The Angel,' the great focus of northerly omnibus traffic, merges into the 'City Road,' which leads past Finsbury Square to the Bank. ISLINGTON, an immense suburb, now grown into part of the metropolis itself, lies to the north, and contains a population of little less than 60,000. In the Liverpool Road is the LONDON FEVER HOSPITAL, removed hither from King's Cross in 1849. The old Church of ST MARY'S, in the Upper Street, was opened in May, 1754; the steeple is more curious than elegant. ST PETER'S CHURCH was built by Barry in 1835, at a cost of £3,407.

CANONBURY TOWER, 17 feet square, and about 60 feet high, is a vestige of the old Manor-House that arose out of the mansion built by Prior Bolton, of St Bartholomew's in Smithfield. Oliver Goldsmith lodged here in 1764, and one of the upper apartments in the tower is yet pointed out as the place where he wrote the 'Vicar of Wakefield.' Not far from Islington Green, in the Lower Road, is the 'QUEEN'S HEAD,' a tavern of modern construction, but built upon the site of a very ancient one that existed till 1829. A portion of the old wainscoted parlour still remains; whilst a tankard, with a curious, but not exactly quotable inscription, recounts the bygone celebrities of the place. A walk through HIGHBURY, noticing its picturesque little church, finished in 1848, and past the Sluice-house, and the New River, to Hornsey Wood House, will give the stranger an agreeable idea of the picturesque character of this vast appurtenance to the mammoth city. The New Islington Cattle Market is close to the New North Road.

Returning to the Angel, and proceeding eastward on the CITY ROAD, first opened in 1761, we must pause to notice the Elizabethan Almshouses, founded by Lady Owen in 1610, and recently rebuilt. They stand on the eastern side of St John Street Road, and furnish habitations for poor old women of the parish of St Mary, Islington, and St James', Clerkenwell, together with a school for poor boys of the same parishes, an equal number from each. Crossing the bridge that spans a branch of the Regent's Canal, we pass the 'EAGLE' on our left, a minor, but generally well-conducted house for operatic entertainments, under the title of the 'Grecian Saloon,' and reach the OLD STREET ROAD, the suburbs of Hoxton and Hackney lying to the north. At the corner is ST LUKE'S HOSPITAL, for lunatics, instituted in 1751, and built by Danes in 1784. No patient is received here who is known to be in possession of means for decent support in a private asylum. The parish church of ST LUKE'S seen further on, is by no means remarkable for beauty. It was built in 1733. BUNHILL ROW should be traversed, for the sake of seeing the large Burial Ground, for nearly two centuries used by the Dissenters as a place of interment. Here is buried, John Bunyan, the well-known author of the 'Pilgrim's

Progress' (d. 1688); George Fox, the founder of the Society of Friends (d. 1690); Daniel De Foe (d. 1731); Isaac Watts (d. 1748); and Blake (d. 1828), and Stohard (d. 1834), the painters, besides others, who, like those we have recorded, have left a reputation as well as a name behind them. In ARTILLERY WALK adjoining, Milton finished his 'Paradise Lost,' and here, in 1674, he died.

The ARTILLERY GROUND is now, as it has been for upwards of two centuries, the exercising ground of the Honourable Artillery Company of the City of London, the old City trained band, formed in 1585, to oppose the contemplated Spanish invasion. When the alarm subsided, the City volunteers discontinued their customary exercises, and the grounds were used by the gunners of the Tower. In 1610 a new company was formed, and the weekly exercise rigidly enforced. On the breaking out of the Civil War, they took part against the king; and though previously held in low estimation, and treated merely as 'holiday' soldiers, they did good service to the Parliamentary cause, especially at the battle of Newbury. Clarendon is forced to admit that they 'behaved themselves to wonder, and were in truth the preservation of that army that day.' Cromwell himself acknowledged their value, and gave the command of them to Major-General Skipton. They then numbered 18,000 foot and 600 horse, divided into six regiments of trained bands, six of auxiliaries, and one of horse. Disbanded at the Restoration, a new company was formed, of which Charles II and his brother the Duke of York became members. Since that period they have led a peaceful life; and, except in 1780, when by their promptness they saved the Bank of England, their appearances in public have been confined to festive occasions. The strength of the Company has gradually fallen off. In 1708, they numbered about 700; in 1720, about 600; and in 1844, only about 250. Prince Albert is their colonel. Now again with rifle volunteer corps forming everywhere under royal and national patronage, this ancient company will probably greatly increase in numerical and effective strength.

From the Artillery Ground Lunardi made his first balloon ascent in 1784.

Returning to Old Street, and crossing GOSWELL STREET, we pass through a narrow thoroughfare chiefly inhabited by brokers, and called WILDERNESS ROW, whence we may extend our perambulations to CLERKENWELL GREEN, part of a region thickly populated by watch and clock makers. Here is the SESSIONS HOUSE for Middlesex, the building dating from 1782, and near it is the Church of St James', Clerkenwell, built on the site of a much older church to the same saint, and originally the choir of a Benedictine nunnery founded about 1100. The present building was begun in 1788, and finished in 1792. In the vaults is preserved the tomb of Prior Weston, the last Prior of the Hospital of St John of Jerusalem. Here also rest the remains of Bishop Burnet.

North of the Green is the Clerkenwell HOUSE OF DETENTION, for receiving prisoners who have not yet had sentence passed upon them. The annual expenditure is said to be nearly £7,000, and the average number of prisoners daily 110. A chapel and school-room are attached to the premises. Hence we may return into St John Street, and so reach Smithfield; or, by permeating the uninviting thoroughfares at the back of Saffron Hill and Hatton Garden, return by way of Holborn. Should the latter, for the sake of novelty, be chosen, the visitor will be able to gather some insight into that colony, which, for the last century, has been the chosen refuge of the lower class of emigrants, and the favourite haunt of those vagrant Savoyards who gain a precarious subsistence by grinding barrel-organs through the metropolis, from sunrise till sundown. Here, too, live the greater part of the image-vendors and modellers, the sellers of cheap earthenware and Birmingham goods, the dealers in broken clocks and umbrellas, and specimens of those in describable traders about the pavement who live by the sale of fruit or fish according to the season. This portion, indeed, is the focus of those scattered rays of itinerant life that penetrate at various periods of the day into every portion of the streets of London, giving a distinct character to its thoroughfares, and colouring, as it were, the stream of daily traffic with the motley hues of metropolitan vagabondism. As such it may, with proper precautions that suggest themselves, form with advantage one of the places visited by the stranger in London.

When Bradshaw wrote this Hand-Book, construction of the Victoria Embankment had yet to commence. Its purpose was to reduce the width of the river on the north bank in order to ease road congestion and also to accommodate new sewage pipes and the Metropolitan District Railway underground. This cutaway shows the section at Charing Cross station with the railway bridge over the river on the right.

Today's Waterloo station is the result of a total rebuild which was not completed until 1922. Prior to that the station consisted of a mishmash of buildings and platforms. This is the main part of the South Western Railway's terminus, with the line to London Bridge extending across the road on the left, *c.* 1900. *(LoC)*

PART FIVE

The South

Crossing London Bridge we now enter the BOROUGH OF SOUTHWARK, one of the most animated parts of the metropolis, from the extent of the business carried on in this extensive locality, and one of the most interesting from its antiquity. On the right is the old Church of ST SAVIOUR'S, erected on the site of the ancient priory of St Mary Overy, and first made the parochial church in 1540. The choir, restored in 1822, and the beautiful Ladye Chapel, renovated in 1832, form the oldest portions of the present structure. Here is a monument to Gower the poet, and contemporary of Chaucer; it was restored by the Duke of Sutherland, a descendant of the Gower family, in 1832. These fathers of English poetry followed each other closely to the grave; Chaucer died in 1400, aged 72,and Gower in 1402, blind and full of years. John Fletcher and Philip Massinger the dramatists are also interred here, but without inscriptions. On the opposite side is the Church of St Olave's, which, by a corruption of names sufficient to puzzle a phonetic philosopher, gave the appellation of Tooley Street to the long straggling thoroughfare that hence leads to Bermondsey, Horsleydown, and the river-side districts.

The spacious terminus of the SOUTHEASTERN, LONDON AND BRIGHTON, GREENWICH, NORTH KENT, and CROYDON Railways, that all converge at this point, is seen at the end of a broad turning that leads from the main road up to the respective stations, the premises are not without some pretensions to ornament; but, what is still better, their arrangements are admirably made to give the greatest possible accommodation to the public without the slightest approach to confusion. The various additions to the original structure have been made from time to time as the increase in the traffic of the respective lines called for their extension, and beneath are spacious vaults under the arches for the stowage of heavy goods.

Close to this cluster of railway stations is ST THOMAS' HOSPITAL, originally founded as an Almonry, in 1213, by the Prior of Bermondsey, and opened as a hospital in 1552. The present edifice, which, since the date of its erection in 1706, has been frequently altered and repaired, consists of three courts, with colonnades between each, and containing 20 wards and 485 beds … we may mention that in 1849 there were admitted, cured, and discharged 4,737 inpatients, and 59,109 outpatients, including casualties, whilst many have been relieved with money and necessaries at their departure, to accommodate and support them in their journeys to their several habitations. In the middle of one of the courts is a bronze statue, by Scheemaker, of Edward VI; and in another is a statue of Sir Robert Clayton, a Lord Mayor of London who gave a considerable amount towards its endowment. The statue was erected before his death, which happened in 1714.

In St Thomas' Street, on the right hand side, is GUY'S HOSPITAL, founded by Thomas Guy, a benevolent bookseller in Lombard Street, who, by various successes in trade and speculation, succeeded at last in amassing a considerable fortune. He made liberal gifts to St Thomas' during his lifetime, and also founded an almshouse, afterwards endowed by his will, for fourteen poor people at Tamworth, his mother's native town, which he represented in several parliaments. He left annuities to his older relatives, amounting to £870 a year; and to the younger, extending to grandchildren of his uncles and aunts, he left stock in the funds, mostly in sums of £1,000 each, to the extent of more than £74,000, besides bequeathing land. To Christ's Hospital he gave a perpetual annuity of £400, to receive, on the nomination of his trustees, four children yearly, who must be his connexions, and there are always applicants. He left £1,000 to discharge poor prisoners in London, Middlesex, and Surrey, at £5 each; and another £1,000 to be distributed among poor housekeepers at the discretion of his executors. The erection of the hospital, the earliest part of which was built by Dance, cost nearly £19,000, and the rest of his personal property, about £219,000, was devoted to the endowment of his hospital. Though seventy-six when it was commenced, the humane founder lived to see the hospital ready to receive its patients, the first sixty of whom entered in January 1725. Guy's Hospital now occupies a site of five acres and a half. Against the stone front of the building, on entering, are the emblematic figures of Æseulapius and Hygeia. In the west wing is the chapel, and opposite, in the east wing, which is the older, is the court-room; in the former was buried Sir Astley Cooper, the eminent surgeon, who died in 1841. In the centre of the first court is the statue of the founder, in bronze, executed by Scheemaker; and in the chapel is a fine piece of sculpture by the elder Bacon, representing Guy in his livery gown holding out one hand to raise a poor invalid lying on the earth, and pointing with the other to a distressed object carried on a litter into the hospital, which is seen in the background. The buildings, which are airy and well suited to promote recovery, contain about 530 beds for inpatients, and there are 50,000 outpatients relieved annually, nine-tenths of whom are on the average cured. Eastward, towards Bermondsey, is a poverty-stricken region called the Maze, and a Roman Catholic Chapel and Convent, where the ceremony of taking the veil may be occasionally witnessed. ST PAUL'S CHURCH, in that district, was finished in 1841.

The old inns in the Borough, with their wide, rambling staircases, and wooden galleries round the inn-yards, are pleasant reminiscences of the ancient days of coach and wagon traffic, and must not escape observation. Many of these have had an existence for centuries, and we have little occasion to remind the reader of Chaucer, that the TALBOT (No. 75) in High Street, was the Tabard 'where Geoffrey Chaucer, knight, and nine-and-twenty pilgrims, lodged on their journey to Canterbury, in 1383.' The sign was changed from the 'Tabard,' which signifies the sleeveless coat worn by the heralds, to the 'Talbot,' is 1677, when a great portion for the present building was erected.

A little further on, at the corner of Great Dover Street and Blackman Street, is the parochial church of ST GEORGE THE MARTYR, built in 1737, on the site of an older one. Over the altar is a painted window, representing our Saviour preaching in the Temple. Here are entombed the remains of Edward Cocker, the author of the once famous, often-mentioned, and yet seldom-seen school-book, 'Cocker's Arithmetic.' It is curious that no map of this parish is known to exist; a fact not more strange and discreditable than that a resolution was passed at a vestry-meeting, held in 1776, 'to sell to Mr Samuel Carter all the parish papers and documents in a lump, at the rate of three-halfpence per pound, he being at the expense of carrying them away.' Kent Street, at the back, so called from its having formed the great road to the country of Kent, is a wretched and profligate part of the Borough. In 1633, it was described as 'very long and very ill-built, and inhabited chiefly by broom-men and mumpers,' and its present character would, if described, be found even more disreputable. On the site of a distillery opposite St George's Church, was the palace of Charles Brandon, Duke of Suffolk, the husband of Mary, sister of Henry VIII, and window of Louis XII. In 1545, this princely edifice was converted by Henry VIII into a Royal Mint, subsequently taken down, and replaced by a number of mean and irregular dwellings. In 1697, the number of houses was 92; in 1830, they amounted to 1,712. Even as early as the time of Edward VI, the Mint had become an asylum for debtors, felons, rogues, and vagabonds of every description, and it was only partially put down by Act of Parliament, at the latter end of the reign of George I. Here were the cheap lodging-houses of the Borough. On an average, each house in winter sheltered 70 persons, and in summer about 30. The usual charge to each person was threepence for the 24 hours. No stranger should trust himself in this locality without an efficient protection, the utmost vigilance of the police being found insufficient to repress the acts of violence and robbery still perpetrated occasionally within its precincts, notwithstanding the improvements which have been made of late years even in this locality.

On the left, reached either through Trinity Square or by the Lane itself, is HORSEMONGER LAND JAIL, the place of imprisonment and execution for the county of Surrey. On the right, at the corner of the Borough Road, is the QUEEN'S BENCH PRISON, the sombre walls of which, fifty feet high, with the chevaux de frize at the top, look grimly down upon the busy thoroughfare beneath. This is a prison of great antiquity, and, for some years past, has been used exclusively for debtors. There are nearly 250 distinct rooms within, and, since the Fleet and the Marshalsea have been abolished, the vacancies have been very rare. It is here that tradition asserts Prince Henry, afterwards Henry V, was sent by the independent Judge Gascoigne, for striking him on the bench. In the Borough Road is the BRITISH AND FOREIGN SCHOOL, and the SOUTHWARK LITERARY INSTITUTION.

Resuming our progress, we arrive at the well-known tavern called the ELEPHANT AND CASTLE, whence omnibuses are constantly arriving from, and departing to, all parts of the metropolis and its environs. The quaint old pile opposite is 'The Fishmongers' Almshouses,' built about 1633; latterly the company have determined on a removal of their hospital to a more open site at East Hill, Wandsworth, where the first stone of a new asylum was laid in June, 1849. The New Kent Road leads to Deptford and Greenwich; the Walworth Road to Camberwell, and the south-westward over Kennington Common to Brixton and Clapham. In Penton Place is the entrance to the SURREY GARDENS and MUSIC HALL, which occupies the site formerly known as the Surrey Zoological Gardens. They were opened for concerts and other entertainments by a company, which, not proving successful, they have only been temporarily occupied for a variety of al fresco entertainments …

Returning by the LONDON ROAD, we may notice at the end some workshops, that till recently formed part of the establishment of the PHILANTHROPIC SOCIETY instituted in 1788 for the reformation of youthful offenders by religious and industrial training. Until the year 1850, this was the place where the operations of the Society were carried on; but the institution is now removed to Red Hill, near Reigate, and the manufactory is transformed into a farm. The farm consists of 133 acres, and has been taken on a lease of 150 years. The number of boys at school generally averages about 100, and they are all destined for emigrants to the British Colonies. Immediately adjacent is the school for the education of the INDICENT BLIND, founded in 1799 … There are about seventy inmates, who are taught to make baskets, cradles, clothes, boots, shoes, mats, and various other articles, which are sold at the school. The present spacious Gothic structure was built in 1837, and is admirably adapted to its purpose.

In the last century St George's Fields, the site of these palaces of philanthropy, was the scene of low dissipation; and here, on the very focus of the 'No Popery' riots of 1780, has arisen the ROMAN CATHOLIC CATHEDRAL. This singular evidence of the mutations to which localities are subject, and striking proof of our advance in liberality of opinion, occupies a large plot of ground at the corner of the Lambeth Road, and nearly facing the eastern wing of Bethlehem Hospital. The building was commenced in 1840, from the designs of Pugin, and was consecrated with great pomp and ceremony on Tuesday, the 4th of July, 1848. The cathedral is dedicated to St George, and is in the later decorated style. It is cruciform in plan, and consists of a nave and aisles, the tower, a chancel, and two chapels; one is dedicated in honour of the Holy Sacrament, and the other in honour of the Virgin, and between them is the high altar. The body of the church is allotted to the laity, and is calculated to seat about 3,000 persons. The principal entrance is in the great tower, intended to be carried up to the height of 320 feet, and over the deeply-moulded doorway is a brilliantly painted window, representing St George, St Michael, and other saints. The arch which opens to the nave is 40 feet high. The cross, an original work of the fifteenth century, was purchased in Belgium, and, restored, forms one of the finest examples existing, quite equal to that of Louvain, and probably executed by the same artist. The range of monastic buildings adjoining, includes a convent for Sisters of Mercy, and a school for 300 children.

Bethlehem Hospital, a noble institution, designed for the reception of those who are suffering from that most awful of human maladies, mental aberration, covers a surface of fourteen acres, and presents a fine exterior, constituting of a centre and two wings about 700 feet in length. Old 'Bedlam,' in Moorfields, having been taken down in 1814, the present structure was raised in St George's Fields, and finished soon after, on the site of a notorious tavern, called 'The Dog and Duck.' A new wing was added in 1839, and since then other portions of the premises have been considerably enlarged. The annual expenses reach nearly £20,000. In the vestibule are the two statues of Raving and Melancholy Madness, which were sculptured by Caius Cibber, and formerly surmounted the hospital in Moorfields. One is said to represent the tall porter of Oliver Cromwell, who was a lunatic at the time. On entering the grand hall, the eye of the visitor is first attracted by the spacious staircase, which ascends from the ground floor to the council-chamber above. On each side, passages run laterally through the building, the one to the right leading to the male, the other to the female ward. Following the former, we are inducted through a long series of galleries, ascended by stone staircases, to the apartments occupied by the patients. The sleeping-rooms contain a low truckle bedstead, with chair and table, light and air being admitted through a small barred circular window at the top. Each door opens to the gallery, affording a promenade 250 feet in length, where the patients can resort for exercise when the weather proves for exercise when the weather proves unfavourable. To the left of the gallery is the dining-room, capable of accommodating about 100 persons. The diet, which is of the best kind, is served on wooden bowls and platters, and is seldom unaccompanied by good appetites. These corridors are preserved at an equable temperature through ever change of season, by the introduction of warm air-pipes and stoves beneath the flooring, so constructed that every patient's room has an equal degree of warmth. Each story has one of these galleries connected with it, from the last of which a stone staircase conducts to the chapel, a spacious but neat apartment, well adapted to the solemn purpose for which it has been consecrated. A curtain separates the male and female auditors, the former occupying the left, the latter the right benches, whilst the pulpit is arranged so as to give the minister a commanding view of his congregation. Not only is strict decorum here is observed, but he most marked attention is paid to the preacher's exhortations, and the responses are followed with apparent heartfelt and unaffected devotion … The workshops are in another portion of the building, where those patients who, from their previous employment, are qualified for their task, may be seen working at their respective trades.

A library is also at the disposal of those who may feel inclined to read and study. The freedom of ventilation, and the establishment of baths accessible to all, must not be forgotten as highly deserving commendation with the other arrangements. A proof of the general health and longevity enjoyed by the inmates may be found in the fact, that Margaret Nicholson, who was confined in the hospital for attempting to stab George III, died here in 1828, after an imprisonment of forty-two years; and James Hatfield, who was confined for a similar offence in 1800, only died as recently as 1841. During the year 1849, there were admitted 150 males, and 194 females; discharged cured, 70 males, and 106 females. The ratio of cures is said to be fifty-nine in every hundred. The general aspect of the patients is that of extreme contentment, excepting, of course, those labouring under particular delusions. Not the slightest restriction is visible throughout, and there are but few whose demeanour is violent enough to require more rigid measures. Kindness is the only charm by which the attendants exert a mastery over the patients, and the influence thus possessed is most remarkable. Whilst the impression left on the mind of a visitor is that of a mournful gratification, it is yet blended with a feeling of intense satisfaction, arising from a knowledge that the comforts of his afflicted fellow-creatures are so industriously sought after, and so assiduously promoted.

At the junction of the London Road with the Blackfriars Road, is an obelisk, standing in the centre of the open ground whence six roads branch off in different directions. It is now considered merely as the indicator of various distances, for few seem to recollect that it was placed there in 1771, to the commemorate the independent and patriotic spirit with which Brass Crosby, Esq., then Lord Mayor, released a printer who had been seized, contrary to law, by the House of Commons, and for committing the messenger of the House to prison, though, for this last daring achievement, he was himself incarcerated in the Tower. Nearly at the corner of the Blackfriars Road is the SURREY THEATRE, originally opened in 1782 as a Circus, by Messrs. Hughes and Dibdin, who conducted it for some time with considerable success, as an exhibition of ballets, pantomimes, and horsemanship.

It was burned down in 1805, and being rebuilt the following year, has, subsequently, proved one of the most attractive of the minor theatres. In 1848, it was considerably improved, being re-embellished, and nearly rebuilt. A short distance from it, in the Blackfriars Road, is the MAGDALEN HOSPITAL, established in 1758 for the relief and reformation of those unfortunate females, who, having strayed from the paths of virtue, and become outcasts from society, may here find a refuge and a home. Since the period of its existence, more than 6,000 poor girls who were admitted, have been restored to their friends, or placed in reputable employments. The committee meet ever Thursday to receive applicants, and Divine service is performed at the chapel twice every Sunday. Few will be deterred from attendance on this last occasion, by hearing that a collection is made previously to admission, for supporting this excellent institution, and for which a small donation is expected from the visitor …

The Waterloo Road, leading to Waterloo Bridge, is a broad, but ill-built thoroughfare, much better than it used to be, but still susceptible of vast improvement. About half-way down, on the eastern side, is the VICTORIA THEATRE, a cheap place of minor dramatic entertainment, and opened as the Coburg Theatre in 1818. On the same side the way, and nearer the bridge, is ST JOHN'S CHURCH, built in 1824. Within the narrow limits of the churchyard lie several of the sons of Thespis, who have furnished in their lifetime many mirthful hours to the public. Opposite, are the vast premises forming the London TERMINUS of the SOUTH WESTERN RAILWAY. The extension from Vauxhall to the Waterloo Road was thrown open July 11, 1848. The advantages of this metropolitan station have been very great, both to mere pleasure-seekers and men of business; and when about to undertake a journey on this most tempting and trustworthy of all the railways, it is felt to be something akin to magic, to be wafted from the very heart of London to the verge of Southampton Water, in less time than one could walk from here to Hampstead; or, enabled to enjoy the enchanting scenery of Richmond and Hampton Court for an expenditure of the same sum that would be absorbed in the most moderate indulgence at a gloomy tavern in town.

The Westminster Road, leading to Westminster Bridge, has at the angle of junction with the Kennington Road the FEMALE ORPHAN ASYLUM, an excellent institution for the reception of destitute female orphans. It was founded in 1758, and incorporated in 1800. From its foundation to the present time nearly 3,000 orphan girls have been sheltered, educated, and fitted for domestic employment. No girl is admitted under eight or above ten years of age, and none remain after they have attained the age of sixteen. The asylum, which contains about 160 inmates, is open to visitors, by special order …

The Kennington Road, leading to Kennington Common and the southern suburbs, is a spacious well-inhabited thoroughfare, with some neat squares and terraces adjoining. In Kennington Lane is the LICENSED VICTUALLERS' SCHOOL, and further on is the principal entrance to VAUXHALL GARDENS, a favourite place of summer resort, from the reign of Charles II to that of Victoria. They were first opened for public amusement by Jonathon Tyers, in June, 1732, and their long career of 127 years was brought to a close only in 1859, when they were sold for building purposes.

From Bethlehem Hospital the road leads direct through Church Street to old Lambeth Church and Palace. To the left are some narrow streets, now traversed by the viaduct of the South Western Railway, and worth looking at as vestiges of the old river side habitations. They are now, for the most part, tenanted by soap-boilers, whitening manufacturers, and the proprietors of bone factories and potteries; the dense smoke vomited forth from the tall chimneys, and the noisome odours resulting from the various processes carried on, by no means contributing to increase the salubrity of the locality.

The old parish church of ST MARY'S adjoins the Palace. The tower, built about the reign of Edward IV (1375), has been lately restored, and other necessary repairs made, from time to time, to ensure the safety of the structure, have materially effaced the outward indications of antiquity is once possessed. Beneath these walls Mary d'Este, the Queen of James II, flying with her infant prince from the ruin impending over their House, after crossing the Thames from the abdicated Whitehall, took shelter from the inclement weather of the night of December 6th, 1688. Here she waited with aggravated misery till a common coach, procured from an adjacent inn, arrived, and conveyed her to Gravesend, whence she bade an eternal adieu to these kingdoms. The interior has no special feature requiring notice, beyond the painting in the south-east window, which represents the full-length figure of a pedlar with his pack, staff, and dog. A pleasant tradition, repeated so often that it has come at last to be believed, relates how the parish received from this illustrious unknown, the bequest of a piece of ground, on condition that the portrait of himself and dog was preserved in one of the church windows; and, to favour its probability, the painting is jealously perpetuated, and to a recent date the Belvidere Road, as it is now called, went by the appellation of 'Pedlar's Acre.' A walk through the churchyard, that thickly-tenanted sepulchre of past generations, will, however, repay the observer for half an hour's meditation among the tombs. Most conspicuous amongst them is the altar-tomb of old John Tradescant, the indefatigable collector of curiosities, who, with his son, rests beneath a monument somewhat incongruously embellished with pyramids, palms, death's heads, and pelicans. He is the first person who ever formed a cabinet of curiosities in this kingdom, and is said to have been at one part of his life gardener to Charles I. we are indebted to him for the introduction into this country of many valuable fruits and flowers indigenous to the East. At his death, in 1652, his collection fell as a legacy into the possession of Elias Ashmole, who removed it afterwards to Oxford, where it is still preserved in the Ashmolean Museum …

Lambeth Palace has been, from a very early period, the London residence of the Archbishop of Canterbury. Close to the church is the picturesque gatehouse of red brick, built in 1500. The hall to which it leads is a spacious structure, 93 feet by 38, and was built by Archbishop Juxon, whose arms are over the door, with the date of 1663. The chapel is the oldest portion of the palace, and was built by Boniface, Archbishop of Canterbury, in 1224. The library now contains about 25,000 volumes, and was founded by Archbishop Bancroft, who died in 1610, and left all his books to his successors forever. It has since been considerably enriched and enlarged. Here are some scarce works of ancient date, and some rare old volumes of divinity. But by far the best known, and most interesting portion of Lambeth Palace, is the LOLLARD'S TOWER at the western end, which is pointed out to later ages as the very prison in which the persecuted followers of Wickliffe were incarcerated. This tower, so fraught with the associations of history and the tales of legendary lore, was built, for £280, by Henry Chicheley, who enjoyed the primacy from 1414 to 1443. A niche, in which was once placed the image of St Thomas, may be noticed in the front facing the river. At the summit is a small room, 13 feet by 12, and about 8 feet in height. This is called 'the prison,' and on the oak wainscoting, which is above an inch thick, several broken sentences and names, in curious antique characters, are inscribed … Eight large iron rings in the wall, to which the prisoners were chained before they were brought to the stake, attest the nature of the apartment, and the cruelties that were practised within it. The gardens at the back, thirty acres in extent, are laid out with great taste, and the tall old trees materially contribute to the picturesque effect of the building, as seen from the river.

Through BISHOP'S WALK, whence across the river an excellent view can be gained of the New Houses of Parliament, and Stangate, a famous spot for boat-builders, we come to the WESTMINSTER BRIDGE ROAD, at the commencement of which is ASTLEY'S AMPHITHEATRE. In 1774, Philip Astley, who is said to have enjoyed the enviable privilege of being the handsomest man in England, erected a booth on this spot for horsemanship and other amusements in the open air. The success of this enabled him to build a theatre, which was thrice destroyed by fire, and thrice rebuilt. The last fire took place in 1841, when the excellent management of Ducrow had raised the establishment to a high rank among its contemporaries; and since then a new theatre has been constructed on a larger scale. The present one will hold about 3,000 spectators, and the arena for the equestrians is 126 feet in circumference. The performances are varied, and generally well sustained.

Crossing the old district of Pedlar's Acre, and proceeding down the Belvidere Road, we shall have an excellent opportunity of noticing the extent of the artificial elevation given to the road when the approaches to Waterloo Bridge were made. Indeed, it hardly needs the occasional incursions of the river to remind the water-side inhabitants, that this now dense and widely-spreading region was once a marsh, and even within the recollection of many living, a flat swampy level, scarcely raised above the surface of the Thames. The great timber yards about here are well worth a visit, and seem in their colossal piles to threatened exhaustion to the forests of Norway and Sweden.

Stamford Street, or the Commercial Road, leading by the water-side, will bring us to the Blackfriars Road. CHRIST CHURHC, built in 1737, stands partly on the side of Paris Garden, one of the ancient playhouses of the metropolis. It seems to have been much frequented on Sundays for bearbaiting, a favourite sport in the time of Queen Elizabeth. Continuing our way along the BANKSIDE, once the scene of our ancestors' dissipation and debauchery, but now chiefly frequented by bargemen and those connected with the smaller river craft, we come to the BARCLAY AND PERKINS' BREWERY, so associated all over the world with the celebrity of London porter. On part of the ground occupied by the adjacent premises, stood the GLOBE THEATRE built 1584, and demolished 1644, and here many of Shakespeare's plays were originally produced. The buildings belonging to the Brewery, which is the largest in the world, extend over ten acres ... Among the host of curiosities to be seen in London, this mammoth establishment is one of the most characteristic and interesting, and should be visited by all who can obtain the necessary introduction. The quantity of malt consumed here, in 1849, was 115,542 quarters; and in the busy season of the year there are about 600 quarters of malt brewed daily. Among the many vats to be seen is one containing 3,500 barrels of porter, which, at the selling price, would yield £9,000. There are 180 horses employed in the cartage department, which are a show of themselves. They are brought principally from Flanders, and cost £50 to £80 each. There are annually consumed by these horses £5,000 qrs. of oats, beans, or other grain, which is bruised; 450 tons of clover, and 170 tons of straw for litter. The manure, spent hops, and other refuse, are let yearly, and the sum paid for 1850 was £75. The lessee employs the railway company to take it from the premises to his farm. On an average, there are weekly 18 tons of stable manure, and 37 tons of refuse, chiefly spent hops, which is about 1s 7d per ton for the manure, and all the rest for nothing. There are now four partners in the house, who conduct every department of it in the most liberal manner, as may be judged when we state that they pay their head brewer a salary of £1,000 per year. In the by-streets between here and London Bridge, some of the walls of WINCHESTER HOUSE, the ancient palace of the Bishops of Winchester, are still visible; and the CLINK, a prison by the Bankside, of the time of James I still perpetuates its name in one of the adjacent thoroughfares.

Hence we cross by the Borough Market back to London Bridge, and so, having effected a complete circuit of the southern portion of the metropolis, return to the point from which we originally started.

And here the Guide resigns his companionship …before, however, finally relinquishing his office, he would again earnestly impress upon the stranger the necessity of once during his stay at least going to Waterloo Bridge of a clear morning to see the metropolis by sunrise. Then will he truly feel with Wordsworth:

Earth has not anything to show more fair;
Dull would be of soul who could pass by
A sight so touching in its majesty;
This city now doth like a garment wear
The beauty of the morning; silent, bare,
Ships, towers, domes, theatres, and temples lie,
Open unto the fields and to the sky,
All bright and glittering in the smokeless air.
Never did sun more beautifully steep
In his first splendour valley, rock, or hill;
Ne'er saw I – never felt – a calm so deep,
The river glideth at its own sweet will.
Dear God! the very houses seem asleep,
And all that mighty heart is lying still.

PART SIX

The Tour Of The Thames

A Complete Steamboat Companion For Summer Excursions,
From Hampton Court To The Nore.

PART I

Up The River – From London Bridge To Hampton Court, Etc.

London Bridge – From the rude wooden structure, with turrets
and roofed bulwarks, that was swept away by the river in 1091, to
the present substantial erection, of which the foundation stone was
laid in 1825, there is a complete series of events associated with this
spot, which would furnish an inexhaustible mine for the materials
of history and romance. Peter, curate of St Mary Colechurch, whose
bones were found beneath the masonry of the chapel in 1832, built
the first London Bridge of stone in 1209. The traitors' heads that were
stuck about its battlements, the lines of houses that overhung the
sides, and were taken down in 1757, the successive calamities of siege,
and fire, and flood that beset it during its existence of six centuries,
all invest the site of these reminiscences with a stirring and enduring
interest. The present bridge was thrown open in 1831, having cost,
with its approaches, nearly a million and a half of money. It is about
100 feet higher up the river than the old one. There are five arches, the
centre of one being the largest of the kind ever attempted: the span in
152 feet 6 inches. The roadway is 52 feet in width. Contiguous to the
bridge are the steamboat piers, that contribute largely to the animated
scene this portion of the river always presents. On the Surrey side

Hammersmith Bridge was designed by Sir Joseph Bazalgette, the engineer credited with solving the 'Great Stink' by creating a new sewer network for London. *(LoC)*

of the Thames, in the vast area now occupied by Barclay & Perkins' Brewery, was the site of the Globe Theatre, so suggestive of the days of Shakespeare and his contemporaries.

Southwark Bridge was commenced in 1814, and completed in 1819. The iron used in its construction was cast at Rotheram, in Yorkshire. It is 700 feet in length, 42 in width, 53 in height, and has three arches, of which the centre has a span of 240 feet. About here may be seen the steam-dredging engines, which maintain the depth of the river, and free it from obstructions. They consist of iron frames, with buckets and cutters, made so as to scoop the bed of the river.

Blackfriars Bridge, which is the next reached, has had its architectural beauty somewhat spoiled by the removal of the balustrades, and the substitution of a plain parapet. The recent repairs cost upwards of

£300,000. It was finished in 1770; is 1,000 feet in length, 42 in width, 62 in height, and has nine arches, the centre having a span of 100 feet. There is a fine view here of St Paul's. The site of the ancient sanctuary of Whitefriars, the 'Alsatia' of James I, is marked out by the huge gasometer of the City Gas Works, seen just above. The Temple Gardens, wherein the roses were plucked that served for the emblems of the York and Lancaster wars, are next observed: the roses have ceased to bloom; but the gardens have been celebrated of late years for the most extensive show of choice varieties of the chrysanthemum, which will richly repay a visit during the months of September and October. SOMERSET HOUSE, which its fine balustrade terrace, next claims our notice.

Waterloo Bridge was commenced in 1809, and opened with great state in 1817, on the anniversary of the battle from which it takes its name. A million of money was expended in this structure, which Canova has pronounced the finest in the world. It has nine arches, each of 120 feet span, and is altogether 1,326 feet in length Buckingham Gate, by the Adelphi Terrace is the last vestige of the stately mansion of the Duke of Buckingham, and was the work of Inigo Jones.

Hungerford Suspension Bridge, by [I. K.] Brunel, is a marvel of modern mechanical ingenuity. Its centre span alone is nearly 100 feet greater than the entire of the Menai Bridge. The weight of iron is 700,000 tons. This is the great central focus of the passenger traffic of the Thames. Passing the mansions in Whitehall Gardens, among which that of the late Sir Robert Peel is prominently distinguishable, we next pass under the arches of Westminster Bridge – This bridge was built in 1750; it is 1,223 feet in length, and consists of fifteen arches, the centre one being seventy-six feet wide. Within the last forty years the repairs have cost nearly half a million of money. It is now being rapidly pulled down, and a portion of the new iron bridge alongside is already open for heavy traffic.

The New Houses of Parliament here present a bold frontage to the river, upwards of 800 feet in length, and are decked with a rich display of architectural embellishments. This parliamentary palace covers an area of nine acres, and has eleven open courts. The Victoria

Tower attains a height of 400 feet, and other towers of less magnitude crown other portions of the building. The interior is redundant with sculptures, paintings, and other decorative embellishments. On the opposite side of the river is Lambeth Palace, the town residence of the Archbishops of Canterbury. The tower next to the chapel is still known as the Lollard's Tower, and there are large iron rings to which those unfortunate persons were manacled still exhibited on the walls. Adjoining is the old parish church of Lambeth, with a tower, lately repaired, of the time of Edward IV, and some curious tombs, for the lovers of antiquarian research. On the Middlesex bank is the Fentinentiary, built about thirty years ago, and designed for the punishment and reformation of prisoners who were formerly sentenced to transportation. It is an octangular building, with an outer wall, enclosing eighteen acres of ground.

Vauxhall Bridge, with a pier affording convenient facilities to passengers, is now encountered, and may be briefly described. It was commenced in 1811, and finished five years afterwards. It is 810 feet long, and has a span of 78 feet for the centre arch. The tall trees seen through the openings among the house-tops, point out the site of VAUXHALL GARDENS, having more than a century's existence as one of our places of public amusement, but with the best days of its celebrity long since passed.

The river now introduces us to various interesting object in rapid succession. To the right lie the new streets, stretching forth towards the modern elegant region of Belgravia, and exhibiting evidence of the wealth and station of the metropolitan colonists advancing in this direction. To the left is 'Nine Elms' with its steamboat pier, clipped of much lively animation since the extension of the South Western Railway to Waterloo Bridge. A little higher stood the Red House, a noted place of resort for pigeon-shooting, and a favourite haunt for Sunday-strolling citizens. Opposite will be noticed

Chelsea Hospital, for invalids in the land service. It was built by Sir Christopher Wren, on the site of an old college which had been escheated to the Crown, at an expenditure of £150,000, and begun in the reign of Charles II, was completed in that of William III. The principal building consists of a large quadrangle, open at the south side; in the centre is a bronze statue of Charles II in a Roman habit. On the east and west are buildings, each 365 feet in length, that contain the apartments of the pensioners. The hall wherein the pensioners dine is situated on the opposite side of the vestibule, and is of the same dimensions as the chapel – 110 feet in length. At the upper end is a picture of Charles II on horseback, a gift of the Earl of Ranelagh. A small gratuity to the pensioners will enable the visitor to see every portion of the building open to the public.

The Botanic Gardens adjacent, belonging to the Apothecaries' Company, were founded by Sir Hans Sloane, and are noted for two venerable cedars that are prominent objects from the river. The Cadogan Pier affords easy access to Cheyne Walk, which, a century ago, was the favourite residence of many persons of distinction. At the upper end stood the palace of the Bishops of Winchester; and the tavern called Don Saltero's Coffee-House still remains, which was once a noted house of entertainment when kept by en eccentric barber named Salter, who had a museum of wondrous rarities, to which Sir Hans Sloane largely contributed. This tavern is said to have been a favourite lounge of Richard Cromwell, son of the great Oliver, and who, when he came here, is described to have been 'a little and very neat old man, with a placid countenance.'

Battersea Bridge, a wretched impediment of wood, has about eighty years of existence to answer for as an obstacle in the way of our river navigation.

Chelsea New Bridge, which forms so beautiful an ornament to this part of the river, connects Chelsea with Battersea Park. On the right lies Cremorne, a favourite place of amusement, with some fine grounds attached; and, across the river, the village of Battersea, with its church, assumes a picturesque effect.

Putney Bridge, built by subscription in 1729, is another wooden structure of equal inconvenience with that of Battersea. Its link together the parishes of Fulham and Putney. Fulham Church has a stone tower of the fourteenth century, partially rebuilt about four years ago. All the Bishops of London, with the exception of Bishop

Porteus, have been buried here since the Reformation. In the palace-garden of the Bishop of London, close by, are many fine forest trees of extreme rarity. The house itself is of brick, was built in the reign of Henry VII, and has a moat surrounding the grounds.

Hammersmith Suspension Bridge is a light and elegant structure, completed by Tierney Clarke in 1827, at a cost of about £80,000. To the left will be seen the village of BARNES, memorable, among other associations, as being the place where Sir Francis Walsingham entertained Queen Elizabeth and her retinue, at enormous expense, though the next year he died at his house in Seething land so poor, that his friends were obliged to bury him privately at night. The church, about a quarter of a mile from the river, is one of the most ancient in the neighbourhood of the metropolis, having been erected in the reign of Richard I (1189). Here lived Jacob Tonson, the bookseller, the founder and secretary of the Kit-Cat Club. After passing CHISWICK, on the Middlesex bank, and the hamlet of MORTLAKE, on the Surrey side, we come toKew Bridge, with its seven stone arches, constructed in 1789, and which sold for £22,000 a few years since.

The Botanic Gardens at Kew are open to the public every day throughout the year from one till dusk. The entrance is from Kew Green. A volume would be required to describe its attractions thoroughly; but, among other rarities shown, may be enumerated the Egyptian Papyrus, the Bread Fruit Tree, the Cow Tree, the Coconut, Coffee, Banana, and a fine Weeping Willow, reared from that which overshadowed the exiled emperor's tomb at St Helena.

Passing the straggling town of OLD BRENTFORD, we soon come within a view of ZION HOUSE and grounds, the seat of the Duke of Northumberland. It was once the residence of Lady Jane Grey, who was thence conducted to the Tower. The ivied turret of Isleworth Church looks well in the landscape. Perch, roach, and dace are to be met with here, except when the tide is flowing; but, for the purpose of preserving the fish in the Thames, angling is prohibited during March, April, and May. The promenade on the banks of the river up to Richmond Bridge is a delightful saunter of a summer's morning. The Richmond and Windsor branch of the South Western Railway crosses the Thames by a handsome iron bridge of three arches.

Richmond Bridge has five arches, of which the central arch is sixty feet wide and twenty-five high. The first stone was laid in 1774, and it was completed in 1777, at a cost of £26,000. Some picturesque snatches of scenery are caught through its arches. The aits, studding the broad stream with willows and poplars, the grounds of Twickenham Park, the hill with its crown of villas, and the terrace gardens sloping down the side, make up a beautiful picture on a sunshiny day. The view from the summit of Richmond Hill has been thus graphically described with equal force and justice: 'Of all that belongs to the beautiful in scenery nothing here is wanting. Wood and water, softly swelling hills and hazy distance, with village spires and lordly halls, are blended in beautiful harmony. From the gently slope of the hill, a vast expanse of country stretches far away, till the distance is closed by the hills of Buckinghamshire on the north-west, and the Surrey Downs on the south-east, and all this intermediate space is one wide valley of the most luxuriant fertility, but appearing to the eye a succession of densely wooded tracts, broken and diversified by a few undulations of barren uplands, and here and there is a line of white vapoury smoke, with a tower or spire marking the site of a goodly town or humble village. In the midst the broad placid river, studded with islets, and its surface alive with flocks of swans and innumerable pleasure skiffs, winds gracefully away till lost among the foliage, only to be occasionally tracked afterwards by a glittering thread of silver, seen as the sun glances suddenly upon it between the dark trunks of the trees; and something of majesty is added to the exceeding loveliness by Windsor's royal towers, which loom out so finely on the distant horizon.' Richmond Park, with its fine oaks and elms, its wide glades and grassy undulations, affords some lovely glimpses of sylvan scenery. On the mound within the enclosure at the end of the terrace, it is said that Henry VIII took his stand to watch for the rocket which was to ascend as a signal of the execution of Ann Boleyn. The picturesque road that leads under the brow of the Park to Petersham is a delicious bit of rurality. On the other side of the bridge is Twickenham, with its ait, that, from the celebrity of its fishy delicacies, has achieved a distinctive reputation as Eel-pie Island. The glories of Pope's Villa and Strawberry Hill have both gone, but a flaunting red-brick villa indicates the site of the one, and a part of the mansion still remains to identify the other. The villas that fringe the bank about here, give a pretty appearance to the windings of the river. It was at Orleans House that Louis Philippe resided when Duke of Orleans.

Teddington is now reached, noticeable chiefly for its lock, so well known to the brethren of the angle. The tide ascends above London Bridge to Teddington, a distance of nineteen miles. The high-water mark is about eighteen inches higher than at London Bridge, and the time of high water is about two hours later. Low water surface at Teddington is about 16¾ feet higher than at London Bridge. Altogether, the tide flows a distance of more than sixty miles from the sea, which is said to be a greater length than it flows into any other river in Europe. This is the first station on the Thames where trout can be taken.

Kingston comes next, with its antique church and Saxon associations. The present bridge has five arches, and was built in 1828, but the old wooden one is said to have been built even prior to that at London Bridge. The vicinity of the railway has given rise to a new town, which is already abundant in villa residences, and has the convenience of handsome rows of shops besides.

Hampton Wick, on the Middlesex side of the bridge, is a capital point for the pedestrian to start from on his way to Hampton Court. One Timothy Bennett, a cobbler of Hampton Wick 'being unwilling to leave the world worse than he found it, by a vigorous application of the laws of his country, obtained a free passage through Bushy Park, which had long been withheld from the people.' There is a print of this humble patriot extant, taken in the year 1752, when he was aged 75.

Thames Ditton is not without charms for the angler, who here finds roach, perch, dace, and chub, to reward his piscatorial exertions, as well as an occasional fine trout or jack. At Moulsey, opposite Hampton Bridge, the 'sullen Mole that runneth underground' finds its way to the Thames.

Hampton Court is now gained. If its Palace does not present its best front to the Thames, it undoubtedly looks charmingly picturesque from it, backed as it is by a magnificent framework of foliage, that sets off the venerable ruddiness of this grand historical building to great advantage. Open every day, except Friday, to the public, it is gratifying to know that thousands of delighted visitors flock here annually; and the fine works of art and glorious scenes of nature that they behold within its precincts cannot but produce a beneficial effect, even on the minds of those least prone to appreciate them. The portion of the Palace seen from the river was built by Wren, for William III …

Hampton Court Bridge is an old-fashioned wooden structure, consisting of ten arches, and was built in 1778. The view from the bridge is extremely pretty, the channel of the Thames being here narrowed by islands, and completely overhung in parts by drooping foliage.

Sunbury, on the Middlesex bank, presents another lock or weir to the river voyager. The church looks very picturesque, and in artistic contrast to the turret of Shepperton Church, seen in the distance beyond. The osier beds that now intersect the river give a varied character to the landscape, and the groups of houses, clustered among the trees, that greet the eye at intervals, furnish some nice bits for the portfolio of the sketcher.

Walton Bridge spans the river soon after. The village is on the Surrey side, just below the bridge. The church is a massive structure, built about the twelfth century, of flints and rough stones intermixed, and in some places covered with plaster. A square tower of substantial aspect rises at the west end. In the interior of the church is a large black marble slab, denoting the resting place of William Lilly, the astrologer. A short distance above the bridge, is Coway or Causeway Stakes, ascribed by tradition to point out the ford at which Caesar crossed the Thames in his march to encounter the Britons. This ford was subsequently destroyed by planting stakes shod with iron in a straight line across the river; the ford or causeway presenting an irregular curve, which the stakes crossed in two places and effectually blocked up. One of these stakes, too heavy or too firmly fixed to be raised, remains still imbedded in the river, and can be distinctly seen when the water is clear and the sunlight falls glancingly upon it. The Wey falls into the Thames a short distance beyond.

Chertsey Bridge next crosses the river. It is of stone, and was built in 1786. The town has been described in another part of this work. About a mile above, on the Middlesex side, is the pleasantly-secluded village of Laleham.

Staines Bridge, with its three flat granite arches, was opened in 1832, by William IV. Staines is on the Middlesex shore, and Egham on the opposite. Northward of the bridge is the city boundary stone, with this inscription: 'God preserve the City of London. A.D. 1280' and here the jurisdiction of the Lord Mayor, as conservator of the Thames, terminates. The Coln flows into the Thames a little above. The famous RUNNIMEDE, where King John signed Magna Carta (June 15th, 1215), is on the north side of Egham, and extends a considerable distance along the bank. Opposite is CHARTER ISLAND, a place well known to picnic providers; and at Ankerwyke, close by, is a yew-tree, now flourishing luxuriantly, though it is said to have been in the enjoyment of a green old age when the memorable compact received the royal signature.

An abrupt curve of the river brings us to the ferry at Old Windsor, and the renowned Datchet Meads, identified so closely with the memory of Falstaff. The station of the Richmond, Windsor, and Staines Railway is at hand, and will furnish a rapid as well as pleasant means of transit back to town. The iron bridge that crosses the river here connects Eton with Windsor, and serves as a link between the counties of Buckingham and Berks. Here, as 'wanders the hoary Thames along his silver winding way,' we obtain a fine view of the terraced heights of Windsor Castle. The terrace is seen to its full extent. King John's Tower, Queen Elizabeth's Gallery, George the Fourth's Tower, the Cornwall Tower, the Brunswick Tower, 100 feet high, and the majestic Keep, soaring in its massive magnificence above all, make up a fine picture, with the verdant slopes that form the foreground. Nowhere, it has been truly said, has man been more lavish of his labour, or more ostentatious of his means; and nowhere has nature been more bountiful of her gifts.

The out-door attractions of Windsor and its neighbourhood are quite as great as those that lie inside the Castle. After such an experience of its beauties as we have indicated, the tourist will be disposed to exclaim with the poet:

The splendid Thames, with all the strength of life.
Its boldest beauty and its sweetest breath,
Peopled with such a world of love and strife,
Upon whose borders grandeur gathereth
Its hundred monuments of fame and pride,
And the link'd sweetness of fair Nature's charms,
Whose lovely landscapes peep into his tide,
And fold their sapphire beauty to his arms

PART II

Down The River – From London Bridge To The Nore

The Thames below Bridge – The characteristics of the river at this point are full of interest. A perfect forest of masts, belonging to ships of all sizes and nations, looms out in the Pool. Colliers, coasters, steamboats, and river craft throng the Thames in every direction; and the fleet of merchantmen daily arriving, and the restless activity seen along the banks, give a Londoner a vast conception of the glories of that commerce which has been the cause of the riches and grandeur of his native city. From London Bridge to Deptford, a distance of four miles, with a breadth across varying from 290 to 350 yards, the Pool is narrowed to a small channel by the mass of ships ranged on each side, and which renders the navigation of this portion sometimes very intricate. The depth of the river varies considerably; the mean range of the tidal influx at London Bridge being seventeen feet. Up to Woolwich, the river is navigable for ships of any burden; to Blackwall, for those of 1,400 tons; and to St Katharine's Docks, for those of 800 tons. The wharfs and granaries along the banks are recognised as the largest in the world.

THE TOWER – After passing Billingsgate, behind which the New Coal Exchange is situated, what was opened by Prince Albert in November, 1849, the Tower becomes the first prominent object on the northern bank of the Thames. It is a large pile of building, including an area of more than twelve acres, and owes its irregularity to having been erected and enlarged by various sovereigns at distant periods of time. Besides being the repository of the regalia, it is now used as a garrison and arsenal. The river view is very fine, and a gateway through which the state victims were conveyed, is peculiarly suggestive of historic fancies, strangely contrasting with the peaceful indications of commerce that now lie scattered around.

ST KATHARINE'S DOCKS, adjacent to the Tower, occupy twenty-four acres, and were opened in 1828. From morning till night this vast scene of commercial action presents to the observant eye a panoramic view of the various vessels trading to all parts of the globe.

THE LONDON DOCKS come next, covering an area of thirty-four acres. In the vaults can be stowed more than 65,000 pipes of wines and spirits.

THE THAMES TUNNEL affords a convenient, as well as curious, communication between Wapping and Rotherhithe. It is 1,300 feet long, and passes underneath the river at the depth of 63 feet. The approach at each end is by a vast circular shaft with a spiral roadway. The entire work was executed in about nine years of actual operation, though the first boring commenced in 1826. The opening took place in 1843.

THE WEST INDIA DOCKS, extending across the northern extremity of the Isle of Dogs, from Limehouse to Blackwall, were opened in 1802, and formed the first establishment of the kind in London. The chief warehouses for import goods are on the quays which bound that enclosure. They are admirably contrived for the reception, preservation, and delivery of goods, and are capable of storing away 170,000 hogsheads of sugar, besides coffee and other colonial productions. The whole space occupied by these docks extends over 295 acres. It is enclosed on every side; all the buildings are fire-proof; and the premises are well guarded by watchmen, so that the system of pilfering formerly carried on here is completely abolished. The nearest end is at Limehouse, three miles from the Royal Exchange, and the other end, half a mile further, is at Blackwall; the expense of cartage was therefore considerable, until the construction of the Blackwall Railway lessened the outlay, by increasing the facility of removal. Some admirable contrivances have been lately adopted, by which the great body of water in the docks is kept always sweet, and by which the constant deposit of mud from the water of the river is carried away gradually.

THE COMMERCIAL DOCKS are on the other side of the river, and were originally intended, and principally used, for the vessels connected with the Baltic and the whale fisheries. Hemp, corn, timber, and iron, are usually stored here in great quantities. The logs of the Canadian and Norwegian forests line its immense area, affording a pleasant shelter for the perch, which securely swim beneath its sombre waters undisturbed, unless when the logs are removed for the purposes of commerce, or when the permission of the directors is obtained for a day's vocation in the 'gentle craft.'

DEPTFORD, with its docks, storehouses, victualling-office, and busy shipyards, next claims our notice. It has been a place for shipbuilding since the time of Henry VIII. A short distance further, and the DREADNOUGHT, the old man-of-war that once captured a Spanish three-decker in Trafalgar Bay, is seen before us. As a marine hospital, the vessel is open for the reception of the sick or disabled seamen of all nations.

GREENWICH we have already spoken of at some length in another 'Excursion,' but it well deserves a few words in addition. The Observatory, that stands out so boldly picturesque from the clustering foliage of the Park, and forms so striking an object from the river, was built in 1675 from the materials of Duke Humphrey's Tower, which previously occupied its site. Precisely at 1 p.m., on every day of the year, a ball attached to a staff on the summit of the Observatory, is seen to fall: byt this all the vessels within sight regulate their chronometers. The Park is rich in sylvan beauty and historical interest...

The whole front of the Hospital, 875 feet long, looks, with its terrace, a magnificent building from the river. The pile consists of four quadrangles, detached from each other. The principal quadrangle is 273 feet wide. West of this part is King Charles's building; on the east lies Queen Anne's building; and to the south are the structures built by Sir Christopher Wren, called, on the western side, King William's, and on the east, Queen Mary's buildings. Besides the four quadrangular piles, which, as it were, constitute the Palace, there is the infirmary, a handsome square brick building, 193 feet in length, and 75 broad, another asylum for the helpless, capable of containing 117 persons, with their attendants; a building opposite this for civil officers of the Hospital; and finally, the Naval Asylum, where a fine model frigate may be seen planted on the grass plot. These are all perfectly arranged for the fulfilment of their designed purpose.

The Isle of Dogs, originally called the Isle of Ducks, from the quantity of wild-fowl that found a resting-place upon it, is now seen on the opposite side; and following the abrupt turn which the river takes, we come to BLACKWALL, at the back of which the East India Docks occupy a large space of ground. The Blackwall Pier, with the handsome terminus of the Blackwall Railway, is always a lively scene, from the constant passenger traffic that animates the spacious area. Wigram's shipbuilding yard is adjoining, and a little further down, the river Lea, under the name of Bow Creek, has its outlet into the Thames.

On the right, after entering Woolwich Reach, is seen Charlton, with its picturesque church; and, on the Essex bank, the new station of the Eastern Counties Railway affords a pleasant summer lounge to those who have no opportunity of proceeding further, or who await the arrival of the Gravesend boats, that call here going and returning. A short distance above, the river Roding flows into the Thames, after a sinuous course, from Dunmow, of 38 miles.

Woolwich is a place for sight-seekers to glory in; and, in another part of this work, the Rotunds, Cannon Foundery, Arsenal, and

Barracks, have been fully described. The characteristics of Woolwich, as visible from the river, have been thus nearly and graphically given: 'The long lines of walls, the closely pressed tide-gates, with the bows of many a noble vessel towering proudly over them from their docks, like sea-monarchs on their thrones, looking down in scorn on the river waves; the high heaps of timber, the huge coiled cables, the church tower in the background the heavy lighters crowded along the shore; the light raking craft, with pennants long streaming in the wind; the well-manned boats, pulled hither and thither by sturdy hands, with an occasional portly form and cocked hat in the stern-sheets; the sun glittering with a playful brightness on the many eye-like windows that break the monotony of what, otherwise, would look like slate-roof barns, belonging to some giant farmhouse; the gloomy hulks, moored along the shore, with the water dashing sullenly against the chains that bind them – all tell us that we are sweeping by that ancient dockyard and those famous shipbuilding slips, where England stores the lightning, and forges the thunderbolts which have enabled her to acquire and keep the rule of the main.' The Arsenal contains every description of missile or warlike implement now in use, and has a furnace for the casting of cannon, in which seventeen tons of metal can be melted at once. The public are admitted free to the Arsenal, Dockyard, and Military Repository, everyday, from 9 till 12, and from 1 till 4; upon an extraordinary pressure of work, admission is suspended, as such visits are supposed to interfere with the progress of labour. A special order is required for foreigners.

The bend of the river is here known as Gallion's Reach, and is plentifully studded with buoys, placed there by the Corporation of London, for the use of Indiamen coming into port. The little bankside tavern, half-way between London and Gravesend, is a conspicuous object on the Kentish shore.

Sir Christopher Wren's hand is unmistakable in the design of the towers at the Royal Hospital for Seamen, Greenwich, as they repeat many of the architectural elements found on St Paul's Cathedral. Part of the Greenwich site is now home to the National Maritime Museum's collection. *(CMcC)*

PART SEVEN

Greenwich

There are no less than four modes of getting to Greenwich, each of them to be severally commended as speedy, agreeable, and economical. They are:

1. By Omnibus from Charing Cross down the New Kent Road.
2. By Greenwich Railway from the south side of London Bridge.
3. By Blackwall Railway, from Fenchurch Street to Blackwall, crossing the river by a steamer.
4. By steamboats from Westminster, Waterloo, Blackfriars, and London Bridges, two companies keep up a constant succession of departures every twenty minutes throughout the day.

For the sake of variety, we shall proceed to describe the journey by water, which, of a fine day, is not only the most agreeable, but, as furnishing an excellent opportunity of seeing the scenery of the Thames, is perhaps most desirable to strangers.

Leaving London Bridge, a perfect forest of masts, belonging to ships of all sizes and all nations, looms out in the Pool. BILLINGSGATE, situated chiefly at the back of that cluster of buildings by the Custom-House, has been since the days of William III the most famous fishmarket in Europe. The CUSTOM-HOUSE, 480 feet in length, was begun in 1813, and finished four years afterwards, at a cost of nearly half a million. It contains nearly 200 distinct apartments, each having a range of communication with the Long Room, which is 197 feet long, and 50 feet high. One hundred clerks are engaged about this room alone, and the principal business of 'clearing' is here conducted.

We next see the TOWER, said to have been built by Julius Caesar, and afterwards reconstructed by William the Conqueror. The last state prisoners here were Thistlewood and his associates, in 1820, for the Cato Street conspiracy. The public have free access from ten till four, sixpence being charged to view the regalia. About half a mile lower down are the warehouses of ST KATHARINE'S DOCKS, which cost one million in construction, and were first opened in 1828. The LONDON DOCKS, close by, opened in 1805, occupy a space of about thirty acres. WAPPING is a well-known resort for sailors, and those connected with maritime pursuits. At Execution Dock pirates were formerly hung in chains. ROTHERHITHE, opposite, is, in its river frontage, only distinguished by a mass of warehouses, and the glimpse we get of the old parish church, where Prince Lee Boo was buried. The TUNNEL, over which we next pass, was first commenced, to afford a subaqueous communication between the two sides of the river, in 1825, and was completed, after much difficulty and expense, in twenty years. Sir I. Brunel was the projector and engineer. The height is nearly twenty-five feet, and the length 1,300 feet. One penny toll is charged for each passenger. Entering the Lower Pool we pass LIMEHOUSE, where the Regent's Canal communicates with the Thames, and have next to notice the WEST INDIA DOCKS, opened in 1802, after an expenditure of £1,200,000, and extending over an area of 204 acres. On the opposite side of the River are the COMMERCIAL DOCKS, after which is passed Earl's Sluice, forming the boundary between Surrey and Kent. DEPTFORD, where the dockyard and its bustling animation gives a lively appearance to the shore, reminds one of Peter the Great, who, in 1698, came to Saye's Court and studied the craft of shipbuilding at the once picturesque retreat of Evelyn, the autobiographist and author of 'Sylva.' But alas for the glories of Saye's Court – its glittering hollies, long avenues, and trim hedges! That portion of the victualling yard where oxen are slaughtered and hogs salted for the use of the navy, occupies the enchanting grounds wherein Evelyn was wont to delight, and on the site of the mansion itself is the common workhouse of the parish. Approaching Greenwich Reach, where large quantities of whitebait are caught in the season, the opening of the river discloses a pretty view of a distant country beyond, and, with a few more revolutions of the paddle-wheel, we are brought to our destination.

Greenwich presents a striking appearance from the river, its Hospital forming one of the most prominent attractions of the place. Here was the palace erected by Humphrey Duke of Gloucester, and by him called Placentia; and here were born Henry VIII and his two daughters, Queens Mary and Elizabeth. Charles II began the present magnificent edifice, and William III appropriated it to its present patriotic purpose, since which time successive sovereigns have contributed to enrich it with various additions. As the first generally seen, we shall begin our description with an account of its interior. The Chapel and Picture Gallery are open gratis on Mondays and Fridays; on other days threepence each is charged for admission. It is as well to remind the reader that the Hospital consists of four distinct piles of building, distinguished by the appellations of King Charles', King William's, Queen Mary's, and Queen Anne's. King Charles' and Queen Anne's are those next the river, and between them is the grand square, 270 feet wide, and the terrace by the river front, 865 feet in length. Beyond the square are seen the Hall and Chapel with their noble domes, and the two colonnades, which are backed by the eminence whereon the Observatory stands throned amid a grove of trees. In the centre of the great square is Rysbrach's statue of George II, carved out of white marble, from a block taken from the French by Sir George Rooke, and which weighed eleven tons. On the west side is King Charles' building, erected chiefly of Portland stone, in the year 1684. The whole contains about 300 beds, distributed in thirteen wards. Queen Anne's building, on the east side of the square, corresponding with that on the opposite side, was begun in 1693 and completed in 1726. There are here 24 wards with 437 beds, and several of the officers' apartments. To the south-west is King William's building, comprising the great hall, vestibule, and dome, erected, between 1698 and 1703, by Sir Christopher Wren. It contains 11 wards and 554 beds. Queen Mary's building was, with the chapel, not completed till 1752. It contains 13 wards and 1,100 beds. The PAINTED HALL, a noble structure opposite the chapel, is divided into three rooms, exhibiting as you enter statues of Nelson and Duncan, with twenty-eight pictures of various sizes; the chief are Turner's large picture of 'The Battle of Trafalgar,' the 'relief of Gibraltar,' and the 'Defeat of the French Fleet under Comte de Grasse.' On the opposite side is Loutherbourg's picture of Lord Howe's victory on the memorable 1st of June 1794, whilst above are suspended the flags taken in the battle. The other pictures up the steps are chronologically arranged, the most prominent being the 'Death of Captain Cook,' the 'Battle of Camperdown,' 'Nelson leaping into the San Josef,' and the 'Bombardment of Algiers.' It may not be generally known that every mariner, either in the royal navy or merchant service, pays sixpence a month towards the support of this noble institution, which has of course, besides, a handsome revenue (£130,000) derived from other sources. The pensioners, who are of every rank, from the admiral to the humblest sailor, are qualified for admission by being either maimed or disabled by age. Foreigners who have served two consecutive years in the British service are equally entitled to the privileges, and the widows of seaman are exclusively appointed nurses. The Hospital was first opened in January, 1705, and now the pensioners provided with food, clothes, lodging, and a small stipend for pocket-money, number nearly 2,500. The number of out-pensioners is about 3,000. The 'Royal Naval School,' for training the sons of seamen to the naval service, is a most interesting institution, administering the best instruction to now about 450 boys.

The 'Royal Observatory,' occupying the most elevated spot in Greenwich Park, was built on the site of the old castle, the foundation stone being laid on the 10th of August, 1675. The first superintendent of the establishment was Flamstead, and he commenced his observations in the following year. It stands about 300 feet above the level of the river. For the guidance of the shipping the round globe at its summit drops precisely at 1 p.m., to give the exact Greenwich time. The noble park is chiefly planted with elms and chestnut trees, and contains 188 acres. It was walled round with brick in the reign of James I. The views from the summit are very fine, embracing perhaps the finest prospects of London and the Thames, the forests of Hainault and Epping, the heights of Hampstead, and a survey of Kent, Surrey, and Essex, as far as the eye can reach. The flitting of the fawns through the distant glades, the venerable aspect of the trees themselves – many of them saplings in the time of Elizabeth – and the appearance of the veteran pensioners, some without a leg or arm, others hobbling on from the infirmity of wounds or age, and all clad in the old-fashioned blue coats and breeches, with cocked hats, give beauty and animation to a scene which no other country in the world can boast.

A small doorway in the south-western extremity of the park brings us out with a sudden contrast on to BLACKHEATH, where Wat Tyler assembled the Kentish rebels in the reign of Richard II, and where Jack Cade and his fellow insurgents are said to have held their midnight meetings in a cavern which still remains, though so choked up as to be considered nearly inaccessible. LEE is about a mile distant, crossing the Heath towards the south. In the old church was buried Halley the astrologer. On the east of Blackheath is 'Modern College,' founded in 1695 for decayed merchants, and now having about forty recipients of its benefits. Following the old Dover road, which, crossing the Heath, leads on to Shooter's Hill, we pass a rustic little hostelry on our left, distinguished by the peculiar title of the 'Sun-in-the-Sands.' Hazlitt, Hunt, and others of our essayists, were often wont to ramble over here; there is the advantage of an open balcony, from which a pleasant view may be obtained of the surrounding country. It is recorded by old Hall, the historian, that King Henry VIII often rode 'amaying from Greenwich to the high ground of Shooter's Hill with Queen Katharine his wife, and many lords and ladies in gay attire.' Several jousts and tourneys took place here in the same reign, at one of which the King himself, accompanied by the Duke of Suffolk, the Earl of Essex, and Sir George Carew, challenged all comers to tilt at the barriers. This was on the 20th of May in the eighth year of King Harry's reign: he got too crass and corpulent for such athletic pastimes afterwards. Shooter's Hill – anciently Suiter'shill, from the number of applicants, doubtless, that came this way to procure places about the court – is 446 feet high, and commands an expansive prospect. The 'mighty mass of brick and smoke and shipping,' as Byron calls the view of London from this point, is well contrasted with the foliage of the wooded country extending towards the south beyond the vale of Eltham. On the summit rises the commemorative castle of Severndroog, built in 1784 by Sir William James, to celebrate the conquest of one so called on the coast of Malabar.

For those who either have seen Woolwich, or who prefer postponing their visit thither for a distant excursion, we can especially recommend a deviation from Shooter's Hill down the inviting green lane at its base that leads to ELTHAM, a pleasant walk of hardly two miles. Here stood anciently one of the most magnificent of England's royal palaces. Anthony Bec, the 'battling Bishop' of Durham, erected the first mansion about the middle of the thirteenth century, and on his death the manor with its possessions fell to the Crown, which is still the rightful owner of the property. John, son of Edward II, was born here in 1315, and was thence called John of Eltham. In the next reign the Parliament was here convened, and Edward IV, after rebuilding it, kept his Christmas here with great splendour in 1482. Henry VII made still further additions, and in his time the Royal Palace consisted of four quadrangles enclosed within a high wall, and encircled by a moat. A garden and three parks were attached, comprising about 1,800 acres, and were well stocked with deer. The many fine old trees that still remain, show how richly wooded this district must have formerly been. All that now remains of this once stately edifice is the Hall or Banqueting Room, which has been for years converted to the plebeian uses of a barn. Nothing can be more interesting than this relic of ancient kingly grandeur. The symbol of the rose, seen on various portions of the building, identifies the Hall as that erected by Edward IV. In 1828 its neglected condition attracted the attention of antiquarians, and the government undertook the work of restoration, to secure the permanence of what remained. The Hall is about 100 feet long, and 60 feet high, and it has been well said 'the taste and talent of ages are concentrated in its design.' The windows have been built up, but the splendid roof is nearly perfect. From the immense length of the beams, sound and straight throughout, it has been considered that a forest must have yielded its choicest timber for the supply, and it is evident the material has been wrought with amazing labour and admirable skill. Some of the walls of the old garden are perceptible to the east of the palace, and there is an ancient dwelling close by worth notice. In 1834 some curious subterraneous passages were discovered. Under the ground-floor was found a trap-door opening into a room underground, ten feet wide, and communicating with Middle Park, where there were excavations sufficient to contain sixty horses. About 500 feet of this passage was entered, and 200 feet of another, which passed under the moat, and was believed, from traditions extant, to lead under Blackheath to Greenwich or the river. In the field leading from Eltham to Mottingham the archway was broken into, but the brickwork could be traced considerably further in the same direction. After leaving the Hall go and see Eltham Church; not that it is architecturally remarkable, but in the church-yard will be found a tomb to Doggett the comedian, who bequeathed the coat and badge still rowed for every 1st of August by the 'jolly young watermen' of the Thames. Hence we can get back to Greenwich, and go home by railway.

Woolwich can be reached either by water, or, as forming a continuation of our present stroll down the road, we can turn off by the sixth milestone and go through Charlton, or take the road to the left at Shooter's Hill. Of course nearly all the interest connected with Woolwich is concentrated in the government establishments, which are acknowledged to be the finest in the world. These, consisting of the Dockyard, Arsenal, and Royal Military Repository, we shall describe in the rotation generally adopted when seeing them. Coming from Shooter's Hill and crossing Woolwich Common, the extensive range of buildings forming the barracks of the Royal Artillery first attracts attention. The principal front extends above 1,200 feet. In the eastern wing is the chapel, containing 1,000 sittings, and the other principal parts of the building are the library and reading-room, plentifully supplied with newspapers and periodicals. The whole establishment affords excellent accommodation for upwards of 4,000 men. The troops, when of parade, present a very animated appearance. The 'Royal Arsenal' will be observed but a short distance off, composed of several buildings, wherein the manufacture of implements of warfare is carried on upon the most extensive scale. On entering the gateway the visitor will see the 'Foundery' before him, provided with everything necessary for casting the largest pieces of ordnance, for which, as in the other branches of manufacture, steam power has been lately applied. Connected with the 'Pattern Room', adjoining, will be noticed several of the illuminations and devices used in St James' Park to commemorate the peace of 1814. The 'Laboratory' exhibits a busy scene, for here are made the cartridges, rockets, fireworks, and the other chemical contrivances for warfare, which, though fill of 'sound and fury', are far from being considered amongst the enemy as 'signifying nothing'. To the north are the storehouses, where are comprised out-fittings for 15,000 cavalry horses, and accoutrements for service. The area of the Arsenal includes no less than 24,000 pieces of ordnance, and 3,000,000 of cannon-balls piled up in huge pyramids. The 'Repository' and 'Rotunda' are on the margin of the Common, to the south of the town, and contain models of the most celebrated fortifications in Europe, with curiosities innumerable. To the south-east of the Repository is the 'Royal Military Academy', for the education of the cadets in all the branches of artillery and engineering. The present building, partly in the Elizabethan style, was erected in 1805, and though 300 could be accommodated, the number of cadets at present does not exceed 160. In going from the Arsenal to the Garrison there will be noticed, on the right of the road, an extensive building forming the headquarters of the Royal Sappers and Miners. On the same side the way is the 'Field Artillery Depot', where the guns are mounted and kept in readiness for instant action. The Hospital is to the left of the Garrison entrance, fitted up with 700 beds, and under the superintendence of the most skilful medical officers. From the Arsenal we proceed to the Dockyard, which, commencing at the village of New Charlton on the west, extends a mile along the banks of the river to the east. There are two large dry docks for the repair of vessels, and a spacious basin for receiving vessels of the largest size. The granite docks, and the Foundery and Boiler-making department, recently added, have been great improvements. Timber-sheds, mast-houses, storehouses, and ranges of massive anchors, give a very busy aspect to the place, which was first formed in the reign of Henry VIII, and considerably enlarged by Charles I …

Though within a short period nearly 2,000 additional houses have been built, the town presents few inducements for a prolonged visit, and has no feature of interest in itself whatever. The old church looks better at a distance than close, and there are few monuments in the churchyard bearing names familiar to the eye and ear. Perhaps, after his visit to the Arsenal, the visitor will feel most interested in that to Schalch, a Swiss, who died in 1776, at the advanced age of ninety years, sixty of which he passed as superintendent of the Foundery there. Indeed, it was to him chiefly that the establishment owed its origin, for he was the cause of its removal from Moorfields, and the improvements made in conducting the operations.

From Woolwich we have the choice of four speedy modes of transit to town:

1. By steamer direct to London Bridge and Westminster.
2. By steam ferry across to Blackwall, and so on by railway to Fenchurch Street.
3. By a similar conveyance to the new station of the Eastern Counties Railway, on the Essex banks of the river, which brings us to Shoreditch.
4. By the North Kent line.

The Woolwich station, eight miles and twenty-one chains from London, is in the close vicinity of the Barracks; the two tunnels between Woolwich and Charlton are, respectively, 120 and 100 yards in extent; and the Blackheath tunnel, near the Morden College, is 1,681 yards long. The excursionist may consult his own convenience for preference of choice.

PART EIGHT

Richmond

Where either train or steamboat will enable us to stop, is just the pleasant point for an excursionist to reach bent upon exercise and enjoyment. The walks by the margin of the river, the leafy luxuriance of the park, the famed view from the hill, and the varied scenery of its environs, through which wind the prettiest green lanes imaginable, all tend to make this 'region of loveliness' attractive beyond the day. Monarchs and monks had a wonderful knack long ago of discovering the prettiest places for a summer retreat round London, and accordingly we find it was a royal residence at a very early period. At Richmond Green, where the only remains of the 'aunciente Palace of Sheen' is to be found, in a gateway at the north-east angle, Kings Edward I and II lived, and the third King Edward died – broken-hearted, it is said, for the loss of his heroic son, 'The Black Prince.' Here, too, died Anne, Richard II's queen, who first introduced the side-saddle for the benefit of succeeding female equestrians. In 1492, Henry VII gave a grand tournament, and here, in 1509, he died. Queen Elizabeth also breathed her last in this regal abode, which, after minor changes connected with royalty, was finally demolished by George III in 1769. Passing through the town, which contains on its outskirts several elegant villas of the nobility, we proceed up the hill to the park, which embraces an area of about 2,300 acres, and is nearly nine miles in circumference. It was enclosed by Charles I with a brick wall, and this became one of the articles of his impeachment. An attempted exclusion of the public, in the reign of George III, caused a spirited resistance from a brewer named Lewis, who, by an action at law, established the right of footway, and since then no further encroachment upon the privileges of the public has been essayed. The umbrageous solitudes of this fine park, and the comprehensive and beautiful views from its summit, extending over the fertile valley of the Thames, and even including the distant turrets of Windsor Castle, have long been the theme of eulogy in book and ballad.

At sunset, when the far-off masses of foliage are sobered down by twilight, and the river, catching the last beams of the sinking orb, gleams through the leafy landscape like a fairy lake, in which every ripple yields a golden sparkle, the scene is truly enchanting. In Richmond Church, a neat structure, partly ancient and partly modern, there are several interesting memorials of the departed great. The first that arrests attention is a marble tablet on the wall, with a medallion head sculptured on it, beneath which is the following inscription – 'Edmund Keane – died May 1833, aged 46 – a memorial erected by his son Charles John Kean, 1839.' Here, too, is the grave of the poet James Thomson, with the Earl of Buchan's copper tablet, the inscription on which time has almost made illegible. He was buried without the wall; but the church having been enlarged to make room for the organ, the wall now passes right across his coffin, cutting the body, as it were, in twain. Near the communion table lies Mary Ann Yates, a celebrated tragic actress, and once the Mrs Siddons of her day, but now her very name appears forgotten. In a whimsical epitaph to a Welsh lawyer, one Robert Lewes, it is recorded to his honour, that he 'was such a great lover of peace and quietness, that when a contention began in his body between Life and Death, he immediately gave up the ghost to end the dispute.' Among the rest may be mentioned, tombs to the memory of Joseph Taylor, the original 'Hamlet;' Dr Moore, the author, and father of the Corunna-renowned general, Sir John Moore; Gilbert Wakefield, the critic; Viscount Fitzwilliam, who founded the Museum at Cambridge; and Edward Gibson, an artist of repute. Richmond has a theatre, firs opened in 1719 by the facetious Will Penkethman, and carried on for some time by Cibber; it was the scene of many of Kean's triumphs in the mimic art; latterly it has been badly managed and worse frequented: but the Prince of Wales having taken up his residence at Richmond as Ranger of the Park, the fortunes of the theatre even may be revived. Near it is 'Rosedale House,' where Thomson lived and died (August 22, 1748), and having lately become the residence of the Countess of Shaftesbury, it is known as 'Thomson's Villa.' Many relics of the poet, and some manuscript portions of 'The Seasons,' in his own handwriting, are here carefully preserved. The summer-house, his poetic study, still exists.

Petersham, reached by a pleasant rural lane leading from the hill, is delightfully situated in the valley beneath, and has some fine springs of water, which are duly taken advantage of by a hydropathic establishment recently formed. Ham House was once a royal domain, where James I, Charles I, Charles II, and James II, the latter by compulsion, occasionally resided. About a mile west from Richmond is TWICKENHAM, near which is TWICKENHAM AIT, or Eel-pie Island, consecrated from time immemorial to the votaries of that esteemed delicacy. Pope's Villa, now demolished, and having a number of villas on its site, has long associated the poet's name with the place. In the village church may be seen his tomb, with a Latin inscription written by his friend Warburton, Bishop of Gloucester, and a more characteristic one beneath, written by the bard himself …

Teddington, two miles further, is well known to the angling fraternity, and here the first 'lock' is encountered in the upward progress along the Thames. It is worthwhile to turn aside from the road, and have a look at the old church, which, though recently modernised, presents in its south aisle a specimen of architectural stability of 800 years back. 'Peg Woffington,' the clever actress and beautiful woman, whose history is of itself a romance, was here buried in 1720, and there are other monuments of remunerative interest and antiquity.

PART NINE

Hampton Court

The situation of Hampton Court, which stands of the north bank of the Thames, about twelve miles from London, is so happily described by Pope, that we cannot resist quoting the favourite passage:

> Close by those meads for ever crown'd with flowers,
> Where Thames with pride surveys his rising towers,
> There stands a structure of majestic frame,
> Which from the neighbouring Hampton takes its name
> Here Britain's statesmen oft the fall foredoom
> Of foreign tyrants and or nymphs at home;
> Here thou great Anna, whom three realms obey,
> Dost sometimes counsel take, and sometimes – tea.

In summing up the points of its early history, we may briefly state, that in the thirteenth century the manor of Hampden was vested in the Knights of St John of Jerusalem. Cardinal Wolsey, its illustrious founder, was the last of the enlightened churchmen of old, whose munificence patronised that style of building; which, originating with the ecclesiastics, seemed to end in his fall. He is supposed to have furnished the designs, and having been commenced in 1515, the building, when finished, was in so magnificent a style, that it created great envy at court. The banquets and masques, so prevalent in the age of Henry VIII, were nowhere more magnificently ordered than here; and, however vast the establishment of the Cardinal, it could not have been more than sufficient for the accommodation of his train of guests. Numerous sovereigns since that time made it their temporary abode; and the last who resided here were George II and his

Queen, since which period various members of the court have occupied
the apartments, the Crown reserving the right of resuming possession.
At present, about 700 decayed gentlemen and gentlewomen, with their
servants, occupy offices connected with the establishment, to which
they are recommended by the Lord Chamberlain. The Lion gate, which
fronts the entrance to the magnificent drives and promenades of Bushy
Park, is the chief avenue; and continuing through the Wilderness, by a
path overshadowed with lofty trees, we find ourselves by the side of the
palace, in front of which extends a long walk, ornamented with parterres,
an exotic shrubbery, and a spacious fountain in the centre. The grand
east front extends 330 feet, and the grand south from 328 feet, from the
designs of Sir Christopher Wren. The grand staircase and the guard-
chamber lead to the picture galleries, to which so many cheap catalogues
furnish descriptive guides, that our enumeration of their magnificent
contents is unnecessary. Suffice it to say, the paintings are about 1,000 in
number. Retracing our steps to the middle court, we may observe, under
the archway, the flight of steps leading to Wolsey's Hall. It is 106 feet long,
forty feet wide, and illuminated by thirteen windows, each fifteen feet
from the ground. On one of the panes of the bay window at the end,
extending nearly to the floor, the young Earl of Surrey wrote his lines
to the fair Geraldine. On each side the walls are hung with tapestry of
the most costly material and rarest workmanship, said to have formed
a portion of the gifts interchanged between Henry and Francis, at the
celebrated 'Field of the Cloth of Gold,' in the centre of the dais there is
a doorway leading to the withdrawal room. The beautiful gardens in
front of the palace have been repeatedly the admiration of all visitors.
They were laid out by William III in the Dutch style, with canal and
watercourses, and the compass and shears were industriously employed
in making birds, beasts, and reptiles, out of yew, holly, and privet. The
private gardens extend from the sides of the palace to the banks of the
river, and contain, besides some remarkably fine orange-trees, many of
them in full bearing, a fine oak nearly forty feet in circumference, and
an ancient elm called 'King Charles' swing.' The large space of ground
on the opposite side of the palace is called 'THE WILDERNESS,' and
was planted with shrubs by the order of William and Mary. Most of

the walks are completely overshadowed, and on a hot summer day a stroll through these umbrageous paths is exceedingly inviting. In this portion of the grounds is situated the MAZE, so constructed that all the parts apparently leading to the centre turn off to a more distant part, and involve the inquisitive adventurer in constant perplexity. Though we are not quite sure that the revelation does not spoil the chief sport, the secret of success in threading this miniature labyrinth is, that after the first turning to the left the right hand should be kept towards the fence the whole of the remaining way. The greatest curiosity, however, is perhaps the famous Vine, which, sheltered and nurtured in a hothouse, is 110 feet long, and, at three feet from the root, is twenty-seven inches in circumference. It bears from two to three thousand bunches of the black Hamburg grape in the season. We may now mention the arrangements made for the reception of visitors.

The State Apartments, Public Gardens, and Picture Galleries, are open daily (Friday excepted) throughout the year, from ten till dusk; and on Sundays after two p.m. The Public Gardens have generally a military band in attendance, and a small fee is expected by the gardener for exhibiting the orangery and the vine.

The Chestnut Avenue of Bushy is world-famous. 'Look across the road,' says a pleasant companion to the spot, 'upon those dark masses of a single tree with thousands of spiral flowers, each flower a study, powdering over the rich green from the lowest branch to the topmost twig. Now you shall have a real reward for your three hours' toil under a lustrous sun. Look up and down this wondrous avenue. Its mile length seems a span; but from one gate to the other there is a double line of unbroken green, with flowers rich as the richest of the tropics contending for the mastery of colour. Saw you ever such a gorgeous sight! Fashionable London even comes to see it; but in the Whitsun week, and during the some twenty days of the glories of the chestnut, thousands come here to rejoice in the exceeding beauty of this marvel of nature, which the art of the Dutch gardeners, whom William of Nassau brought to teach us, have left as a proud relic of their taste.'

We hence recommend the excursionist to proceed across Kingston Bridge, erected in 1827, to KINGSTON, a distance of not much more than two miles, and take a train homeward by the South Western Railway …

PART TEN

The Crystal Palace

The Crystal Palace stands upon the heights of Penge, the most remarkable work of its kind the world has ever witnessed, appealing to appreciation of the wonderful with a force unknown in this country, and unrivalled in any other. Versailles is not nearly so marvellous a sight as that brilliant fabric which rears its glittering bulk upon the Surrey hills, within view of the metropolis. It is a work fit to take rank with the noblest and greatest in the world.

The building, the park, the waterworks, the garden inside and out, the fine art collection – all, more or less, surpass what could be hoped for or desired.

This marvellous works of commercial enterprise and human ingenuity has now so far reached perfection as to realise all the anticipations that had been formed during its progress. What was said of it on its first pillar being raised has become a demonstrated truth, as the structure has grown into maturity, and we here behold a building which, for the excellence of its objects, the magnitude of its design, and the triumph of its execution has no equal in the world. Former ages, it is true, have raised palaces enough, and many of them surpassing magnificence. We have heard of the Hanging Gardens of Babylon, the colossal temples of Egypt, and the gorgeous structures of Nineveh and Persepolis; many have seen the scattered fragments of Nero's Golden Palace on the Palatine Hill, and the vast ruins which still speak so eloquently of the grandeur of Imperial Rome; but these were but raised by the spoils of captive nations and the forced labour of myriads of slaves, to gratify the caprice or vanity of some solitary despot. It is to our own age that the privilege has been reserved of raising a palace for the people – the production of their own unaided and independent enterprise. We find here the greatest amount of instruction, combined with the largest amount of amusement, the highest utility blended with the highest refinement, and, as an educational institution, as well as an enchanting recreative resort, the Crystal Palace will every year strengthen its claims upon the patronage of the public, and more triumphantly attest the genius and indefatigable energy of its founders.

The origin of that peculiarly appropriate style of architecture, which has now become so familiar to the eye, is worth remembering. A few years ago, a party of naturalists proceeding in a boat up some unexplored river in South America came suddenly upon a floral specimen which filled them with amazement and delight. They beheld peacefully floating on the waters a lily of such gigantic proportions that its petals could not be embraced by the outstretched arms, and whose boat-like leaves were able to support the full weight of a man.

After the Great Exhibition at Hyde Park had finished, the Crystal Palace was resited at Sydenham, South London, in an enlarged form. It was destroyed by a terrible fire on 30 November 1936. *(CMcC)*

Extraordinary as this discovery was considered at the time, no one could imagine the train of events to which it was destined to give rise; that the sudden surprisal of that Brobdignagian flower in its native wilds, where for thousands of years it had bloomed unseen by man, would be the immediate cause of a crystalline structure – yet so it proved.

When the Victoria Regia Lily was brought to this country and removed to the princely grounds of Chatsworth, it was found necessary to build a conservatory purposely for its accommodation. This conservatory was constructed by Mr Paxton, of glass and iron – the first of its kind ever erected, and this little house of glass was the first fruits of that mother-thought which reared the gleaming arch, and stretched the vast arcades upon the emerald sod in Hyde Park, and which has since ornamented all the important capitals in Europe and America with palaces of crystal such as we only read of in old fairy tales.

The Crystal Palace estate was originally called Penge Park, and is situated in the parish of Battersea, partly in Surrey and partly in Kent. A finer site could not possibly have been chosen. Standing on the brow of a hill rising some two hundred feet above the valley through which the railroad passes, the Crystal Palace is visible for miles away in every direction. The grounds form an irregular parallelogram, about half way between the Sydenham and Annerley stations, having a frontage towards the railway of 1,800 feet, and facing the New Road, Dulwich Wood, a frontage of 3,000 feet, giving a magnificent panoramic view of London, and the high grounds of Middlesex from the galleries on the Dulwich side, and of the beautiful undulating scenery of Kent on the Penge side. The entire area consists of about 289 acres, and the carriage drive round the park and grounds is nearly two miles. The building covers a space of 20 acres, and is, from end to end of the nave, 1,608 feet, and from side to side, 384 feet. It is intersected by three transepts, the central one being 384 feet long and 120 feet wide. The two end transepts are each 336 feet in length and 72 feet in width, and the whole length of the palace, from end to end of the wings, is 2,000 feet. These wings are each 600 feet long, and terminate in towers 100 feet in height. The chief transept is about 200 feet in height, and has five tiers of galleries; the end transepts, three tiers. Five hundred tons weight of glass have been consumed in the roof and sides, and the cubic contents of the building are estimated at 40,000,000 feet – about one-fourth more than that in Hyde Park, and forty times more than Westminster Hall, the largest hall in England.

With reference to the distinctive dimensions of the Palace at Sydenham and the one in Hyde Park a few figures will assist us in drawing a comparison between them. The length is 1,608 feet, or less by 240 feet than the building of 1851. It is broken by three transepts instead of one, of which two are 136 feet in height from the garden, with a span of 72 feet, and the third 200 feet, with a span of 120 feet. The extreme breadth of the building is 384 feet at the transept, or 72 feet less than the Palace in Hyde Park, and this breadth is apparently further diminished by the arched roof which now runs the full length of the whole building. The diminution of the length and breadth is in some measure compensated by the capacity of the two wings, which stretch on either extremity 567 feet. These extend into, and as it were, enclose the Italian terrace garden. There is also an additional basement story, which goes by the appellation of Sir Joseph Paxton's tunnel.

This basement story or tunnel contains apparatus for warming the building by rows of furnaces and boilers, and an iron network forming fifty miles of steam pipes. It extends from end to end of the building – a distance of 1,608 feet, and is 24 feet wide. There are about thirty boilers arranged in pairs along the tunnel at regular distances.

Conveyances to the Palace – No undertaking, however wonderful, will be largely visited for pleasure which demands a sacrifice of some three hours to reach or to leave. The noble site, the unrivalled view, the splendid gardens and fountains will spread their attractions in vain on the heights of Penge unless the bulk of the people of London can get there as quickly, as cheaply, and as pleasantly as they can get up or down the river. The Company have done all they possibly can to facilitate the passage of visitors at a distance to and from the palace, the new west-end railway materially aiding those residing west of London. The trains start punctually from the London Bridge and Wandsworth Stations at the times advertised in the official bills; but special trains are put on always as occasion may require.

The shortest route from London, by carriage, is by the Elephant and Castle, Camberwell, Denmark Hill, Herne Hill, and Dulwich. The ordinary entrances from the road are at the South and Central Transepts. Entrances are also provided opposite Sydenham Church, and at the bottom of the Park, below the Grand Lake and Extinct Animals.Omnibuses leave Gracechurch Street for the Crystal Palace at intervals from 10 in the morning. An omnibus also leaves the Paddington Station at a quarter to 11 a.m. Also one from the Kings and Key, Fleet Street, at 12 o'clock, and one from the Green Man, Oxford Street, at the same time. Omnibuses leave the City for Camberwell every ten minutes. Conveyance can also be procured from Peckham and Clapham.

A complete system of omnibuses correspondence, or direct conveyance, was introduced by the London General Omnibus Company between the following districts and the Crystal Palace Railway Station at London Bridge: Hammersmith, Chelsea, Putney, Brompton, Westminster, Paddington, Bayswater, St John's Wood, Holloway, Hornsey-road, Islington, Hampstead, Kentish Town, Barnet and Finchley, Stoke Newington, Clapton, Hackney, Bethnal Green, Kingsland, Hoxton, Newington Causeway, and Kent-road. Through Tickets, including omnibus to and from the Station, Railway to the Palace and back, with admission to the building, were issued at the Omnibus Company's Offices; but the advantages of this system not being duly appreciated, after a trial the plan was abandoned.

As a general guide to the visitors, it will be convenient to remember that one half of the building is devoted to ancient art, architecture, and sculpture, and that the other half, that facing the garden is appropriated to all the various forms of modern art, architecture, inventions, improvements, and manufactures, together with a well-arranged Picture Gallery, which now contains nearly 1,000 pictures, by ancient and modern artists. There are some exceptions to the rule, where exigencies of space have modified the arrangements, but this will serve as some clue to guide the stranger through the beautiful labyrinth, in the apparent intricacies of which he will find himself at first bewildered. The very brilliant and fairy-like aspect of the place, as it reveals itself suddenly to the eye, will produce an impression, of itself calculated to absorb the utmost attention a visitor can bestow on his first becoming acquainted with the interior, and the multitude of objects around him will seem to baffle all attempts to discover the nature of their arrangements. So admirably, however, have the different compartments been designed, that a very little consideration will soon enable the public to reach that in which they may be especially interested, and the multiplicity of claims upon our notice will only serve to elicit from us additional tributes of admiration. It is emphatically the triumph of artistic design as well as of artistic construction.

The Sydenham dinosaurs: Sculptor Benjamin Waterhouse Hawkins built thirty-three life-size dinosaurs, using iron skeletons covered with a combination of brick and cement, to create the 'Dinosaur Court' at the Crystal Palace Park which opened in 1854. The Victorians were fascinated by the discovery of fossils, although this 'Paleoart' at Sydenham is generally considered to be rather inaccurate by modern standards.

Acknowledgements

I am grateful to the following for providing images: The Library of Congress (LoC), Campbell McCutcheon (CMcC), A. Parrot, Johnny Greig, Clickos/Dreamstime and Man vyi. Unless otherwise stated new photography is by the editor, John Christopher.